MORE THAN
CONQUERORS

From the painting by Sir Henry Raeburn

Sir Walter Scott

MORE THAN CONQUERORS

BY
ARIADNE GILBERT

Illustrated

Essay Index Reprint Series

BOOKS FOR LIBRARIES PRESS
FREEPORT, NEW YORK

STANDARD BOOK NUMBER:
8369-1036-2

LIBRARY OF CONGRESS CATALOG CARD NUMBER:
68-58791

PRINTED IN THE UNITED STATES OF AMERICA

TO MY MOTHER

And all others who have fought and conquered
without a shot

"Fight on, my men," Sir Andrew sayes —
"A little I'm hurt, but yett not slaine,
I'll but lye downe and bleed awhile,
And then I'le rise and fight againe!"

TO MY READERS

This series of biographical sketches, published in *St. Nicholas*, was written for young people. Why have a preface at all, then — a thing young people never read? Well, the preface is a sign-post to their elders to warn them not to follow the road unless it tempts them with its windings or its friendly shade. Yet I hope the book is not distinctly juvenile. I have tried not to " write down " to my young readers.

No short sketch can pretend to be a complete " life." The best it can do is to leave a general impression of the man, to entice the reader to look further, and to know his hero better. But young people will not read tomes! And some older people have not the patience to read a long life in several thick volumes, even to make a friend.

The facts in these sketches are, of course, gathered from books and articles already published — a library of " lives and letters "; but they have been gathered lovingly and painstakingly, and combined in a new way. I acknowledge, as I put my labors into your hands, that I have used all sources freely. I hope I have given credit honestly. Only the combining is my own. And if I have succeeded in putting my readers into sympathy with my heroes, it is because I was first in sympathy with them, myself. It is like sharing friendships. To spoil your taste for trivialities, grow intimate with great men. Here is an invitation to hear them talk, to read their letters, to have them for life-companions. Through intimate companionship you will see their few weaknesses and their great strengths, their conquering struggles and their brave cheer.

"A biography," said Phillips Brooks, "is indeed a book; but far more than it is a book, it is a man. . . . Get the man, his hates, his loves, his dreams, his blundering hopes, his noble, hot, half-forged purposes, his faith, his doubt, get all of these in one vehement person clear before your eyes." And Phillips Brooks, a preacher, calls biographies the best sermons.

But these "best sermons" fall, like many other sermons, on heedless ears, unless they are intimate. In Boswell's book of supreme biography, the man is there — all of him. We see him, we hear him; he talks, he thinks, he acts, he even prays. If Johnson is laughable, as he tweaks off a lady's shoe at dinner or wipes his greasy fingers on the back of a dog, from his lounging-place in a coffee-house, he is also lovable as, almost without being conscious of it, he turns his house into a home for the homeless and gets complaints instead of thanks. By showing all sides of the man, Boswell has left us an immortal work of intimacy.

But turn from biography in general to this group of heroes in particular, and consider them guests in your house, made welcome not only for their great nobility, but for all their little personal ways. Emerson has his pie for breakfast and Beethoven his superb self-made coffee,— sixty beans to a cup. Phillips Brooks's voice, a little off the tune, rings out lustily while he takes his morning bath. Leave Stevenson's old hat on the peg, he hates to wear a new one; and arrange for Scott to ride horseback and Saint-Gaudens to swim. Perhaps Agassiz will spend the whole day in a bog hunting for turtle eggs. And so each is contentedly following his own hobby, and you are contentedly amused thinking of the great variety of natures that have come together under your roof.

Only through books can all these great men be your guests. Of different nations and of different callings, these conquerors were not all contemporaries, though all were famous within the last hundred years. A large proportion of them are American, for which an American does not apologize. Washington and the noble Robert E. Lee should have been included had I not limited myself to the heroes of peace, to conquerors not ranked by the world as soldiers.

The whole book should ring with the time-honored wisdom that " stumbling-blocks may become stepping-stones," and with that sturdy determination inscribed on the head of an old pickaxe, " Either I will find a way or make one."

Before us is a noble company of " hallowed failures " and difficult conquests. Brooks and Emerson failed in the school-room; Livingstone, in the pulpit; Thackeray wrote because his drawings were refused;

TO MY READERS

Scott turned to novel-writing because Byron had beaten him at verse. Out of the loss of early hope and love, Irving found sunlight enough to fill his old-bachelor home with other people's children, and with laughter; and Lamb, with his storm-driven sister always beside him, made himself a *hiding-place from the wind.*

There is a legend that the birds were created without wings and that their first wings were burdensome. The little creatures chirpingly begged to be freed from the new weight. They complained that the wings were too heavy for them to raise. Yet only by learning to lift their burdens did they gain the power to fly.

ARIADNE GILBERT

Plainfield, N. J., July 8, 1914.

CONTENTS

LIST OF ILLUSTRATIONS

I

BEETHOVEN

"Dædalus, though enclos:d in the labyrinth, invented wings which carried him into the air; oh! I also will find such wings."

Ludwig van Beethoven.

MORE
THAN CONQUERORS

I

THE DEAF MUSICIAN

IT was over a hundred and thirty years ago. The
neighbor across the way from the Beethovens,
who was standing in front of his comfortable home,
saw Ludwig, Carl, and Johann Beethoven turn in at
their gate and bravely help their staggering father up
the steps. He watched them solemnly. "Herr van
Beethoven has been drinking again," he thought.
Many times after that, he saw the same sight — the
three Beethoven boys almost lifting that sagging burden into the house.

But what wonderful music came through the open
door across the way! At his best, Herr van Beethoven sang beautifully. Ludwig, when he was only
four, had sat at the harpsichord in his father's lap,
rapt not in the fascination of flying fingers, but in
satisfied love of the music. Then Herr van Beethoven
had stopped, and, letting the baby hands take their turn
on the cold, white keys, had felt with a thrilling, bound-
ing confidence that no ordinary child touched the in-

3

strument. Out of it stole the same melody as his own. And so, when Ludwig was only four or five his father began his musical training, and later a big man named Pfeiffer, who lived with the Beethovens, gave him regular lessons. As the oldest son and a possible genius, Ludwig was to have his chance. While the Beethoven boys were playing, Herr Pfeiffer would come to the door and thunder, " *Ludwig, komm' ins Haus*"; and the child, sometimes crying, would stop his fun and stamp into the house to that dull practising. At times, they say, his teacher had to use something harsher than his big, harsh voice.

But once in doors Ludwig was not miserable; he handled the keys with love. Sometimes Herr Pfeiffer would pick up a sweet-voiced flute, and, standing there beside the boy, he too would play. And the people going by would stand still, and perhaps even Carl and Johann would stop their games to listen, too, for they were German boys, and music made them happy.

One day, the neighbors heard that the Beethovens had sold their linen and their silver service; another day, that much of the furniture and table-ware had been sold. Frau van Beethoven grew paler and paler, and the father kept on drinking. Sometimes Ludwig would go away to play at public concerts. At that time, no one knew that Herr van Beethoven, in order to gain a large audience, reported the child a year younger than he really was. He was such a little fellow for his age that this was easy to believe. When, " aged six," he was advertised to give a series of concerts in Cologne, he was really seven. But he was only ten when he made a concert tour through Holland with his mother, and he was only fourteen when he was appointed assistant to the court organist.

People used to love to have him " describe the character of some well known person " on the piano. He could do with the piano what a painter does with his brush.

Before Beethoven was out of his teens, his brave, good mother died. " There was once some one to hear me when I said ' Mutter '," thought the lonely boy. Before long, his father, who was less than a cipher, lost his position through drink, and so Ludwig was made head of the family, with the weight of his brothers' education and all his father's debts.

Hoping to have his genius recognized and perhaps to take a few lessons, he went from Bonn to Vienna to play before the great Mozart. But Mozart was absorbed in composing an opera; he did not want to be bothered. He looked at the short young man with the " snub nose " and thought little of him; heard him play, and still thought him commonplace. In fact, he believed that Beethoven had learned his pieces by heart just to show off. Then, on fire with disappointment, Beethoven asked Mozart to give him a subject, and, just as an author might make up a story on a given subject, he sat down and played a wonderful piece of music. The older genius was astounded. " This youth will some day make a noise in the world ! " he exclaimed.

Another story is told by Gelinek, a musical young Austrian who went one evening to a party where he and Beethoven played.

"How did the affair go off?" asked Gelinek's father the next morning.

"Oh, I shall never forget yesterday! The devil is in the young man. I never heard such playing. He improvised on a theme I gave him in such a manner as I never even heard Mozart. Then he played some of his own compositions, which are wonderful and magnificent beyond everything; he brings out of the piano tones and effects we have never dreamed of."

"What is his name?"

"He is a short, ugly, cross-looking young man," Gelinek continued excitedly, "whom Prince Lichnowski brought here from Germany some years ago, to learn composition from Haydn, Albrechtsburger, and Salieri; his name is Beethoven."

Before Beethoven was thirty he began to grow deaf. Think of it! Think of a painter losing his sight; never again to see the changing beauty of cloud and river; the chasing light on a field of waving grain; or the sparkle in a baby's eyes. It was as heart-breaking for a musician to grow deaf as for a painter to be struck blind. "The noblest part of me, my sense of hearing, has become very weak," Beethoven wrote in sorrowing confidence. "Please keep as a great secret what I have told you about my hearing." Then followed years of torment mingled with terrible sensitiveness, even to the point of running away for fear people would learn that he was deaf, and show pity in their faces. It was not possible for him to say: "Speak louder, shout, for I am deaf." "A feeling of hot anxiety" overwhelmed him, and at the same time a pathetic wistfulness, when he thought that perhaps his companions could hear "a distant flute" or a "shepherd singing." When he went to concerts, he had to lean forward close to the orchestra to get the sound. This sealing of his dearest sense must have made him feel like "a house half-ruined ere the lease be out."

With time, in spite of all his doctors, the humming in his ears grew worse. In vain he tried hot baths and blistering. At last, his deafness drove him to ear-trumpets, written conversations, and, saddest of all, terrible crashing discords,— an agony to those who heard.

It would be both impossible and misleading to systematize a life of Beethoven. Eccentric genius that he was, his life had next to no system. Though many of his days were much alike, domestic explosions of one kind or another broke into them and kept him harried and confused. We must think of him as seldom at peace. His youth was spent in the city of Bonn; his manhood in or near Vienna, with some of his summers at Baden. For reasons to be explained later, he was constantly changing lodgings. He never married and he never had a home, in any real sense, though his great, affectionate heart would have dearly loved one.

Now fretted by small suspicions and petty wants, now upborne by the power of great emotion, he was a wonderful combination of pygmy and giant. Judged by his letters, the veriest trifles made up life; judged by his music, life was too vast for our poor human groping. And so, one person called him "a growling old bear"; another, "the cloud-compeller of the world of music." Almost as helpless as a child, in some respects, he expected his friends to look after all sorts of things: wrote to Ries for half a dozen sewing needles, and to the ever patient Zmeskall for quills, a watch, a barometer, the cost of re-vamping his servant's boots, at last: "Please send me for a few hours the looking-glass which hangs next to your window; mine is broken;" and even: "Send me at once your servant."

If ever a man needed a guardian it was Beethoven. Wholesome Frau Streicher, the wife of one of his friends, did all she could to help him in his many domestic difficulties. "Yes, indeed," he wrote her, "all this housekeeping is still without keeping, and much resembles an *allegro di confusione.*" To her, the poor man turned for dusters, blankets, linen, scissors, knives, and servants; and to her he complained of having to "carry in his head so many pairs of trousers, stockings, and shoes."

"Man stands but little above other animals, if his chief enjoyments are limited to the table," Beethoven would often say. Under inspiration, for days to-

gether, he " forgot all about time and rest and food."
On the other hand, when he did eat, he was particular.
He generally made his own coffee for breakfast, allow-
ing sixty beans to a cup, and counting them as precisely
as if coffee was all important. Not only was he, like
most other Germans, very fond of soup, but he thought
himself the highest authority on that great subject,
and would argue hotly on the best way to make it.
" If Schindler had declared a bad soup good, after
some time he would get a note to this effect: ' I do
not value your judgment about the soup in the least, *it
is bad,* " — or perhaps a savory sample to prove Beethoven's knowledge. Indeed, Germany's mighty composer made very superior soup!

" There is music in running water," says Van Dyke.
To Beethoven there surely was; but his landladies
must have regretted it. If, for any reason, he could
not go out of doors, he had a way of creating inspiration of his own. He would go to the wash-bowl,
" pour several jugs " of water over his wrists, and
dabble there till his clothes were drenched. If this had
been all, no one else would have cared; but often, in
his absent-minded rapture, he poured out a great deal
more water than the bowl would hold, and, before long,
buxom old Frau von R——, who roomed below him,
would find her ceiling dripping. To her there was no
" music in running water ", and she took pains to say
as much to the landlady. And then there would be
one more change of lodging for Beethoven. Often,

when he moved, he would leave part of his things behind, and sometimes he was paying for " two, three,
and at one time four, dwelling-places at once."

" He has three sets of apartments in which he al-
ternately secretes himself," said a friend —" one in
the country, one in the town, and a third on the ram-
parts."

One day, a ten-year-old boy was taken to see Beethoven and this is his memory of the visit:

" We mounted five or six stories high, . . . and were
announced by a rather dirty-looking servant. In a
very desolate room, with papers and articles of dress
strewn in all directions, bare walls, a few chests, hardly
a chair except the rickety one standing by the piano,
there was a party of six or eight people. Beethoven
was dressed in a jacket and trousers of long, dark
goat's hair. They at once reminded me of ' Robinson
Crusoe ', which I had just been reading. He had a
shock of jet-black hair, standing straight upright."

Beethoven called his servants, who came and went
continually, by such names as: " horrid animal ", " old
child ", " big swine ", " thief ", " witch ", and even
" devil." " Nany has quite changed since I threw
half-a-dozen books at her head," he wrote proudly.
But, humbled all too soon: " Would you undertake
now to advise me how I can generally get comfortable
meals at home? The servant lost a pair of socks out
of the last washing." And then he begged for " a
good cook able to patch shirts." Too often he was
" out at elbows." Doubtless his servants did not love

him; but doubtless many of them were at fault. One
of them used the " Grand Mass " to wrap up Beethoven's boots and shoes and kitchen kettles. When
he found it, several pages were not only rumpled
and dirty but torn in half.

But at last came the " quick-sailing frigate ", to be
his housekeeper,— and the servant who drank and
stole, and the one who made a face when Beethoven
asked her to bring up wood, and the one who could
" no longer see, smell, or taste ", so that his " poor
stomach was always in danger ", all were forgotten
in the peace of her capable reign.

And so, the frets were lost, some of them, and the
great musician could still be his giant self.

When Frau Streicher was in Baden, Beethoven
wrote to her. " If you wander through the mysterious
fir-forests, think it was there Beethoven often poetized,
or, as it is called, composed." " Strolling among the
mountain clefts and valleys " with a sheet of music
paper in his hand, he would " scribble a lot for the
sake of bread and money — daub-work for the sake
of money ", so that he might " stand the strain of a
great work."

Never understood, that great, mysterious soul with
its tremendous inner struggles must have suffered in-
curable loneliness. Indeed, Beethoven was doubly
solitary — through deafness and through greatness.
In all seasons and in all weathers, beneath the open
heavens, he sought society in winds and lightning, as
well as gurgling brooks and restful moonlight. Away

into the woods he would go. The hurry of business, the clatter of wagons and of many feet — these things suffocated his inspiration. Solitude gave it life. Tempests filled him with power; clouds with their faraway peace; but not even in his greatest music could he utter it all. And so he had the pain, not only of loneliness, but of being forever unsatisfied. After his deafness came on, he could not hear the wind in the pine-trees, or the singing bird that soared up, up into the blue; but he could see the green boughs bend, and watch the joyous flight, and he could *remember*. In his little note-book, he would feverishly jot down his ideas, waiting a while to let the melody and its variations settle, in all the perfection of the gift. Then at dusk, half-afraid that it might all slip away, his hat gone and his bushy head bowed, he would stride home through the city streets, seeing and hearing no one, not even his best friends.

"Just Beethoven!" they would laugh, getting out of his mad way. "Only his body is in the world!" or some such thing. Though he had lost nothing in the woods but his hat, very likely strangers thought he had lost his wits. On the contrary, he had found a wonderful something that made his heart swell. In that heart a great symphony struggled for creation and release, and all the elements of earth and sky cried out to be immortalized in music.

"God has a few of us whom He whispers in the ear;
The rest may reason and welcome; 't is we musicians know."

When Beethoven reached home, he dashed in, and, keeping his hat still on (if he *happened* not to have lost it) and throwing his coat anywhere, he rushed to the piano. There, leaning low over the keys, to catch all the beauty his deafness would allow, he played rapturously, not knowing who or where he was, not knowing, above all, that a crowd had gathered outside the forgotten open door to hear the great free concert.

Just as his eccentricity scattered his servants and enraged his landladies, so it broke out on his friends, his orchestra, his pupils, in a hundred hot-headed actions. We laugh; but the common world laughing at a towering genius is like a sparrow scoffing at an eagle's flight: the strong-winged bird that soars so high moves over the ground with none of the sparrow's grace. Yet we will laugh!

They say Beethoven " seldom laid his hands upon anything without breaking it: thus, he several times emptied the contents of the inkstand into the neighboring piano."

His friends had to be very patient and believing. Von Breuning, Ries, and Schindler were repeatedly tested by his shifting trust and suspicion. There would be a terrible word-explosion or a letter of the never-speak-again kind, and then " warm out of the heart ", but in abominably illegible handwriting, would gush a little note begging for forgiveness and the same old place in their affections. It was a fragment of the child left in him. " I fly to you, . . . Your contrite, faithful, and loving friend, Beethoven." "I know I have rent thy heart." Then, after pages of penitent pleading: "Now perhaps thou wilt fly back into my arms." Notes of two successive days read: "Do not come any more to me. You are a false fellow"; and "You are an honorable fellow. . . . So come this afternoon to me." One day he calls Schindler "arch-scoundrel", later, "Best of Friends" or "Trust-worthy one, I kiss the hem of your coat." This is one unique invitation: "You can come to midday meal, bring your provisions with you — be ready — we are ready."

Once, in the middle of a public concert, when his orchestra had not pleased him, he stopped, quite as if he was giving a lesson, and shouted, "Begin again! From the beginning!" The orchestra obeyed. He never treated a lord with a whit more respect than a peasant. When Duke Raimer came late to his music lesson, Beethoven revenged himself on the young man's fingers.

"Why are you so impatient?" asked the Duke.

"You make me lose my time in the anteroom and now I cannot get patient again," answered Beethoven. After that, Duke Raimer never kept him waiting. As we can imagine, the tediousness of counting his pupils' time wore terribly on the great composer. He did it for bread. But rather often he excused himself, on the ground of illness, from lessons to the Archduke Rudolph. "Your Imperial Highness", he called him, or oftener "Y. I. H." The same old reason crept again and again into his profoundly respectful letters. We must remember, however, that Beethoven suffered for years from rheumatism, indigestion, and finally from dropsy. He seems never to have been really well.

Just as eccentric in public as in private, when he led an Orchestra, he would make himself smaller and smaller to compel softened sounds. Then, as he wanted the sounds louder, his head would " gradually rise up as if out of an abyss; and when the full force of the united instruments broke upon the ear, raising himself on tiptoe, he looked to be of gigantic stature, and, with both his arms floating about in undulating motion, seemed as if he would soar to the clouds. He was all motion, no part of him remained inactive."

Few things are more irritating to musical people than drifting attention. It is as if, sensitive to every thought and feeling, the power to play leaves the musician's hands if his listeners are not with him. A frivolous audience scattered the great Beethoven's inspiration like wind-blown leaves. And he could not recall it! As a rule, though, he did not care to; he gave way to justified impatience. One day, during a duet by Beethoven and Ries, some young people began to talk and laugh in the next room. Suddenly Beethoven stopped, grabbed Ries's hands from the piano, and, springing to his feet, exclaimed, " I do not play for such swine!" No one could persuade him to finish the piece.

" You prelude a great while; when are you going

to begin?" was his tart comment when Himmer com-
peted with him in improvising. It sounds bitter and
conceited, but Beethoven was equally hearty in his
appreciation and in offers of assistance. "Truly in
Schubert dwells a divine fire," he said. He admired
the "scene-painting" of Rossini; but particularly the
work of Mozart, Bach, and Handel. And he was un-
stinting in his praise of "The Messiah." "Handel
is the greatest composer who ever lived," he sweepingly
declared. "I could uncover my head and kneel upon
his grave." One letter, practical, loving, tender, he
wrote to help raise money for Bach's daughter, who
was "aged and in want." He asked earnestly for
help —"before this daughter of Bach dies, before this
brook dries up, and we can no longer supply it with
water." (*Bach* is German for brook.) Beethoven
was apt to make puns in his letters, just as he was apt
to begin them with a bar of music.

With his hands too full of his own work, he wrote,
nobly and freely, "With pleasure, my dear Drieberg,
will I look through your compositions, and if you
think me able to say anything to you about them, I
am heartily ready to do it." And he wrote to a little
girl of eight or ten who "raved over him": "If, my
dear Emilie, you at any time wish to know about something, write without hesitation to me. The true artist
is not proud, he unfortunately sees that art has no
limits; he feels darkly how far he is from the goal.—
I would, perhaps, rather come to you and your people,
than to many rich folks who display inward poverty."

Just such a democratic spirit as this ruled his life. Passion and pride moved him to all sorts of unexpected acts. He refused to take off his hat to royalty. When his brother Johann wrote him a letter signed Landowner, Beethoven signed his answer Brain-owner. When he was asked in court to prove his right to his title of nobility, he said, raising his rough head grandly and flashing his brilliant little eyes, "My nobility is here and here," and he pointed to his head and heart. In his warm hero-worship he had dreamed that Napoleon meant to make France a republic, and he intended to dedicate his "Heroic Symphony" to him. But, just as he was completing it, he heard that the Emperor had been crowned. With mingled passion and disappointment, he tore off the title page bearing the word "Bonaparte", and flung the whole thing to the floor. "After all, he's nothing but an ordinary mortal!" he exclaimed bitterly. And so, though the original manuscript still bears faint traces of the fallen hero's name, it was published merely "To the Memory of a Great Man."

As Louis Nohl says, the march in this symphony gathers into one picture "the glad tramp of warlike hosts, the rhythm of trampling steeds, the waving of standards, and the sound of trumpets."

To Beethoven, the greatest element in music was spiritual. Not only did he long to lift the audience heavenward, but every one of the orchestra too. His own feeling was so immense that he judged the best musical performance as nothing if it had no soul.

" Read Shakespeare," he said to some one who wanted to play. Those who would interpret Beethoven must be full of poetry. For that reason, those who are mere piano gymnasts, no matter how good, had better try shallower compositions.

There is the music of imitation, and there is the music of feeling. One of Beethoven's early teachers had complained, in despair: " He will never do anything according to rule; he has learnt nothing." But even then the young genius was *feeling* something no follower of rules could teach. Before him lay a conquest of sound so glorious that strong men would bow their heads and sob aloud at its power.

> " Like a mighty heart the music seemed,
> That yearns with melodies it cannot speak."

Sir George Grove said of Beethoven's " Funeral March ": " If ever horns talked like flesh and blood, they do here." That solemn march stirs us to the depths. But hard labor had gone hand in hand with feeling. Though Beethoven could neither play nor write formally, he often worked for years on a piece of music, changing, cutting, and improving. They say that of his Opera " Fidelio " he made as many as eighteen different versions.

He had the power of imitation, too, though that was not his greatest strength. As we can see the sunlight flash on the leaping fish in Schubert's " Trout ", so we can see a heavenly shimmer in Beethoven's " Moonlight Sonata." His " Pastoral Symphony "

" After all, he's nothing but an ordinary mortal! " he
exclaimed bitterly

carries us from the scene by the brook, through the gathering of the peasants, a thunder-storm, a shepherd's song, and a final rejoicing. We hear the murmur of the brook and the mutter of thunder; the violins make flashes of lightning; the flute, oboe, and clarinet mimic the nightingale, quail, and cuckoo. One part of the Symphony pictures "a rustic merry-making, the awkward, good-natured gambols of peasants", and one old fellow who sits on a barrel and is able to play only three tones.

The great, lonely composer gave and craved much love. But no friend, no *one* ever held a place in his heart equal to his nephew Carl's. At eight, the boy had been left by his father's will to his Uncle Ludwig, and immediately that uncle assumed all a father's responsibility and love. His one great thought, aside from music, was Carl. Much of his music, even, was written to get money for the boy's education. We follow the uncle through all his early hopes. Believing he saw scientific genius "in the dear pledge intrusted" to him, he sent the boy to a fine school and gave him, besides, lessons in drawing, French, and music. For years he chose him the best tutors, watched over him like a mother, sent his clothes to the wash, measured his feet for goloshes, and called him all kinds of pet names: "lovely lad", "my Carl", "dear little rascal", "best ragamuffin", "dear jewel", but, oftenest of all, "my son." How willingly he adjusted his own program to suit the boy's convenience! He believed he found in the handsome little fellow all

the things he longed for: honor, tenderness, affection;
and he vowed to do his "best for him to the end of his
life" and leave him everything after death. "O
God," he sighed, "hear my prayer for the future, to
be together with my Carl." "The stem is still pliable,
but, if time is lost, it will grow crooked in spite of the
guiding hand of the gardener."

And the time of crookedness came.

To those who read Beethoven's letters, even the awful, increasing deafness seems less cruel than Carl's
ingratitude. The empty-hearted fellow had no loyalty. As he grew older, he grew calculating and defiant. It is not too hard to say that he loved his uncle's
money, not his uncle. At twenty, he was publicly
expelled from the University, and later sent to prison,
his uncle getting him out and securing him a commission in the army. With all this, the selfish nephew
even begrudged Beethoven his society. The "father,"
in his wistful loneliness, wrote him the most pathetic
letters. From him, helpless, dependent, pleading, came
requests for shaving-soap, razors, newspapers,— little
comforts like that, and then: "Whenever you can on
Sundays, do come. I would, however, not keep you
away from anything, if I were only sure that the Sunday is spent well without me" . . . But . . . "I
should be so glad to have a human heart about me in
my solitude."

How often the great composer must have looked,
from his sick-room window, into the street so welcom-

ing to Carl! The long days lagged by, and many
suns set gloriously behind the trees; but Carl did not
come. What Beethoven wanted most of all was that
the fellow should be straightforward; that he should
deceive him in nothing; that there should be confidence
between them. Carl's life, however, would not bear
the clear, straight gaze of any honest eyes; he knew
it; and so he stayed away.

Meanwhile, " in his remote house on the hill," the
" Solitary of the Mountain " fought out his final conquest. On his writing-table stood his framed motto:
" I am all that is, all that was, and all that shall be:
no mortal man hath my veil uplifted." " He had
learned in suffering what he taught in song." His life
had been one battle after another, all the way: the child
Ludwig had begun by caring for a drunken father and
shouldering big debts; the man had driven himself
through humdrum lessons. Then came the approach
of closing deafness, and, in the darkness of desperation, Beethoven had looked up and said: " Art, when
persecuted, finds everywhere a place of refuge;
Dædalus, though enclosed in the labyrinth, invented
wings which carried him into the air; oh! I also will
find such wings." Lonely for Carl and hungry for his
own music, he said to himself: " Poor Beethoven,
there is no external happiness for you! You must
create your own happiness." " O God, grant me
strength to conquer myself," he prayed. And so he
determined to give to others what he, himself, could

not get — a wonderful rapture of sound; he would not leave this earth till he had revealed what lay within him.   For this, he had been made by God.

His tempestuous fight ended March 26th, 1827, after a long illness.   He died in the midst of a great thunder-storm.   None of his dearest friends were with him. The flinty Carl was not there; Von Breuning and Schindler had gone out on errands.   Beethoven's clock stopped, as it had often done when it lightened. But the warring elements had been the composer's life-long friends, and often before had carried his soul above this little world.   In the midst of the flashes and the rumbling, he thought, " I shall hear in heaven." He might have thought that he would be immortalized on earth!   Twenty great composers bore Beethoven to his last sleeping-place, and twenty others carried torches in the great, somber procession.   " No mourn-ing wife, no son, no daughter wept at his grave; but a world wept at it."

II
LAMB

" ' We are not of Alice, nor of thee, nor are we children at all. The children of Alice call Bartrum father. We are nothing; less than nothing, and dreams'— and immediately awaking, I found myself quietly seated in my bachelor armchair, where I had fallen asleep, with the faithful Bridget unchanged by my side."

Charles Lamb.

II

PARTNERS IN PLUCK

TO little Charles Lamb everything around him
must have seemed old. He lived in an old
house in an old street in the old city of London. All
his books were dingy and queer. He was ten years
younger than his sister, Mary, and eleven years
younger than his brother, John; and next to his
brother and sister and father and mother, the best
friends he had were old Mr. Salt, old Aunt Hetty,
and his Grandmother Field. But there is a sort of
gentle tranquillity about old surroundings that the
shine of newness cannot give,— and as for old people, what little boys to please other little boys will do
as much as a grandmother?

Charles was born in a small room in the Inner
Temple in the year of our American Revolution.
When he was still very little, before he knew much
more than the alphabet, he would curl himself up
in a corner with the "Book of Martyrs" on his lap
and read its grim pictures of wonderful people who
preferred to die rather than give up their religion.
Charles felt a fascinated awe in the pictures of burn-
ings at the stake. With his little hand laid boldly

on the flames, he thought them hot and glowed with
holy pride that he, too, was dying for his faith.

When Charles and Mary visited in the Hertford-
shire country, they had a beautiful time, for they
were partners in play before they were partners in
pluck. Sometimes they went to see their Great Aunt
Gladman at Mackery End[1]; sometimes, Grandmother
Field at Blakesware. When Charles was six or
seven, Mary was sixteen or seventeen, and so she was
old enough to take him on short trips.

How fresh the fields looked after murky London!
They were full of sparkling flowers. The sun and
grass and sky seemed all new-born. It must have
been Mackery End which Mary described in " Mrs.
Leicester's School ": " hens feeding all over the
yard " and " little yellow ducklings with a mother
hen. She was so frightened if they went near the
water." Then she told how the good-natured spotted
cow let the children stroke her during the milking,
and how, though they hunted for hens' eggs, they
were never allowed to rob the birds. It was probably Aunt Gladman who said the " little birds would
not sing any more, if their eggs were taken away
from them." " A hen," she said, was " a hospitable
bird, and always laid more eggs than she wanted, on
purpose to give them to her mistress to make pud-
dings and custards with." In currant and goose-
berry time, old Spot, the shepherd, used to come in
from sheep-shearing to toast his face and feet by the

[1] Mary is Bridget Elia in Mackery End.

crackling fire, while the crickets chirped in the chimney-corner, and the room was filled with flickering light. Beautiful, peaceful Mackery End!

In one of Charles's Elia Essays we have the Blakesware picture,— lonely, but full of child-content. Grandmother Field was the paid housekeeper of the old mansion, and probably her thin little grandson, with the wistful brown eyes and queer stammer, was hardly noticed by the great people of the house. But their indifference could not cage his soaring imagination. The little boy dreamed long dreams. Everything, indoors and out, was his, as if he had been sole heir: the tapestried bedroom, the Marble Hall with its mosaics and " stately busts ", the faded banner on the stairs with glory in its tattered folds. His was the fruit-garden, with its " sun-baked southern wall " and " murmuring pigeons "; his, the dear old gallery full of family portraits. How he and Mary loved to roam there,— she wishing for a fairy's power to " call the children down from their frames to play."

From the magic of this Blakesware world, the children crept back into the dusky corners of their London home. In a few years Mary began to take in sewing for a living, and Charles was sent to " The Blue Coat School," called, too, " Christ's Hospital."

Though this school was for poor boys, it bore no brand of Charity. Instead, every boy felt proud to be in a school as honored as it was old. For one thing, he could not get in without some kind of " pull,"— as we should say to-day; that is, some man with money, had to vouch for his character, and promise to pay damages, if necessary, to the amount of $500. (Where boys play together, something does *sometimes* get broken.) A written statement was sent with each boy saying that his father was too poor to educate him. Probably Charles Lamb got into Christ's through his father's employer, Samuel Salt.

Within the last few years the fine old school has been moved from the heart of London, to the more open country; but in Lamb's day any one could have seen the Blue-Coat Boys playing in the solemnly-neighbored courtyard, with Newgate Prison opposite, Christ Church on one side, and an old burying-ground on the other. Perhaps, since ball was forbidden, Charles played battle-dore and shuttle-cock, and we can imagine him running about, hatless like the others and like them wearing a long blue coat something like a wrapper, a broad white band for a collar, bright yellow stockings, and a red leather belt into which he probably tucked the awkward skirt that *would* cling round his ankles when he ran. Below the skirt came strong, brown corduroy trousers, and below them, the long, slim, yellow legs looked even longer and slimmer than they were.

From the noisy crowd we might have singled out Lamb's best friend — a quiet boy, Samuel Taylor Coleridge. They were "new boys" together. Coleridge was two years older than Lamb, and brighter in almost every way. "The inspired Charity boy," they used to call him. But young Lamb had no such

nickname. Though he, too, could turn his Latin into
graceful English, except for this, the most striking
things about him were his thoughtful brown eyes
and his bad stutter — which was never wholly cured.
Coleridge, on the other hand, was positively brilliant.

In outward circumstances, however, he was less
happy than Lamb. His family lived too far away
for him to go home, like Charles, for the half or
whole holidays, and he had no Grandmother Field.
His best fun came through excursions to the New
River when the boys would "strip under the first
warmth of the sun, and wanton like young dace in
the streams."

At the Blue Coat School their appetites were
" damped ", not satisfied. To Coleridge every day
had its dish. Monday brought the faithful return
of tasteless "blue milk porritch"; and Saturday,
" pease soup, coarse and choking ", while young Lamb
on home holidays could vary his diet with " a slice of
extraordinary bread and butter from the hot loaf of
the Temple "; and sometimes Aunt Hetty, Lamb's
second-mother — or third, if we count motherly little
Mary, would " toddle " to school to bring him good-
ies. As she seated herself on the " old cole-hole
steps ", opened her apron, and took out her " bason ",
Coleridge would stand enviously by, " feeling alone
among six hundred playmates," and Lamb, though he
liked the gift, would feel just a little ashamed of the
giver; and, years later, bitterly ashamed of that shame.
Once he gave an old beggar the " six-penny whole

plum-cake " which Aunt Hetty had brought, smoking hot. He cried about it afterwards, not wholly for the cake, though he was not above the love of cake, but because he had cheated her; she had never saved her pennies for that old man, but in her generous love, had planned for small Charles Lamb to eat that cake. And he knew it.

If he was going to give his cake away at all, he might better have given it to one of the other boys instead of to that lazy beggar. There was one poor little fellow at school who used to save the scraps of meat left on the plates, carry them to his room, and hide them there. One " leave day " two of the other boys, who had already condemned him as half-ghoul, half-miser, saw him glide, solitary, through the great gate, carrying something in a blue-checked handkerchief. Too curious to resist, they slunk after him, through the gate, down the street, and up the four dark flights of stairs of an old house. There they found the boy's father and mother, hungrier than himself. From that day, to the credit of the boys at Christ's, the half-miser was counted as a hero.

From Coleridge, Lamb, Leigh Hunt, and others, we get combination pictures of some of the teachers at this school. The Rev. Mr. Field " came late of a morning; went away soon in the afternoon; and used to walk up and down, languidly bearing his cane, as if it were a lily." During his classes the school-room had the soothing air of " summer slumbers." Not so, stout little Boyer, with his " close and cruel " eye, condemning spectacles, and hands "ready for execution." Boyer was known by his wigs: "one, serene, smiling, fresh powdered, betokening a mild day"; the other, "old, discolored, angry", threatening storm.

"Od's my life, Sirrah," he would roar, "I have a great mind to whip you." Then, after waiting long enough for the culprit to "forget the context", he would yell, "*and* I WILL *too!*"

This is Lamb's and Hunt's picture. Coleridge, with more zeal for learning, found Boyer as sensible as he was severe. He was a keen, though merciless critic of compositions: "Harp? Harp? Lyre?" he would demand. "Pen and ink, boy, you mean! Muse, boy, Muse? Your nurse's daughter, you mean! Pierian spring? Oh, aye! the cloister-pump, I suppose!"

One day, when Coleridge had just come back from his holidays, Boyer found him crying. "Boy! the school is your father! Boy! the school is your mother! Boy! the school is your brother! Boy! the school is your sister! the school is your first cousin, and your second cousin, and all the rest of your relations! Let's have no more crying." Wouldn't any boy be convinced by such sympathetic tenderness?

With time, however, all these school troubles grew smaller and smaller, to vanish, at last, entirely, or to be remembered dimly, as mere jokes; while one thing won at school would last forever — the beautiful friendship of Lamb with Coleridge. "Oh, it is pleasant," Lamb said years later, "as it is rare, to find the same arm linked in yours at forty which at thirteen helped it turn over the Cicero."

Lamb's days at Christ's Hospital ended when he was only fourteen. Then his old friend, Mr. Salt, got him a position at the South Sea House. Here, beginning at a salary of about two dollars and a half a week, he stayed for three years. When he left the South Sea House, it was to work at a weary, monotonous clerkship in the East India House. For the first three years in this position, Lamb had no salary at all; it was considered privilege enough to learn the business. Once learned, however, his work was very fairly paid, and he was raised steadily and generously.

Though the office took his hours, it could not take his heart. Devotion to his home and family, particularly to his sister Mary, was his very life, compared to which his business, his love of books, and even his friends were of small account. And so, to understand him at all, we must think of him as at home; and a sad, hard place it was — to bear that name. Besides Mary, there were his father, once merry, but now an old man too feeble to work; his invalid mother, unable to walk; his brother John, who, though he had had some business success, chose to live independently and to enjoy life by lightly shirking its responsibilities; and old Aunt Hetty, bringer of his boyhood's plum-cake. Aunt Hetty had a small income; but, except for that, all the money that came into the Lamb household was earned by Charles's bookkeeping and by Mary's sewing. The oldest brother had left home,

without once offering to help. For the two who
shared the load, it was a long, dreary struggle: for
him, the desk all day and wearisome games of cards
with his father at night; for her, nerve-wearing indoor life with two infirm old people. (She even slept
with her mother.)

As the nettling littlenesses of house- and needle-
work grew more and more irksome, Mary weakened
in unseen ways. Still she endured until one day, September 22, 1796, when Charles was only twenty-one,
there came a sudden, violent breakdown,— a fearful
tragedy — which one may dimly imagine from
Lamb's short letter to Coleridge, the only friend to
whom he could turn in his overwhelming grief: "My
poor dear, dearest sister in a fit of insanity has been the
death of her own mother. I was at hand only in time
enough to snatch the knife out of her grasp. My
poor father was slightly wounded, and I am left to
take care of him and my aunt. Write as religious a
letter as possible, but no mention of what is gone and
done with. With me, 'the former things are passed
away,' and I have something more to do than feel.
God Almighty have us all in His keeping!"

How his friend longed to take him away from
London and the ever-depressing walls of his "home"
to the uplifting hills of the lake region! "I wish
above measure," he wrote, "to have you for a little
while here; no visitants shall blow on the nakedness
of your feelings; you shall be quiet, and your spirit
may be healed. I charge you, my dearest friend, not

to encourage gloom or despair. You are a temporary sharer in human miseries that you may be an
eternal partaker of the Divine Nature."

But of course Lamb could not make the proposed
visit. There was for him no little holiday; there could
be no hours under the strengthening hills; or in the
sound companionship of his best-loved friend. Not
even for a few days could he drop the burden. He
must act,— stand at the wheel and steer. He took
Mary to a private asylum at Islington, and, when business hours were over, made a home, as well as he could,
for his father and Aunt Hetty. For a little while
Aunt Hetty visited a rich relation, but she was soon
returned as " indolent and mulish."

It was a heavy weight and a fixed weight for a young
man just out of boyhood; but he bore it, and perhaps
only the one friend knew how his heart yearned sometimes for his sheltered youth. But he must be a man
now, and a man for life. And so, back to that " thorn
of a desk " all day and the dull games of cards at
night.

Imagine ourselves going with him some morning to
the East India House, to the office where he clerked
for the best hours of his life.

" I notice, Mr. Lamb," comments one of his supe-
riors, " that you come very late every morning."

" Yes, but just see how early I go," is Lamb's logical
answer.

Another day, one of the heads of the department
asked:

" Pray, Mr. Lamb, what are you about? "

" Forty, next birthday."

" I don't like your answer."

" Nor I your question."

De Quincey has given us the best description of the circumstances under which Lamb worked. He sat on a high stool at a high desk, railed in — in a kind of pen, with five other " quill-driving gentlemen "— from the main room. When De Quincey called, Lamb's first greeting was an unforgettable smile. Then, so as not to converse from a height, he began to dismount, turning his back as one would to come down a ladder, assuring De Quincey that he was not going to " fly ", and laughing heartily as he made his steep descent.

Though he says comparatively little about his business, even to his best friends, it is easy to imagine how tedious he found it,— that young man, with his love of merriment, his strong impulse to write, his quivering fear of home disaster, all mixed up in mind and heart. No wonder that his " spirits showed gray before his hair "; no wonder if he found the single days at Christmas and at Easter too brief to commemorate the seasons, and the one week of summer too short to repair his strength. Frequently, like many business-men of to-day, he had to stay at his office till almost seven o'clock every day for a week or so, " starving . . . without my dinner," and often, then, some young man hanger-on,— one of many to feel Lamb's charm,— would walk home with him. " The burs stuck to him," and, though " they were good and loving burs," he would have been as comfortable burless. "I am never C. L., but always C. L. & Co.," he exclaimed. Young would-be writers pestered him. "One of them accompanies me home, lest I should be solitary for a moment; he at length takes his welcome leave at the door; up I go, mutton on table, hungry as a hunter . . . knock at the door . . . in comes somebody, to prevent my eating alone!—a process absolutely necessary to my poor, wretched digestion. Oh, the pleasure of eating alone!—eating my dinner alone! let me think of it."

Meanwhile, old Mr. Lamb, who had been sitting round through all the empty day planning Charles's evening full of cribbage, could hardly wait for his son to finish his meal, and, if the younger man showed the least reluctance to begin those "repeated games" would grumble out, "If you won't play with me, you might as well not come home at all."

Within three years after Mary's necessary exile, Aunt Hetty and Mr. Lamb both died, and then Charles, who was perfectly fearless for himself, brought his sister back home. So it was that they wrote the "Shakespeare Tales", as well as much else, in partnership — she managing the comedies, and he, the tragedies,— the work being divided so as to keep her mind only on happy things. In some of their other books it is hard to tell where he laid down the pen and she took it up. Meanwhile even the wearisome business life was turned by Lamb into something sunny. Little by little he dropped into writing for the papers,—

poems or bits of prose,— anything that darted into
his mind. " The very parings of a counting-house,"
he said, " are in some sort the setting up of an author." The " Old Benchers of the Inner Temple,"
the " South Sea House," and the " Superannuated
man " are nothing but descriptions of the old men he
knew on the street or in the office. Piece together his
essays and his letters and there is his autobiography
— half sad, half playful. He takes our arm, in his
intimate friendliness, and with him we laugh and re-
flect over all the little things that make the mighty
world. Finding interest in trifles was one of his great
gifts. He turned the common things of every day
into literature and made them live. His " works "
shine on our book shelves,— a ten-volume set; but
these were really his " recreations." He who first
wrote hiding behind the name of " Elia ", called his
works " the ledgers in the office." " There is nothing
of the author about me but hunger."

Some lives brim with variety, others with drudgery.
Aside from the over-shadowing gloom, whatever novelty there was in Charles Lamb's life he put there by
his own sparkling interpretation. Of course, if frequent movings and change of address meant novelty,
he had that. Mary's illness sometimes forced a move.
As she grew older, her breakdowns lasted longer and
came closer together. But neither of these partners in
pluck would let the sunlight of the present be dimmed
by a future cloud. Though both were all awake to
cruel facts, they were both all alive to the need of joy-

ousness. After each of her recoveries, she seemed
better in every way,— as if the absence of the mind had
kept its temple fresh.   She had a quick wit, clear brain,
and particularly strong memory.   Healing brought
with it marvelous serenity and new vigor.   She
wanted and needed work, and, as the brother and sister worked together, she sagged no more than he.   He
spoke of her as a " prop." In their " sort of double
singleness ", the partnership was as sweet as it was
solid.   Charles said they were as inseparable as " gum-
boil and tooth-ache."   They shared letters and they
shared friends; they shared reading and writing and
vacation.   After wandering about the old grounds of
Oxford and Cambridge in the holidays, they were full
of imaginary learning.   " Mary rode home triumph-
ing as if she had been graduated."

Office and home then made up Lamb's humdrum
days — dull enough they were, all of them, in the eyes
of dull-hearted hundreds.   Boil down the bare facts
and we have his thirty-six years in business as a common clerk, " chained to the desk's dull wood," his
browsings of leisure moments in old book-stores and
old print-shops, evenings spent in reading, writing,
smoking, card-playing, and talking,— cozy evenings
with fire-light and candle-light and Mary; and — that
was all,— that, and the fun and the pathos and the
measureless fidelity with which the old bachelor
watched over the old maid who was at once his care,
his chum, his treasure, and his life.   His greatest conquests were lowly ones.   At twenty-one, he began a

Charles Lamb

life-long campaign to conquer domestic difficulties. The giant Atlas held up the sky; this slim little man went about his day's business with a rainbow somewhere underneath his coat, that two hearts — and often many more — might grow strong in its promise.

The gloom overhanging him must not darken this sketch. He would not have wished it to. He smiled back at the blue sky above his head and he buried life's pathos in humor. Lamb's friends would take any amount of teasing from him. They laughed, and felt no hurt. He was like a bee bearing honey but no sting; or, as he said of another, "All his whips were rods of roses."

When Martin Burney lounged back from a visit to the veal-pie and seated himself at the card table, Lamb quietly commented,

"M-Martin, if d-dirt was trumps, what a hand you'd hold!"

"Charles, have you ever heard me preach?" asked Coleridge.

"I've never heard you do anything else," came as swiftly as the stutter would allow.

And when Wordsworth said, "I believe I could write like Shakespeare, if I had a mind to try it", "Yes, n-nothing is w-wanting but the m-mind," was Lamb's equally keen answer.

"You rascally old Lake poet," he once called Wordsworth, and it is whispered that another time he even pulled Wordsworth's nose!

When Hazlitt's little boy was born, Lamb wrote:

"Well, my blessing and heaven's be upon him, and make him like his father, with something a better temper and a smoother head of hair."

He and Mary made a fine team at teasing. Even when she had grown to look like a Quakerish old lady, he would slap her on the back, like a boy comrade. Though she was strikingly feminine, with her soft voice, small hands, busy with sewing or knitting, gray gown, and snowy kerchief, and though she was little and bent and had grown deaf, he treated her with a kind of tender roughness, as if, a "boy man" himself, he was afraid she might begin to feel old. Once when some one, out of courtesy, placed a comfortable arm-chair for her, he exclaimed, pulling the chair away:

"Don't take it, Mary. It looks as if you were going to have a tooth drawn."

One day he wrote a letter for her, explaining (sure that she would read his explanation): "The truth is, she writes such a pimping, mean, detestable hand, that she is ashamed of the formation of her letters." The words go "staggering up and down shameless as drunkards in the day-time. Her very blots are not bold like this (illustrated by a bold blot), but poor smears" (illustrated by a smear). He called himself, though, "the worst folder-up of a letter in the world, except certain Hottentots, in the land of Caffre, who never fold up their letters at all."

Don't imagine that Mary failed to fire back her fun. Laughingly she wrote of Charles's ear for music (or lack of it):

"Of common tunes he knows not anything
Nor 'Rule, Britannia' from 'God save the King.'"

Meanwhile, the outside world shared the humor of
the Lamb fireside. For a while, at sixpence a piece,
Charles furnished jokes for a paper; but he hated this,
as almost any one would — six jokes a day — out of
the air, out of nowhere, price 75c: "Reader, try it for
once, only for one short twelvemonth," he sighed.
The joy of wit is that it is unstudied, unmeasured,
unpaid for. When it becomes a little package "seven
lines" long, it is spoiled. It was a mercy that Lamb
could turn out this commercialized humor and still
keep his spontaneity!

One day when he was returning from a dinner, the
stage-coach made a short stop at Kentish Town.

"Are you full inside?" inquired a feminine voice.
Lamb stuck his head out of the window:

"Yes, I am quite full inside; that last piece of pud-
ding at Mr. Gillman's did the business for me."

One of the bright chapters in Lamb's story tells
how, at the age of fifty, one April day in 1825, he
came home from the office "For Ever," honorably
discharged and pensioned for faithful service. This
surprise of liberty was as great as it was joyful:
"Every year to be as long as three — to have three
times as much real time in it!" Yet, being Lamb, he
missed his old office cronies and was half-homesick for
the peg where his hat used to hang. He called himself rather sadly "A Superannuated Man."

Whether we look at his life before or after this

retirement, one thing is true of it always: *He had time for people* and, unless they belonged to the immortal family of bores, he had a heart-welcome for them too. They might be only the "dim specks" of humanity, the grimy chimney-sweeps. But what then? They were children, feeling cold and hunger, loving the smell of sassafras-tea, and the taste of sizzling sausages, and knowing what to do with an unexpected coin or the savory dinners which Lamb and his friend Jem White beamingly served. We imagine how the dusky youngsters grinned at the feast, and how, when someone, Lamb himself probably, took a tumble in the street, one little face twinkled with mirth,— with "joy snatched out of desolation."

Perhaps it was the *people* of London, from its sweeps to its pastry-cooks, that made Lamb love it as he did: "O, her lamps of a night! All her streets are pavements of pure gold. A mob of men is better than a flock of sheep." Although, when he and Mary visited Coleridge, he learned to love the towering mountains —"Skiddaw and his broad-breasted brethren, all dark with clouds upon their heads,"— as a rule he was not "romance-bit about nature." He loved to scoff at Coleridge and Wordsworth, with their passion for sky and hills, and declared that he was "more fond of mensects than insects."

Among his whimsical letters decorated with blots and smears,— and one of them was written in alternate red and black ink,— we find invitations for "mensects" to dine: "Leg of Lamb, as before, hot at 4. And the heart of Lamb ever"; and "Turkey and contingent plumb-pudding at four (I always spell plumb-pudding with a *b*, *p-l-u-m-b*, I think it sounds fatter and more suetty."

During their last years, Mary could not bear company, but during many previous ones she was a gracious hostess to the strange but interesting group that straggled in for their Wednesday or Thursday evenings. Tables for four were scattered about the room, and "whist" was salted with racy conversation. At about ten o'clock, Becky spread a white cloth for the supper of cold meat and porter and smoking baked potatoes, and, soon after, Hazlitt would drop in from a concert, Kenney, from his successful new comedy, and lovely Fanny Kelly, still fresh after an evening of acting. Meanwhile Mary moved gently among them, with a smile as winning as her brother's. She was a master of the *Live and Let Live Creed*, and as little disturbed by the rings of smoke as she was by the hearty cheer.

While the Lambs laughed at affected people, such as the woman who *would* talk French because they did n't understand it, they sympathized with all sorts of others. Mary's heart was half of many a kindness, though the *action* mainly had to come from Charles. His sympathy was of the practical kind that found a man a job, and tried to work up a little school for a woman. Scores of benefits to scores of people are written in the heart's indelible record. For years he gave an annual sum of $160

to one of his old teachers, one who had taught him
when he was a very *little* boy, and he was faithful in
this till the day she died.   His spontaneous giving
showed itself in countless ways, from ready money
for beggars,— the value of the coin unnoticed,— to
the open gate through which he urged a hungry donkey to graze on the Lambs' front lawn.

Leigh Hunt, if no one else, knew that Lamb was
no fair-weather friend.   When Hunt was imprisoned
in Surrey Gaol for his published ridicule of the Prince
of Wales, Charles and Mary were among his most
faithful visitors.   They seemed to choose the gloom-
iest days to bring their sunlight in.   Hunt wrote:

"When the sad winds told us rain would come down,
 Or snow upon snow fairly clogged up the town,
 And dun yellow fogs brooded over its white,
 So that scarcely a being was seen towards night,
 Then, then said the lady yclept near and dear,
 Now, mind what I tell you — the L——s will be here."

The "near and dear lady" was Mrs. Hunt.   Perhaps the Lambs came to see four-year-old Thornton
as much as his parents.   They so loved children!
No matter how bright the ever mirthful father could
make his prison, it was a prison for all that, and
no place for a little boy's home.   Feelingly Lamb
wrote:

"Gates that close with iron roar
 Have been to thee thy nursery-door;
 Chains that chink in cheerless cells
 Have been thy rattles and thy bells."

Lamb's love of walking, added to his love of children, often led him twenty-two miles from London, to a girls' school kept by Miss Betsy and Miss Jane Norris. "His head would suddenly appear at the door in the midst of lessons, with 'Well, Betsy! How do, Jane?' 'Oh, Mr. Lamb!' they would say, and that was the end of work for that day." He would tell the girls stories and generally either stay to dinner or eat some bread and cheese in his favorite seat in a tree. Then with a troop of children to the village shop. Leaning over the lower half of the Dutch door, he would beat his cane or umbrella on the floor, demanding, "Abigail Ives! Abigail Ives!"

"Ah, Mr. Lamb," in a delighted voice, "I thought I knew your rap."

"Yes, Abigail, and I 've brought my money with me. Give these young ladies six pennyworth of Gibraltar rock." Then Mrs. Coe, who tells these stories of her childhood's friend, goes on to explain that "Gibraltar rock was Abigail Ives's specialty and six pennyworth was an unheard of amount except when Mr. Lamb was in the village. It had to be broken with a hammer!" We can imagine how the little storekeeper grew to look forward to his coming — the slim gentleman in rusty black, with the noble head and the "immaterial legs", the green umbrella under his arm, and the exhaustless wealth in his pocketbook. Would n't the children of to-day like to have him interrupt their school, with his holidays, his stories, and his candy! Whenever Hazlitt's little girl expected Lamb to visit her father, she would run into the street, stop any stranger she met, and exclaim, gleefully, " Mr. Lamb is coming to see me! " Charles and Mary used to throw books into a strawberry-patch for a certain boy to find.

It does not surprise us that these partners, with the hearts of a father and mother, adopted, in their old age, a young Italian orphan, Emma Isola. In a letter to Mrs. Shelley, Lamb joyfully describes her youthful struggles to learn Latin and her still greater struggles to write poems: " I am teaching Emma Latin to qualify her for a superior governess-ship. Her prepositions are suppositions; her concords disagree; her interjections are purely English ' Ah! ' and ' Oh! ' with a yawn and a gape in the same tongue; and she herself is a lazy, blockheadly supine. As I say to her, *ass in praesenti* rarely makes a wise man *in futuro*." Then in a letter to Dibdin, " Emma has just died, chok'd with a Gerund-in-dum. On opening her, we found a Participle-in-rus in the pericardium; " and to Hood, " Inclosed are verses which Emma sat down to write (her first) on the eve after your departure. What to call 'em I don't know. Blank verse they are not, because of the rhymes; rhymes they are not, because of the blank verse; heroics they are not, because they are lyric; lyric they are not, because of the heroic measure. They must be called Emmaics."

It took far more generosity to give Emma away on the day of her wedding, than it took to give her a home. The brother and sister were older now and needed her youth and mirth. If you can own, to read and re-read, only one of Charles Lamb's essays, let it be that exquisite hint of the hopes of his heart, "Dream Children." It is too perfect to be mangled by quotation or interpretation; — the only thing for us to do is to read it as a whole, to be silent, remembering and imagining, and then read again.

"Saint Charles!" exclaimed Thackeray when he read one of Lamb's letters; and Thackeray, from the hidden sadness of his own life, understood only too well Lamb's loyalty and cheer. But Lamb would have winced under any such title as Saint. His faithfulness was of the instinctive, doglike kind that did not recognize itself. If a halo had been made to fit him, he would probably have said it pricked! And he would have been the very last to want his virtues magnified. Hiding nothing but his goodness, in the open book of his life he has engraved his faults and weaknesses, as if to invite our condemnation. We love or despise him according to what we are. Some, shaking their heads, sigh out: "Lamb must have been very irreligious. He hardly ever entered a church except when it was empty!"

But didn't he find silent worship there? Didn't he read his Bible, and say, "No book can have too much of silent scripture in it"? He shuddered at those who "make a mock of holy things." Is *life* no argument of faith?

Dissect him further and perhaps you say, " He smoked and drank too much."

Yes, self-condemned, he bade one hundred farewells to tobacco, but one hundred and one welcomes. He called himself a " fierce smoker ", " a volcano burnt out, emitting only now and then a casual puff." Then, sadly and passionately,— of liquor: " Out of the black depths could I be heard, I would cry out to all who have but set foot in the perilous flood."

The charitable deal gently with a self-claimed fault. At first he smoked with the hope that it might relieve his life-long stammer. It did smooth his speech for a time, and wine seemed to smooth it even more. With his sociable temperament, he shared what he offered to his friends, but they could drink more than he and still be perfectly sober. This tendency to be easily unbalanced by liquor was probably part of the family taint of insanity that showed itself in his grandfather and father and Mary and once in his own early manhood. So it was that Mary hated to see him take another glass and that he had " no puling apology to make " for himself.

A few years before Lamb died he wrote to a friend, " I shall go and inquire of the stone-cutter, that cuts tombstones here, what a stone with a short inscription will cost; just to say, ' Here C. Lamb loved his brethren of mankind.' " Two days after Christmas, in 1834, and a few months after Coleridge's death, Charles Lamb slipped quietly away. Before the end, he had been " brave enough and loving enough to live

with his sister at the Asylum." The plain stone in
Edmonton churchyard, to the memory of Charles and
Mary, does not bear the inscription Charles laughingly
chose. Inconspicuously cut at the base of the stone, on
which a quaint jingle tries to suggest his nature, are the
words, " Restored by a Member of the Christ's Hospital School." So the boys of the Blue Coat School
remember him still, and other boys, and all the world.
No one can pity him. He was too rich for that. In
sweetness and strength, in mind and in friendships, in
all the things that make money worthless, he had a
wealth that almost any one might envy. His was a
hard, steady pull; but he sang vigor into his muscles;
and he kept the covenant with himself to guard his
" *best* friend " to the end, saving enough money for
her care if he should be the first to go. And he was.
Mary outlived him twelve years.

Lucas has described one sweet memorial. Long,
long after the tall grass had grown over the resting-
place of these partners, a Blue Coat Boy walking on
a London street, stopped and turned at the unexpected
words, " Come here, boy. Come here." A perfect
stranger, bareheaded and old, stood on a door-step
and was beckoning to him. The boy went. Oh,
plumb-cake and Gibraltar rock! hot sausages for
hungry sweeps! and sixpences for numberless small
waifs! the gentleman had slipped a five-shilling
piece into the little welcoming hand, " In Memory of
Charles Lamb."

III
SCOTT

Time and I against any two."

Sir Walter Scott.

III

BELOVED OF MEN — AND DOGS

ABOUT the time of our American Revolution, in the pasture of a certain Scotch hillside, we might have seen a blue-eyed baby boy, lying among the flocks of nibbling sheep and looking quietly at the moving clouds, or reaching for a bit of pink heather. Because his right leg had been lamed by a bad fever, so that he could not run or even creep, he was taking a queer remedy. Dr. Rutherford had said that if young Walter could live out-of-doors and lie in the " skin of a freshly killed sheep ", he might be cured. So, there he was at Sandy Knowe, in the kindly care of his grandfather, and placidly companioned by all these pasture playfellows.

From the power either of the Scotch breezes or of the warm sheep-skin coat, the child grew strong. First he began to roll about on the grass, or crawl from flower to flower, and, by and by, he learned to pull himself up by a farm-house chair, and, finally, with the help of a stick, to walk and run. No doubt he was a great pet with the warm-hearted Scotch neighbors, and no doubt they brought him things to play with and flowers to love long before he could clamber over the rocks and get the sweet honeysuckle for himself. He used, wistfully, to watch for the fairies to dance on the hills, and he had a secret fluttering hope that sometime, when he fell asleep on the grass, he might be carried away to fairyland. One day he was left in the field and forgotten — till a thunder-storm came up. Then his Aunt Jane, rushing out to carry him home, found him sitting on the grass, clapping his hands at every flash of lightning, and crying, " Bonny! Bonny! "

It is no wonder that such an out-of-doors baby loved animals. On the hills, they huddled round him in woolly friendliness. His Shetland pony, no bigger than a Newfoundland dog, used to go with him into the house. One day, the child, sobbing pitifully, limped to his Grandfather's farm-house and sat down on the steps. A starling lay in his lap, its stiff little feet stretched out beseechingly, its brown feathers quite cold. The bird, which Walter had partly tamed, was dead. By and by, the child's passion subsided; but the " laird " who had hushed the starling's singing was not forgiven so soon, and the Scotch laddie had to take a long gallop on his pony to cool his aching head.

As Walter would play contentedly among the rocks for hours, or ride his pony without tiring, so for hours he would listen, in rapt imagination, to Aunt Jane's ballads, until he could repeat whole passages by heart. Stretched on the floor, with shells and pebbles drawn up in order, he would fight the battles or shout forth the rhymed stories to chance visitors. " One may as well speak into the mouth of a cannon as where that child is," exclaimed the parish preacher, with some disgust, for, after Walter learned to read, he was even more excitable. From one of Mrs. Cockburn's letters we can imagine the six-year-old boy reading the story of a shipwreck to his mother. " His passion rose with the storm. He lifted his hands and eyes. ' There's the mast gone!' he exclaimed wildly. ' Crash it goes! They will all perish!' "

From the time he was six, he read ravenously; and it was owing to his wide reading that one time, when he was only fifteen, he became, for a few moments, the center of a group of learned men. It was when the poet Burns visited Edinburgh and had shown great interest in a picture of a soldier lying dead in the snow with a dog keeping patient watch beside him. Beneath the picture were some beautiful lines, but neither Burns nor any of those learned men knew who their author was, until young Walter Scott, who happened to be present, whispered that the lines were by Langhorne. Then Burns turned to him with glowing eyes and said: " It is no common course of reading that has taught you this; " adding, to his friends: " This lad will be heard of yet."

How proud the lad felt! How wistfully joyful in the warmth of the great poet's praise; and then how suddenly forgotten when, only a few days later, Robert Burns passed him in the street without a glance! Scott's moment of fame had vanished.

At school, however, he held the fame of the play-ground. Though he was lame, he was one of the best fighters and one of the readiest fighters among his fellows; and he was the very best story-teller. At recess, those who did not join in the running games crowded round the bench at his invitation, "Come, slink over beside me, Jamie, and I 'll tell you a story." And so, now reciting whole pages by heart, now filling in from his own wild imagination, the boy Scott carried his playmates into a "wonderful, terrible" world. "I did not make any great figure in the High School," he tells us. "I made a brighter figure in the *yards* than in the *class*." However, he was never distinguished as a "dunce", as some have thought; but simply as an "incorrigibly idle imp." (See Scott's own foot-note to his autobiography.)

Dr. Adam, however, by praising the lad's appreciation of Virgil and expecting him to do well, made him feel that Latin was more a pleasure than a task.

Though Scott merely dabbled in foreign languages, he devoured English romance. English poetry, too, such as Shakespeare's plays, Spenser's poems, and, dearest of all, Percy's wonderful collection of ballads, flew away with his fancy into a dream-world. Before he was ten, he had painfully copied several note-books full of his favorite ballads, most of which he could recite from beginning to end.

Meanwhile, he was growing more and more to love natural beauty. Like Irving, he longed to paint, and only gave up his efforts to do so with sad reluctance.

Great crags and rushing torrents filled him with a reverence that made his " heart too big for his bosom." And when he found an old ruin and could crown that ruin with a legend, his joy was complete. Handicapped by lameness, Scott rode wonderfully, even as a little boy, and was always joyously daring. Almost to the day of his death, he would rather leap the trench or ford the flood than " go round."

Moreover, as he said, he was " rather disfigured than disabled by his lameness," so that he managed, limpingly, to wander far, often twenty or thirty miles a day. In rough cap, jacket, and " musquito trousers ", and carrying a long gun, he used to wade into the marshes to shoot ducks, or to fish for salmon by torch-light —" burning the water ", befriended by his pack of dogs. A bold cragsman, he took no account of passing hours, sometimes even staying out all night. " I have slept on the heather," he tells us, " as soundly as ever I did in my bed." Little enough patience his father had with such " gallivantings." " I doubt, I greatly doubt, sir," Mr. Scott would scold, " you were born for nae better than a gangrel scrapegut." [1]

After leaving school, Scott, like many other authors since his day, was apprenticed to the law. " A dry and barren wilderness of forms and conveyances," he called it; but it was his father's profession, and, though the out-of-doors boy disliked the drudgery and detested the office confinement, he loved his father and wanted

[1] A strolling pedlar.

to be useful. We can easily imagine how he "wearied of the high stool", and how glad he was to see daylight fade and to go home to read exciting stories by a blazing fire. Great credit, then, is due him for the five or more years that he persevered at the dull law, and much to his master, Mr. David Hume, who fitted him for that profession. Law study not only gave Scott system, but also training in persistence.

And yet it was largely the effortless education and entirely the self-education that made him an author. His real studies, he tells us, were "lonely" and "desultory", "driving through the sea of books like a vessel without pilot or rudder", or, according to Lockhart, "obeying nothing but the strong breath of inclination." On his long walks and reckless rides, he was educated by the wind and sky, and by the rough people whom he has made immortal. He knew, personally, the charming beggar of "The Antiquary"; and he had seen in his youth "some who knew Rob Roy personally" and who had found him, like the English Robin Hood, "a kind and gentle robber." In "The Pirate" he immortalized an actual old sibyl "who sold favorable winds to sailors"; in "Guy Mannering," a real gipsy, with her "bushy hair hanging about her shoulders" and her "savage virtue of fidelity"; and in "The Heart of Midlothian" he glorifies the simple Jeanie Deans in "tartan plaid and country attire."

The old warriors of the highlands were more than willing to fight their battles over again for Scott, and he used to say that the peasants of Scotland always expressed their feelings in the " strongest and most powerful language." He found more solid fun in talking with the " lower classes ", whose superstitions were almost a faith, than in spending hours with the more conventional people of his own rank. What to some was idle gossip, to him, was living history. " He was makin' himself a' the time," said an old Scotchman, " but he didna ken maybe what he was about till years had passed. At first, he thought o' little, I dare say, but the queerness and the fun." The " Minstrelsy of the Scottish Border " is an echo of his rambles, and " The Lady of the Lake," a " labor of love " in memory of Loch Katrine.

All of his interests widened rapidly; society, law, love, soldiery, all came to have their claims. At twenty-two, he began to apply his legal knowledge by acting as counsel in a criminal court, and so valiantly did he defend an old sheep-stealer that the man received the verdict " not guilty."

" You 're a lucky scoundrel," Scott whispered to his client.

" I 'm just o' your mind," came the happy answer, " and I 'll send ye a mankin (hare) the morn, man."

Though Scott was less successful in defending a burglar, he was thanked for his efforts; and lawyer and condemned had a long, chummy talk in the prison-cell about the little, yelping dogs and the clumsy, rusty keys that were the burglars' worst enemies.

Before Scott was twenty-five he fell in love with a

"lassie" who was later betrothed to one of his own best friends. Scott thought his heart was broken; but it was "handsomely pieced", as he said a few years later, though the "crack remained" to his dying day.

In the meantime, he lived the life of a man of action.

In February 1797, when all Scotland feared the invasion of the French, his fighting blood rose to the call, and with many other young men he volunteered to serve. Too lame to march, he helped to organize a troop of cavalry of which he was made quartermaster because of his dependableness. The fighting spirit of his childhood had never died. His mother always said that if he had not been a cripple he would have been a soldier. That means we should have lost him as an author. And so we have to thank his first great handicap, lameness, for the two hundred volumes he gave the world.

Besides training a regiment on Portobello sands, astride his big black horse, Lenore, Scott's army life forced him to rise at five to drill. In addition to this, his business as Clerk of the Sessions, undertaken in 1806, demanded at least four or five hours a day for six months of the year, during which time he had to make a daily change from soldier's uniform and spirit to clerk's gown and brain.

Though now his time was closely packed with hard work, these years were holidays compared to his later struggles. Before long, he was combining the duties of lawyer and quartermaster with those of county sheriff, "speculative printer", and author. Let us get a little into the heart of the man, however, before we study him as an author, or visit him at Abbotsford.

When Sheriff Scott was compelled to judge a poacher, Tom Purdie, his human nature softened before the victim's plea of poverty and hunger, and he took Tom into his own employ as shepherd. Nothing could have been more characteristic of him. He loved to help people. Among the friends whom he helped to his own disadvantage, Hogg is conspicuous. I suppose that rough peasant took more thankless help than will ever be known. He had a way of accepting assistance as his right; and seemed as unconscious of any indebtedness as he was that his muddy feet had no place on Mrs. Scott's chintz sofa, where he stretched himself full-length the first time he called. Scott bore with all such peculiarities because he enjoyed Hogg's humor and rustic charm; and, though, years later, Hogg repaid Scott's kindness by bitter jealousy, the greater man proved his greatness by his loyalty. When he heard that "The Ettrick Shepherd" was very sick in an "obscure alley" in Edinburgh, he paid for the best medical care; and no doubt did him many unrecorded services. Scott's own memory dismissed such things about as soon as they were done. Now he wrote sermons for a tired minister; now he created a place for William Laidlaw, dictating gipsy stories for him, and then writing:

"*Dear Willie:* — While I wear my seven leagued boots and stride in triumph over moss and muir, it would be very silly in either of us to let a cheque twice a year of £25 make a difference between us." Just at that time, however, Scott's " seven-league boots " were losing their giant stride. And yet, when he could least spare it, he furnished the unlucky Maturin with £50.

One more story of his friendships, a fine example also of quick wit: There was a poor German named Weber, who, though he had a passion for strong drink, had won this great author's loving pity. One day, when Weber had been sitting at Scott's table, apparently as friendly as ever, he suddenly charged Scott with insulting him, flew into a rage, and produced a pair of pistols. With perfect coolness, Scott asked him to lay the pistols on the table, saying that it would be too exciting for Mrs. Scott and the children to hear the noise of shooting, and that, if Weber would stay to dinner, the duel could be fought soon after, out-of-doors, and strictly according to rule. With that, he quietly picked up the pistols, locked them in a drawer, and stepped for an instant from the room to despatch a messenger. Weber stayed to dinner, seeming perfectly rational; but that night he proved to be a hopeless maniac. To the end of his life he was supported by Scott in a New York asylum.

These stories suggest some of the costs of friendship — costs never entered in the accounts of the noble spender's heart. Yet we must remember them, later, in our reckoning of Scott's great business failure.

Let us look, first, however, at Scott the author, and Scott the home-maker.

His literary life may be divided into two parts of

eighteen years each. During the first eighteen years,
a period of joy, he wrote poems; and during the last
eighteen years, novels. As every one knows, Lord
Byron's striding popularity made Scott give up verse.
We get this from his own frank admission that he
" would no longer play second fiddle to Byron "; and,
" Since one line has failed, we must just strike into
something else." Certainly his last poem, " The Lord
of the Isles," was not equal to " The Lay of the Last
Minstrel ", " Marmion ", or " The Lady of the Lake."
Scott himself called it a failure; but, whether it was
a failure or not, we are glad that something made the
great man, with all his hidden powers, turn to prose.
We are as glad Byron beat him at poetry as we are
that lameness hindered him from being a soldier.
Step by step, through handicaps and failures, the buried
genius of the man is found. In his warm admiration
for Maria Edgeworth's Irish tales, he had once mod-
estly thought that he might write stories of Scotland.

One day, when Scott was looking in a drawer for
fishing-tackle, he came on the roughly written sheets
of " Waverley ", begun many years before. As he
read those unfinished pages, he wanted to go on with
the romance; and so, to those first discarded sheets,
we owe the whole set of the " Waverley Novels."
For years, their authorship was a mystery. Book
after book came out " By the Author of Waverley,"
while the puzzled world called him " The Great Unknown " or " The Wizard of the North." He never
accounted for his disguise except by saying it was his

"humour." No doubt he felt more confident in his "Coat of Darkness"; for, while he was sure of his reputation as a poet, he was merely trying his hand at prose.

And yet many think to-day that he was a greater novelist than poet. During the time that he was editing his "Complete Edition", one per cent.,— one in every hundred,— of all the people in Edinburgh were at work in the making and selling of his books. In those two hundred volumes he could say truthfully, "I have tried to unsettle no man's faith", and of them he could humbly hope that, "if they did no good, at least they would do no harm." But they did do good. It is good to entertain and rest a tired world. Scott carries us into another realm,—"to society, if not better than our own, at least more interesting." His books ring with horses' hoofs and the sound of the trumpet. Like himself, they are full of fight; his people have throbbing hearts and blood and muscle.

If you have never thrilled with the "Stranger, I am Rhoderick Dhu" of that heroic law-breaker; or, with Rebecca, dared Brian du Bois Guilbert to advance one step farther toward that dizzy parapet; or cried over Kenilworth, if you are a girl; or acted Ivanhoe and Rob Roy, if you are a boy,— then you have missed something that belonged by right to your youth. I remember how the child-gang in our neighborhood used to act Scott; the boy-leader was Robin Hood, and the fat boy, with the largest appetite, was Friar Tuck.

Many love history more through Scott than through any other medium; perhaps it is not the most authentic history, but it is history gloriously alive. And many more have learned from him to be tender to the "under dog." It may be a real dog, like Fangs; it may be a court fool, or a gipsy, or some member of the once-despised race of Jews; but Scott will always make you "square" to the "fellow who is down." He may even make you love someone whom the rest of the world has forgotten to love.

Rich in sympathy and tingling with courage as the "Waverley Novels" are, they were written, most of them, at a great price,— not of money but of effort. Before entering on Scott's life of darkening struggle, however, let us see him in the glow of peace. Some years after his marriage, we find him quietly settled at Abbotsford with four happy children round him.

It would be interesting to visit the place where most of those wonderful novels were written. Scott had bought the farm of one hundred and ten acres in a rough condition. Many of the trees growing there to-day were planted by his hands, and he and Tom Purdie used to tramp over the place on windy days to straighten up the young saplings. Little by little the farm changed to a noble estate, beautiful without and within, and the Abbotsford of to-day, robbed of its master, is more like a museum than a home. The footsteps of sight-seers echo through its great rooms,— their walls enriched with suits of armor, with tapestry, and relics; and their floors so slippery you can "almost skate on them." There is the portrait of Scott's great-grandfather, Beardie, that loyal Tory who refused to have his beard cut after Charles I was executed; and there is a portrait of Scott's son, Walter, who died of India fever just after being made Colonel. The grim armory speaks of many battles; the relics recall many stories. Among these are a brace of Bonaparte's pistols; the purse of Rob Roy; a silver urn given to Scott by Byron; and a gold snuff-box given him by George IV.

From the time of Scott's first land purchase, the estate grew from one hundred and ten acres to fifteen hundred. If we had gone to Abbotsford with merry-hearted Irving, during Scott's lifetime, and even before he was made Baronet, we should have seen it less as the great castle, which it is to-day, than as a " snug gentleman's-cottage " beaming from the hillside above the Tweed. The branching elk-horns over the door gave it the look of a hunter's lodge; but the scaffolding surrounding the walls, and great piles of hewn stone, hinted a grander future. As Irving entered, " out sallied the warder of the castle, a black greyhound, and, leaping on one of the blocks of stone, began a furious barking." This was Hamlet. " His alarm brought out the whole garrison of dogs — all open-mouthed and vociferous." Then, up the gravel path limped the master of the house, moving along rapidly with the help of a stout walking-stick. We can almost see him — his broad, freckled face and sandy hair; his eyes " sparkling blue " under the old white hat; his

big figure dressed in a dingy green shooting-coat and
brown pantaloons; and his worn shoes tied at the
ankles.   By the master's side, with great dignity, jogs
the gray stag-hound, Maida, trying to display gravity enough for all that yelping pack.   It would
hardly be a welcome without this gathering at the
gate.

"Come, drive down, drive down, ye 're just in time
for breakfast," urges Scott, and then adds, when Irving explains that he has had his breakfast, "Hoot,
man, a ride in the morning in the keen air of the Scotch
hills is warrant enough for a second breakfast."

And so, with Irving, we see the great "minstrel"
at his chief meal, and with Irving we are expected to
eat huge slices of the sheep's head and of the big brown
loaf at Scott's elbow.   Of course, at the table, there
is no discussion of the children; but a short visit dis-
plays their natures: Sophia, joyous and musical;
Anne, quiet; Walter, his father's pride because he is
such a fine shot; and Charles, a lovely boy of twelve.
Scott said there were just three things he tried to teach
his children: "to ride, to shoot, and to speak the
truth."   And when they rode he taught them to think
nothing of tumbles.   "Without courage there can be
no truth," he would say, "and without truth there can
be no other virtue."

The dogs are allowed in the dining-room: Maida,
beside Scott; the pet spaniel, Finette, with soft, silky
hair, close to "Mama"; and a large gray cat, stealing about with velvet steps, expects delicate bits of

breakfast from all the family, and cuffs the dogs in a friendly way with his paw.

After breakfast, they all set out through the sweet, rough country, Scott limping rapidly ahead as usual, pointing out the badgers' holes and sitting hares (which he is always the first to see) while the dogs beat about the glen, barking and leaping, or boundingly answer the call of the ivory whistle that swings from their master's buttonhole. The little terriers, Pepper and Mustard, are as excited as Maida is dignified. Snuffing among the bushes, they have started a hare, and Hinse, the cat, joins the chase in hot pursuit.

By and by a shower springs up, and Scott shares with Irving the tartan plaid which Tom Purdie has been carrying. And so the two great men, congenial as old friends, snuggle under the Scotchman's warm shelter; and while rain soaks the pink heather and mist folds the hills, they talk of trees and nations, homes and dogs, now and then matching each other's legends. Their hearts are in wonderful harmony. Irving tells Scott of the grand American forests, and Scott answers: "You love the forests as much as I do the heather. If I did not see the heather at least once a year, I think I should die."

So cordial and out-doorish is our host, so ready to guide in our rambles, "overwalking, overtalking, and overfeeding his guests", as his wife used to say, that we may easily forget his business in life, or that he has anything else to do but entertain. But Scott rose, presumably, this day, as all others, at five o'clock and was writing away rapidly by six, so that he "broke the neck of the day's work before breakfast." This was his regular program. While he bathed and dressed, his thoughts were "simmering" in his brain, so that he dashed them off "pretty easily" when his pen was in his hand. With no interruption except breakfast, he worked steadily till eleven or twelve. By this system, very rarely broken, he could afford a ride after lunch, and, at one o'clock, rain or shine, he could mount his big horse for a gallop over the hills. The pictures he saw on these rides are in his books, and so is the joyous out-door spirit. One of his first poems, "Marmion," was practically written on horseback, the lines coming into his brain while he trained his regiment, raced over the moors, or plunged through floods.

And just as he would not let his work cheat his outdoor life, so he would not let it cheat his children or his friends. When Irving visited him, he had to excuse himself after breakfast to correct proof; but often he wrote in a room filled with people. Perhaps he used manuscript sheets the same size as letterpaper, so that he might write his books and yet seem to be writing a common letter. The shouts of his children playing marbles or ninepins around him, or his dogs sleeping at his feet or even leaping in and out of the open window, could not interrupt his thought, though occasionally the father stopped to tell a story to the pleading pets who talked, or to give an affectionate pat to those who only looked their love.

And then his active hand drove on, laying aside sheet after sheet.

Let us stop a few minutes to speak of Scott's affection for all his dumb friends. It cannot easily be exaggerated. Of his horses, neither Captain nor Lieutenant nor Brown Adam liked to be fed by any one but him. When Brown Adam was saddled and the stable door opened, he would trot to the " leaping-on stone " (a help to his lame master), and there he would stand, firm as granite, till Sir Walter was well in the saddle, when he would neigh trumpetingly and almost dance with delight. Under Scott's hand, he was perfectly trustworthy; but he broke one groom's arm and another's leg with his wild capers. The beautiful snow white horse, Daisy, proved less faithful than Brown Adam. He was as full of jealousy as he was of life. When Sir Walter came back from a trip to the Continent, he found Daisy had changed toward him. Instead of standing still to be mounted, he "looked askant at me like the devil," said Scott; "and when I put my foot in the stirrup, he reared bolt upright, and I fell to the ground." For any of the grooms the horse stood perfectly; but Scott tried, again and again, always with the same result. At last he had to give Daisy up. When some one suggested that the snowy animal might have felt hurt at being left in the stable, Scott said: "Aye, these creatures have many thoughts of their own. Maybe some bird had whispered Daisy that I had been to see the grand reviews at Paris on a

From the painting by Sir Henry Raeburn

Scott and one of his "Friends"

little scrag of a Cossack, while my own gallant trooper was left behind bearing Peter and the post-bag to Melrose."

Among Scott's dogs, his earliest friends were his bull terrier, Camp, and two greyhounds, Douglas and Percy. These used to race over the hills beside their galloping master, and nose round in the bushes while he stopped to fish. Of the three, Camp had most perfectly his master's confidence. Scott used to talk to him just as if he were a human being; and the servant, setting the table for dinner, would say: " Camp, my good fellow, the Sheriff's coming home by the ford," or: " The Sheriff's coming home by the hills," and, even when Camp was old and sick, he would pull himself up from the rug and trot off as nimbly as his strength would let him, to meet his master by the Tweed or the Glenkinnon burn.

Dear old Camp! He was buried by moonlight in the garden just opposite Scott's study-window. " Papa cried about Camp's death," Sophia Scott told Irving. Indeed, we all know that the affectionate master felt so bereft that he broke an engagement at dinner that evening and gave as his perfectly honest excuse " the death of a dear old friend." Other spots on the estate remind us of other dogs. Maida's grave at Abbotsford is between Sir Walter's bedroom window and the garden. There is a life-sized statue with the head raised as if looking toward the window for his master's face. The Latin inscription means:

" BENEATH THE SCULPTURED FORM WHICH LATE YOU
    WORE,
SLEEP SOUNDLY, MAIDA, AT YOUR MASTER'S DOOR "

Percy was buried not very far away with the epitaph:

" HERE LIES THE BRAVE PERCY "

Scott had one dog, a Highland terrier, that sometimes grew tired of the chase, or " pretended to be so,"
and would whine to be taken up on his master's horse,
where he would sit as happy as a child. And there
was a large wolf-greyhound which had posed for so
many artists that he would get up and saunter out of
the room at the sight of brushes and a palette — por-
trait-painting was a great bore!

One last story, and we must leave Scott's kennels
and stables for a closing study of the man himself.
One clear September morning, boys and girls, dogs
and ponies, Scott, Laidlaw, Mackenzie, and many
others set out for a day's fishing. Maida gamboled
about the prancing Sibyl Grey who tossed his mane in
glee at the thought of a day's sport. Just as the joyous party was ready to gallop away, Anne Scott shouted
delightedly: " Papa, Papa, I knew you could never
think of going without your pet." At her merry laughter, Scott turned, and there, in the roadway, frisking
about his pony's feet, was his little black pig. It took
only a moment to lasso the eager little grunter, and
drag him away from the sportsmen; but Scott said,
with mock gravity:

"What will I do gin my hoggie die —
My joy, my pride, my hoggie?"

That pig was as ridiculous in his claim for a place in
the inner circle as the hen that cackled for intimacy, or
the two donkeys which used to trot to the edge of the
pasture bars, and stretch out their long, hairy noses
for a "pleasant crack with the laird."

After the dreadful business failure, however, Scott
had little time for any of this playfulness. We need
not postpone the sad story any longer, though we want
to make it as short as possible. The crash came in
1826. Within six months of each other fell his
two greatest sorrows: his wife's death and this business collapse. In the partnership with James and
John Ballantyne, whom Scott had known at school,
Sir Walter had furnished nearly all the capital, and
the Ballantynes had been made responsible for the accounts. It did not seem to occur to either of the
brothers to keep the great author informed of the business situation, and Scott, who was overtrusting, did
not demand an exact statement. There was, besides,
a complication with Messrs. Constable, a publishing
house in which the greater portion of Sir Walter's fortune was involved. Things are as tangled to the reader
as they were to the business partners. Failure, which
they did not know how to help, was closing round
them. Both the Ballantynes seemed to postpone the
evil day of facing facts. Scott might have examined
the accounts; he should have; but he was not warned,

and he did not suspect how serious the debt was, till, with Constable's failure, the crash came, and all were ruined. Let us tell the truth: Scott was blind; he was unbusinesslike; he was overhopeful; he was extravagant. He was always too ready to make loans, and far too ready to spend money on his life-hobby, his dear estate of Abbotsford. But, when he realized his dilemma, he came to the fore with a majesty of honor seldom, if ever, equaled in history. He refused all props, the loans urged by his friends; the offered pensions. "Now he worked double tides, depriving himself of out-door exercise altogether." "This own right hand shall work it off," reads his diary, though into that same diary creeps a note of discouragement: "I often wish I could lie down to sleep without waking. But I will fight it out if I can." On his sundial, he carved with his own hand: "I will work while it is yet day," and his brave motto was: "Time and I against any two."

The natural question comes, why did he not sell Abbotsford? It had grown to be a magnificent place. Well, he did. He quitted the estate, leaving orders for sales of his entire collection of paintings, relics, and furniture; but it was the pride of his life, the home for which he had worked all his days, and which he had dreamed would belong to his children. As he said, his heart clung to what he had created; there was hardly a tree that did not owe its life to him. In 1830 his creditors gave him back fifteen thousand pounds' worth of his own books, furniture, and relics; he and his children returned; and again the place was beautiful, though there was little time to enjoy it.

Working at fearful pressure, the out-of-doors Sir Walter shut himself from savage hills and roaring streams, while his horse whinnied for him in the stable, and his dogs lay restless at his feet. Over page after page he raced, not stopping to dot an i, or cross a t, punctuating by a hurried dash, or not at all, and spelling, like Stevenson, with perfect carelessness. If, with a mental microscope, we can find a blessing in this agonizing business failure, it is in the fine collected edition, with its charming introductions, part of " Woodstock," " The Fair Maid of Perth," " Anne of Geierstein," " The Life of Napoleon," and " Tales of a Grandfather." But the effort of these works cost Scott his life.

He wrote till his fingers were covered with chilblains and his brain was threatened with exhaustion. He had always been a rapid writer, and undeterred by sickness. " Guy Mannering " was struck off in six weeks at Christmas-time; " Ivanhoe " was dictated in great pain and punctuated with groans,— Scott's amanuensis, Laidlaw, begging him to stop. " Nay, Willie," came the heroic answer, " only see that the doors are fast. I would fain keep all the cry as well as all the wool to ourselves." One morning before breakfast he finished " Anne of Geierstein ", and, as soon as breakfast was over, set to work on his " Compendium of Scottish History." In a little over a week, immediately following the news of ruin, he

wrote one whole volume of " Woodstock "; the entire
book was written in less than three months. To these
facts, literature gives no parallel. There was no waiting for inspiration. Conquering moods and weather,
Scott made himself work at set times. Perhaps the
drudging law, at which one time the young man had
written a hundred and twenty folio pages without stopping for food and rest, trained into him this wonderful tenacity. The life-habit of work may have
made this cruel need of work less irksome. But " a
single season blanched his hair snow white."

All must not be told. Let us spare ourselves the
painful details of the battle. We need to know not so
much how deep the sword-thrust or how our hero lost
in blood, as the heart of the man, the thing that made
him will to fight and die for honor's sake. The failure
that darkened, ennobled his life. Scott, the man, was
even greater than his books. As with anxious watch
we follow the struggle, twice we see him fall. But he
rises again, gropingly reattacks his labor, and writes
on, in spite of blood " flying to his head," a fluttering
memory, and stiffened hands.

Haggard and thin, with hesitating steps and words,
he would try to tell a story in his old, merry way, and,
before he reached the point, would stop " with the blank
anxiety of look that a blind man has when he has
dropped his staff." " How gladly," says his diary,
would he have compounded for " a little pain instead
of the heartless muddiness of mind."

In October 1831, the doctors absolutely forbade

work. Following their advice, he went to Italy, with
the lame hope of cure. But not the blue sky of Naples,
nor any sun-filled breeze could take the place of his
dour Scotland. With all its roughness, the land of the
thistle was the land of his heart. The buffeting wind
of a lifetime, the bleak hills cloaked in mist, the water
of the Tweed rushing over its white stones — he needed
them all. "Let us to Abbotsford," he begged.

And so they took him home. As they traveled, he
showed little interest in anything but far-off Scotland.
His sad eyes waited for his own trees, the plentiful
heather, the climbing gorse that painted the hills with
gold.

As they journeyed on, he grew more and more sure
that his debts were all paid; and his friends, knowing
how he had struggled, never told him that this was not
quite true.

"I shall have my house, and my estate round it,
free, and I may keep my dogs as big and as many as I
choose, without fear of reproach." So he comforted
himself.

When, about the middle of June, they reached London, Sir Walter was too weak to go on without rest.
Outside his hotel, gathered begrimed day-laborers with
the awed question: "Do you know, sir, if this is the
street where he is lying?" By careful stages, early in
July, he traveled on, crossed the last salt water, and
was tenderly lifted into a carriage for the last drive.
Unawake as he had been to everything else, the well-
known roads and foaming streams roused his memory:

"Gala Water, surely — Buckholm — Torwoodlee" he murmured expectantly.   When, above the trees, they saw Abbotsford towers, he grew more and more excited, and when they crossed Melrose bridge over the Tweed, it took three men to hold him in the carriage. Pitifully weak though he was, he wanted to run to meet his home.   Then, trembling, he saw Laidlaw; then his dogs, trying to kiss him with noses and tongues and paws, and to tell him how much they had missed him.   They were very gentle, though, as if in their loving hearts they knew the days of rough comradeship were over.   Scott smiled and sobbed together at their welcome.

For a few days he lingered, to be wheeled about in a chair among his roses or under his own dear trees. Sometimes his grandchildren tried to help push.

"I have seen much," he would say again and again, "but nothing like my ain house — give me one turn more."

"My dear, be a good man . . . be a good man. Nothing else will give you any comfort when you come to lie here."   This was his farewell to Lockhart, a few days before he died.

"Shall I send for Sophia and Anne?" Lockhart gently asked.

"No," with his old brave calm.   "Don't disturb them.   Poor souls!   I know they were up all night. God bless you all."

The end came with its peaceful relief, September 21, 1832.   It was a beautiful day.   Through the open

window streamed warm sunshine, and the Tweed sang
on that soft, old music that would have suited its sleeping master better than the most wonderful requiem.

They say the line of carriages that followed Sir
Walter to Dryburgh Abbey was over a mile long.
But perhaps his heart would have been more pleased
by the host of yeomen who followed behind on horseback; the villagers, with heads uncovered, gathered
in sorrowful black crowds to say good-bye to the
" Shirra ";[1] or even the little act of one of his horses,
which drew him on that final day. It halted of its
own accord, at the end of the climb, on the very spot
where horse and master had so often stood to view the
steadfast hills.

[1] Sheriff.

IV
IRVING

" If I can by lucky chance, in these days of evil, rub out one wrinkle from the brow of care, or beguile the heavy heart of one moment of sadness — I shall not have written entirely in vain."

Washington Irving.

IV

"PLEASE, your Honor, here 's a bairn was named after you." Lizzie, the Scotch nurse, pushed into the shop, dragging a short-legged boy by the arm till they were close to the President's side. " Here 's a bairn was named after you," she repeated encouragingly. And then President Washington knew what she meant, and laid his hand on the child's tumbled hair in blessing. The boy who received that blessing was Washington Irving. He lived near-by, at 128 William Street, below Fulton Street, in New York City. Eight children were crowded into that two-story city house : William, Ann, Peter, Catharine, Ebenezer, John, Sarah, and Washington. Over the brood presided a stern father, with his " Catechism " and " Pilgrim's Progress ",— and a gentle mother who loved and understood.

Doubtless, as the years advanced, that mother knew that her youngest child, Washington, would learn, like all other children, from every source that claimed his interest. Though he was taught hardly more than his alphabet, in the queer little school in Ann Street, he was taught much else by life in the city. He used to " haunt

the pier-heads in fine weather " to watch the ships
" fare forth " with lessening sails; and there at the
wharves, from the smell of salt water, the call of sea
birds, and the flapping canvas, he was learning a love
of adventure, and was even planning to sail away as
his father had done before the War. At home, he
trained himself to the hardships of a sailor's life by
eating salt pork, fat and greasy,— a thing he loathed;
and by getting out of bed at night to lie on the hard
floor. Monkey-like, he was learning to climb from
roof to roof of the city houses for the pure fun of
dropping mysterious stones down mysterious chimneys,
and clambering back, half giddy, but chuckling at the
wonder he had roused, for he was always a roguish
lad. From the queerly-dressed Dutch people, with
their queerer language, he was learning that there
were other lands besides his own. From the high-
vaulted roof of Trinity Church, with its darkness and
beauty and deep-swelling music, he was learning that
there were other religions than the strict Scotch Pres-
byterianism of his father. He even learned, in time,
that dancing and the theater, both forbidden by that
father, had their own charms; and he secretly took
lessons in the one and let himself down from the attic
window to go to the other,— always timing himself
exactly, to be back at nine for prayers. And then upstairs again and off, by the wood-shed roof, to the
ground — and the play.

"Oh, Washington, if you were only good!" the
dear impulsive mother used to say. And, yet, in her

secret heart, she must have felt that the child was
"good" who was always sweet and sunny and loving.

Perhaps it was because she shared his thirst for adventure that she won his confidence. Not allowed by
his father to read "Robinson Crusoe" and "Sindbad
the Sailor", Washington used to read them at night
in bed, or under his desk at school. He liked those
books better than his book of sums; such stories carried him into the wild world of his longing, and partly
quenched his thirst for adventure — a taste that lasted
a lifetime.

In 1800, when Irving was seventeen, he made his
first voyage up the Hudson to Albany. In those days
a journey from New York to Albany was like a
journey to Europe to-day. Washington's older
sisters,— Ann and Catharine, who had married young,
were living near Albany, and he was to visit them.
Boy-like, he packed his trunk at the first mention of
the trip; but, as the sloop would not sail without a certain amount of freight and a certain number of pas-
sengers, he unpacked and re-packed many times before
her cargo was ready and the wonderful journey began.

To almost any one, that first sail through the Hudson Highlands is a dream of beauty; to Irving, it was a
marvel and a rapture. The stern mountains, crowned
with forests; the eagles, sailing and screaming; the
roar of "unseen streams dashing down precipices";
and then the anchoring at night in the darkness and
mystery of the overhanging cliffs, and drifting asleep
to the plaintive call of the whip-poor-will — it was all

new to the worshiping city boy, who had never left
the New York streets before, except to wander in the
woods with dog and gun.

That journey was the beginning of his many travels.
Though he went into Mr. Hoffman's office the next
year to study law, he did not continue long at the
work. An incessant cough soon developed into con-
sumptive tendencies, and, in July 1803, his employer,
who loved him like a father, invited him to join a party
of seven on a trip to Canada.

The hardships of this journey, however, were a poor
medicine. Beyond Albany, they traveled mainly by
wagons, over roads so bad and through woods so
thick, that they often had to get out and walk. " The
whole country was a wilderness," writes Irving. " We
floated down the Black River in a scow; we toiled
through forests in wagons drawn by oxen; we slept in
hunters' cabins, and were once four-and-twenty hours
without food; but all was romance to me."

Naturally, when he returned home, his family found
him worse rather than better. Accordingly, feeling
that something must be done to save him, the older
brothers put their money together — William, who was
best able, giving the greatest share — and engaged his
passage on a ship sailing for Bordeaux, May 19, 1804.
" There's a chap who will go overboard before we get
across," hinted the captain, eying Irving suspiciously.

On ship, his sleeping-quarters were in the cabin with
sixteen others "besides the master and mate." " I
have often passed the greater part of the night walking

the deck," Washington wrote to William; and again:
"When I cannot get a dinner to suit my taste, I en-
deavor to get a taste to suit my dinner." His letters
breathe a spirit of gaiety and are hopefully full of his
own physical improvement, for he was never a man to
complain. His worries were for others. Of his sister
Nancy's health he wrote: "I wish to Heaven I had
her with me . . . The rude shocks of the Western winters she has to encounter are too violent for a delicate
constitution that is at the mercy of every breeze."

And yet his trip was not all joy: now we read of his
Christmas at sea, in a dull, pouring rain, with the captain snoring in his berth; now of a "villainous crew
of pirates" who attacked the ship.

After Irving reached port, life, like the sea, seemed
smoother; but now he fell a prey to the tempting dis-
tractions of travel. His greatest fault was, no doubt,
a lack of steadiness of aim. Like a bee, he flew from
flower to flower, wherever honey seemed the sweetest.
To be sure, he had gone abroad for his health; but his
brothers, who had sent him, expected him to turn the
time and money to some definitely good account. For
a short time the art galleries in Rome fired him with
an ambition to "turn painter", for he loved wild
landscapes and color, declaring that "cold, raw tints"
gave him rheumatism. This art craze, however,
amounted to a mere temporary dabbling, like his study
of two other subjects. Though his expense-book gives
account of two months' tuition in French and of the
purchase of a Botanical Dictionary, we do not picture

Irving as studying either French or botany very hard
His social instincts were a real impediment to any
study. William, in bitter disappointment, declared
that he was scouring through Italy in too short a time,
" leaving Florence on the left and Venice on the right "
for the sake of " good company." In fact, the younger
brother's bump of sociability was very large. In
Paris, according to his diary, he went to the theater
five nights in succession; we do not imagine that he
went alone. In London he met Mrs. Siddons and the
Kembles. Fascinated with foreign life and foreign
people, he hated the student side of travel, and was
frankly tired of palaces and cathedrals. All his countries were *peopled*. That is why " Bracebridge Hall "
and the " Sketch Book " are so alive.

We are not surprised, then, to find that on his return to New York he plunged into society life
though he still continued his life as an author, begun
before he went to Europe. As a partner of Paulding
and of William Irving, he issued in twenty numbers a
series of brilliant and original papers called " Salma-
gundi." These were reprinted in London, in 1811.

While Irving was abroad, the harsh news of his
father's and his sister Nancy's death had come, so
that on his return we must picture him as living alone
with his mother in the old house (now torn down) on
the corner of William and Ann Streets. There he
wrote his "Letters of Jonathan Oldstyle ", " Sal-
magundi ", and " History of New York by Diedrich
Knickerbocker."

Right in the midst of this work came the most terrible bereavement of Irving's life. Under the encouragement of his employer, the fatherly Mr. Hoffman, Irving had attempted to continue the study of the law. Through Mr. Hoffman's friendship, too, and the openness of his hospitable home, the young man had learned a great deal on another subject. He had learned to love Mr. Hoffman's young daughter, Matilda. She was hardly more than a beautiful child, but he loved her for all that she was, and for all that she promised to be. Just when their love was happiest, however, Matilda caught a terrible cold and within two months died. That sorrow lay too deep for any of Irving's family or any of his friends to touch. During her last days of fevered delirium, when he was constantly with her, her soul had shown itself even more beautiful than it had ever seemed in health; and he never found words to utter his grief. He was twenty-six when she died, and she was only seventeen. But through all his long, lonely life, he cherished her dear love; and after his death, there was found among his treasures a lovely miniature, a lock of fair hair, and a slip of paper bearing her name, "Matilda Hoffman." Through all his travels he had taken her Bible and prayer-book with him, and through all the years, her memory. "I was naturally susceptible," we read in the memoranda, "but my heart would not hold on."

No one could have written of this faithful strength of love more beautifully than Thackeray in that gem of an appreciation, "Nil Nisi Bonum": "He had loved once in his life. The lady he loved died; and he, whom all the world loved, never sought to replace her. I can't say how much the thought of that fidelity had touched me. Does not the very cheerfulness of his after-life add to the pathos of the untold story? To grieve always was not his nature; or, when he had a sorrow, to bring all the world in to condole with him and bemoan it. Deep and quiet he lays the love of his heart, and buries it; and grass and flowers grow over the scarred ground in due time."

Nearly thirty years after Matilda's death one of Mr. Hoffman's granddaughters, who was rummaging in a drawer for music, found a piece of faded embroidery. "Washington," said Mr. Hoffman, "this is a piece of poor Matilda's work." But Irving had grown suddenly grave and silent, and in a few moments had said good-night and gone home.

That Irving tried to lift the clouds from his own spirit is proved by his continuing, in the midst of his sorrow, his "Knickerbocker's History",— a book rippling and sparkling with merriment. "In his pilgrimage through the lanes and streets, the roads and avenues, of this uneven world," writes Irving, "the author refreshes himself with many a secret smile at occurrences that excite no observation from the dull trudging mass of mortals." He, himself, was Diedrich Knickerbocker, and it was he who "would sit by the old Dutch housewives with a child on his knee or a purring grimalkin on his lap." If some of the Dutch

were nettled by his picture of their ways, others saw
that he was writing in " pure wantonness of fun ", and
that none of his laughter left a sting.   Years later,
however, Irving wrote: " It was a confounded im-
pudent thing in such a youngster as I was, to be med-
dling in this way with old family names."

Yet this special gift of finding fun in little things,
and interest in nothings, filled his days with life.   Except for wide traveling, there were few events to light
his lonely way.   The warmth of his family affections
was always one of the sweetest and strongest things
in his nature: now he was helping Ebenezer and his
many children; now bolstering Peter with money loans,
always offered with that graciousness that was a part
of his generous delicacy.   " We certainly understand
each other too well to have any consideration for the
laws of *meum* and *tuum* between us," he would say,
" or for either of us to care on which side the opportunity of profitable exertion lies."   He seems to have
had a constant fear that Peter would not " share his
morsel with him "; he begs him not to be " squeam-
ish ", and pleads: " When you were in prosperity you
made it a common lot between us."   " I send you a
couple of hundred pounds to keep you in pocket-money
until the boat begins to pay better. . . . Let it be as it
should be, a matter of course between us."   " Brotherhood," he believed, " is a holy alliance made by
God, . . . and we should adhere to it with religious
faith."

He and Peter and Ebenezer formed a merchants'

firm, to which Washington, though he detested the
"drudgery of regular business", lent his time and interest till it was firmly on its feet. This required him
to live for a few months in Washington, D. C. His
spirit now, as in all his other travels, was the same.
"I left home determined to be pleased with everything, or if not pleased, to be amused."

On his return to New York the following spring,
he went into bachelor-quarters, with his friend
Brevoort, on Broadway near Bowling Green. It was
a jovial time, free and peaceful, but broken, with the
peace of the nation, by news of the War of 1812.
Irving, adventuresome and loyal, joined the Governor's
staff posted at Sackett's Harbor. His letters of that
time are full of "breastworks, and pickets of rein-
forced militia", but also of his own good health, "all
the better for hard traveling", and of "love to Mother
and the family."

Soon after the news of the victory of New Orleans
and the tidings of peace, Irving sailed for Europe,
little dreaming that he would stay for seventeen years.
He had expected to return in a short time and settle
down beside his dear old mother for the rest of her
life. These plans and hopes, however, were suddenly
broken by the news of her death in 1817. That was
the saddest event of his travels; the happiest was his
friendship with Scott.

At Abbotsford, Scott made Irving more than welcome, and found in him a kindred spirit. They were
both glad, hearty, natural men who loved out-door

life in the same boyish way. Besides this, Scott
found that Irving was a man who needed nothing explained — a man who could tramp with him through
his own Tweedside, and understand all its beauty.   We
can imagine how welcome the Scotchman's cordiality
was to Irving's fireside heart!   To be included as part
of Scott's home, not only by the father and mother
and four children, but by the cat, the packs of barking dogs, and the noble horses — that was what Irving
loved; for, in spite of his outward cheer, he suffered
from the loneliness of the inner self.   As he said, he
was not meant to be a bachelor; and when he writes
letters of blessing on the wives and children of
Brevoort and Paulding and others of the "knot of
queer, rum old bachelors" (for seventeen years
brought many changes), there is an undertone of
pathos in the music.   "You and Brevoort have given
me the slip . . . I cannot hear of my old cronies, snugly
nestled down with good wives and fine children round
them, but I feel for the moment desolate and for-
lorn."   "Heavens! what a haphazard, schemeless
life mine has been, that here I should be, at this
time of life, youth slipping away, and scribbling
month after month and year after year, far from
home."

That is all he *says* and he puts it jestingly then;
but the unsaid thoughts lie deep.   "Irving's smile is
one of the sweetest I know," said a friend, "but he can
look very, very sad."

We do not forget that forty years after Miss Hoffman's death, Irving had her miniature repaired because the case was *worn out*.

But enough of the hidden sadness of this *partner of the sunlight*. Let us go with the companionable Irving on his travels, and go in his spirit — as conquerors of loneliness.

Perhaps, like him, we shall yawn in palaces and shift restlessly on the "cursed stone benches" of the Tuileries, but we shall love the Hartz Mountains because their forests are like our own American forests and we shall love the columns of the vast cathedrals that reach upward like the dear old trees of home. What a mongrel tongue — of English, French, and German — Irving talks to the driver of the *diligence;* and what humor twinkles from his eyes at the "garrulous old lady" who shows us Shakespeare's home.

A rapid journey ours must be, a journey of seventeen years in part of an hour; and yet we must have time for slow steps in the silent Abbey — the most hallowed spot of all England — and time to bow our souls in reverence while the "deep-laboring organ" rolls its music up to Heaven. And we shall need time to enjoy the English Christmas as Irving enjoyed it. "While I lay musing on my pillow," he writes, "I heard the sound of little feet pattering outside of the door, and a whispering consultation. Presently a choir of small voices chanted forth an old Christmas carol, the burden of which was

> 'Rejoice, our Savior He was born
> On Christmas day in the morning.'

I rose softly, slipt on my clothes, opened the door suddenly, and beheld one of the most beautiful little fairy groups that a painter could imagine. It consisted of a boy and two girls, the eldest not more than six, and lovely as seraphs. They were going the rounds of the house and singing at every chamber door; but my sudden appearance frightened them into mute bashfulness. They remained for a moment playing on their lips with their fingers, and now and then stealing a shy glance from under their eyebrows, until, as if by one impulse, they scampered away, and as they turned an angle of the gallery, I heard them laughing in triumph at their escape."

Friendly and glad, Irving was heartily welcomed into the English home — to family prayers and church and the Christmas dinner with its wassail-bowl. And when he left that brother-land, with what a kindly feeling did he grace its memory to the world! How he has made us see its grass-plots and hanging blossoms and "little pots of flowers." And what a benediction he sheds in his "Peace be within thy walls, oh England! and plenteousness within thy palaces." "Do not destroy the ancient tie of blood." "We have the same Bible, and we address our common Father in the same prayer."

So much for his books of English travel; his books on Spain are no less charming. In fact, Spain must have been even more fascinating to a man of Irving's imagination; to the mind that conceived the mystic dwarfs and "wicked flagon" of Rip Van Winkle, and the headless horseman of Sleepy Hollow. Spain was a land rich in legend as well as steeped in beauty. The roads were infested with robbers. Every Andalusian carried a saber. There was often a lantern hidden beneath his cloak. Here and there a cross by the roadside or in a worn ravine, told where some muleteer had been murdered. And there was a subterranean stable where lived a goblin horse.

Sometimes, as Irving rode through this threatening country, " the deep tones of the cathedral bell would echo through the valley." Then " the shepherd paused on the fold of the hill, the muleteer in the midst of the road; each took off his hat and remained motionless for a time, murmuring his evening prayer."

" Who wants water — water colder than snow? " came the carrier's cry as they neared the city. The shaggy little donkey, with water-jars hung on each side, was all too willing to wait.

Arrived at the Alhambra, Irving found it at once a fortress and a palace, every stone breathing poetry and romance. " A little old fairy queen lived under the staircase, plying her needle and singing from morning till night." The Andalusians lay on the grass or danced to the guitar, and everywhere were groves of orange and citron and the music of singing birds and tinkling fountains. It was an enchanted palace. In the evening, Irving took his lamp and, in a " mere halo of light ", stole dreamily through the " waste halls and mysterious galleries." There were no sounds but echoes. Everything, even the garden, was deserted.

Nevertheless the scent of roses and laurel, the shimmer of moonlight, the murmur of hidden streams, had made the garden a fairy-land, only it was a fairy-land where flitting bat and hooting owl were much at home. To Irving, the owl had a vast knowledge of " astronomy and the moon ", and Irving respected the knowledge which he could not share. In short, the Alhambra just suited his fancy; and when, as he said, the summons came to return into the " bustle and business of the dusty world ", that summons ended one of the pleasantest dreams of his life —" a life perhaps you may think, too much made up of dreams."

But poets should not be bound, nor birds caged; nor do we need to take the poet at his own low estimate. Given to hospitality, and consequently open to many interruptions, inclined to postpone, and hating the labors of rewriting, Irving was, nevertheless, a hard worker. Those seventeen years were not all dreams. To them we owe " The Legend of Sleepy Hollow ", written " by candle-light in foggy London "; " Bracebridge Hall," dashed off in Paris in six weeks; and "Rip Van Winkle," which was not, as some have supposed, drawn from life, but was an imagined picture: when Irving wrote that story, he had never visited the Catskills; he had merely seen them from the river on his boyhood's first journey. To these years, too, we owe a longer, harder work than any of the rest —" The Life of Columbus." When the poet Longfellow took his early morning walks in Madrid, he often saw Irving writing at his open study-window at six o'clock; he had risen at five to work on the "Life." "I must make enough money," he would say to himself, "to be sure of my bread and cheese."

As a rule, however, Irving had a great indifference to money-getting. Perhaps this will partly account for his rare generosity, though I think generosity was in his blood. With his customary faithfulness, he gave the "Sketch Book" to his old publisher, Moses Thomas, even at the risk of loss. Utterly without envy, he pushed Bryant's work before the public, popularized Scott in America, gave plots to Poe, and, most generous of all, resigned, in favor of Prescott, his whole scheme for writing on the Conquest of Mexico, though Irving had hugged the hope of such a work since childhood, and had definitely written on it for over a year. Perhaps, blessed with eyesight himself, he thought he would do his blind friend this service. At all events, without consulting any one, he burned his own manuscript. It was a great sacrifice, but Prescott never knew.

Imagine how hard it was for such a warm nature as Irving's to be misjudged by his best friends. But he was misjudged. Some went so far as to think that those seventeen years spent abroad were a proof that he did not love his country and home; whereas Irving was all too weary of foreign society. He was, to quote his letters, "tired of being among strangers"; "sick of fashionable life and fashionable parties"; bored at having to "dress for court"; and altogether weary of mingling in all the "littleness and insipidity

of city life." If ever there was a home-loving man it
was Irving. During those seventeen long years he felt
himself

> "Strange tenant of a thousand homes
> And friendless with ten thousand friends."

He called it what it was, "a poor, wandering life."
"I have been tossed about 'hither and thither' and
whither I would not; have been at the levee and the
drawing-room, been at routs and balls, and dinners and
country-seats, been hand and glove with nobility and
mob-ility, until like *Trim*, I have satisfied the senti-
ment, and am now preparing to make my escape from
all this splendid confusion."

But the world did not understand. The newspaper
attacks hurt him. At last criticism became too keen
for his sensitive nature to bear. Then began for him
" sleepless nights and joyless days ", with the sharp
thought that the " kindness of his own countrymen was
withering towards him." Even Brevoort and Paulding, even his brothers, began to chide him with not
wanting to return.

When he did stand before them once again, however,
with his truth-telling, sunlit face, they questioned his
love no more. Irving's return to New York was
heralded by a dinner in his honor. Now Irving, as
Moore said, had never been " strong, as a lion ", though
he was " delightful, as a domestic animal." He himself said it was " physically impossible for him to make
a speech." A manuscript under his plate did not help

at all. When, at a dinner in England, he had been announced with loud cheers, he had simply responded: "I beg to return you my sincere thanks." And now when, before his fellow-countrymen, the toast was proposed, "To our illustrious guest, thrice welcome to his native land," the shy author who hated speech-making, could only stammer and blush. "I trembled for him," said one of his friends, "until I saw him seize the handle of a knife and commence gesticulating with that; then I knew he would get on."

"I am asked how long I mean to remain here," Irving said. "They know but little of my heart and feelings who can ask me that question. I answer: 'As long as I live!'" He hesitated, stood still, and looked about him, the old genial smile beaming from his dark gray eyes. Then a rousing cheer told him that he had won again the trust of all, and he sat down, satisfied — a tired exile welcomed home.

Except as Irving was twice sent to Europe by our nation, once to England as secretary of legation, and once as Minister to Spain, he did stay home all the rest of his life. It is as a home-maker and a home-lover that he was happiest and best known, and no part of life was so sweet to him as the life at Sunnyside. Let us visit him there in his own little house among the trees. Though the house is small, and already filled with his nieces, there is always room for one more. We take the train from New York for Irvington, near Tarrytown. Sunnyside, a ten-acre farm, bought by Irving in 1835, is only about ten minutes' walk from

Photograph by Brown Brothers

"Sunnyside".—The home of Washington Irving

the station.   The grounds look out on the blue Hudson. There is a cove and a cozy beach, and a spring "welling up at the bottom of the bank."   A stony brook, shaded by trees, "babbles down the ravine, throwing itself into the little cove."   On the rock at the edge of the lawn, Irving often sits, resting in his love of the shining river, and building his "castles at seventy" as he did at seven.   The house described by Irving, is a "little old fashioned stone mansion, all made up of gable ends, and as full of angles and corners as an old cocked hat."   It used to be called "Wolfert's Roost" (or Rest) and over the door is an old motto meaning "Pleasure in Quiet", a motto that was written in its master's heart.

Though you may not find any of the old Indian arrow-heads about the place, nor Brom Bones's pumpkin in the garden, you will find the spirit of Wolfert's Roost unchanged.   Crickets skip in the grass; humming-birds whirr among the trumpet-vines; the phœbe-bird and wren have built under the eaves.   The thick mantle of Melrose ivy, which almost hides the eastern end of Sunnyside, grew from one of Scott's slips. Very lately Irving built the near-by cottage for his gardener.

Within, Sunnyside is plainly furnished; there are not even many books.   Everything, however, looks comfortable and made for use.   For instance, the writing-table is a mass of disorder.   It is one of the sweet elements of our welcome that nothing is changed to receive us.   As part of the family, we will have row-boat picnics on the Tappan Zee. We can perch by Irving on the old stone wall and chat with "Uncle Brom", or see Jesse Merwin — the original *Ichabod Crane* in his old school of tough little Dutchers. We can visit Irving's "tree encircled farm." Those two elms on the lawn were planted by the author's own hands; he carried the saplings on his shoulder. The fruits and vegetables, he will tell you, were raised at "very little more than twice the market-price." Out in the pig pen is Fanny,— a fat pig of "peerless beauty", named for Fanny Kemble, the actress. Purring thunderously, Imp will come and rub his silky head against you, and Toby will bark a greeting and dash away to the other pets. There are cows and setting geese, cooing pigeons, and " squadrons of snowy " ducks. Dandy and Billy, the old coach horses, are as "sleek as seals" and "Gentleman Dick", Irving's saddle-horse, puts his cheek against his master's and lays his head on his shoulder. Though Irving will say nothing about it, perhaps you will notice that the saddle hanging near is an old one, furbished up. The father of so many borrowed children could not afford a new saddle.

"Dick now and then cuts daisies with me on his back; but that's to please himself, not me," laughs Irving, patting the horse's glossy side; and perhaps he may add that Gentleman Dick has thrown him once. It was after a second accident, when Irving was seventy-two, that his nieces forced him to sell this

"Gentleman that had proved no Gentleman." "Poor
Dick!" Irving said. "His character was very much
misunderstood by all but myself."

That word "all" covered a big household. Irving's
dearest brother, Peter, had died; and so had William
and John; but Ebenezer, now growing very deaf, and
his sister Catharine made their home at Sunnyside, and
there were six adoring nieces who kept Irving "almost
as happy" as if he were "a married man."

To see how happy he was, we should have visited
him at Christmas when "The Tappan Zee was covered
with sparkling ice and the opposite hills with snow,"
and when holly reddened the hearth of Sunnyside.
Then, indeed, the cottage rang with shouts, while the
king of the cottage tiptoed round to be first with his
"Merry Christmas", acted a jovial Santa Claus, and
filled all the stockings with presents. "Children who
do not believe in Santa Claus are too wise to be
happy," he used to say. "When I was a child, I believed in Santa Claus as long as I could, until they put
snow-balls in my stockings."

His understanding of children was wonderful.
Once when he had amused two fretful little things on
a long train journey, the mother thanked him with
"Any one can see you 're the father of a large family."
There are two delightful stories of Irving and the
boys who robbed his orchard. One day a little fellow
came up to him with winning secrecy and said: "I 'll
show you the old man's best tree, if you 'll shake it

for me." "Agreed!"—"By George, Sir," laughed
Irving, "if he did n't take me to the very best tree on
my own place!"

Another time, when he came unexpectedly on an
apple squad, he said, picking out the leader, "Boys,
these are very poor apples. I know a much better
tree." Then he led them on, skulking in the shadows
and dodging the gardener, in true boy style.

"Be quiet! Keep near the hedge!" he cautioned.

"We're afraid the old gentleman will catch us."

"He's not there now. There, the best tree's just
beyond the hedge."

The prickly hedge tore the boys' trousers and faces
and hands, but the seekers were too near their Hes-
perides to be daunted.

"Now, boys, this is the tree I spoke of, and I am
the owner of it—Mr. Irving." There was a pause,
during which the boys intently studied the grass.
"Don't be afraid," Irving went on, "I sha'n't punish
you; the prickly hedge has done that. I only wish
that when you take my fruit, you would come to me
and ask for it." He gave them a genial, forgiving
smile, and was gone, the dear old man with the heart
of a boy and the immortal spirit of play.

Up to the very end of life, at seventy-six, he could
laugh at pain and sleeplessness, and at weariness of
mind and body. Let no one underrate the heroism of
those last years — the hard work wrought with aching
hands. With the press dogging Irving's heels, the
"Life of Goldsmith" was written in sixty days.

"Are you sure it does n't smell of apoplexy?" asked
the doubting author, for "self-criticism was apt to be-
set him and cuff him down at the end of the work when
the excitement of composition was over." He spoke
of his writings as "literary babblings" or as "water
spilt on the ground." Many times during the composition of the "Life of Washington"—his last work—
he was at the point of putting it into the fire. His
letters and journal show that writing had become a
"toil of head and fagging of the pen." "I am still
muddling with the 'Life of Washington'," we read.
"It lags and drags." Often he would be scribbling
in his study at half-past twelve at night, long after the
family were in bed and asleep, or he would "rise at
midnight, light his lamp, and write for an hour or two."
If he rested in the evening, with the girls sewing round
him, it was because he had "passed the whole morning in his study, hard at work" and had "earned his
recreation." Feverish and full of fears, he thought:
"I must get through with the work I have cut out for
myself. I must weave my web and then die." The
belief that he might not live to finish the "Life" became a torment; and when, near the end, he sank into
a kind of delirium, he was possessed with the idea that
he had a "big book to write before he could sleep."

Through those last years, though he made a pitiful
struggle for sleep, asthma and nervousness combined
against him, except when he slept from pure exhaustion. Now we read that he got "a little sprinkling
of sleep"; now that he had taken "sleeping potions

enough to put a whole congregation to sleep." And
still he made merry. Turning to one of his nieces,
he said: "I am apt to be rather fatigued, my dear,
by my night's rest," and again, as he took up his
candle: "Well, as the ghost in Hamlet says, 'The
time has come when I to sulphurous and tormenting
flames must render up myself.'"

Besides this sleeplessness, Irving had an aggravated
form of sickness that had warned him years before in
Paris: a lameness of the ankles hindered walking and
an inflammation of the wrists hindered writing.
Without doubt Irving injured himself standing out-
doors in the cold and wet while the builders were en-
larging Sunnyside. Cheerful as ever, the dear old
bachelor refused "to be bullied by a cold"; and of
course the home must be enlarged that it might hold
more people. He still hoped to be

> "Once more able
> To stump about my farm and stable."

And he did manage to hobble round, wearing his customary old slouch hat and muffled in a big gray shawl.
Once when his lameness was at its worst, he spoke of
getting well: "I shall feel like a boy with a new
coat who thinks everybody will turn round and look at
him and say, 'Bless my soul, how that gentleman has
the use of his legs,'— one cannot help being puffed up
a little on having the use of one's legs." As a kind
of benediction on surgeons and dentists he exclaimed:
"May their good deeds be returned upon them a

thousand-fold! May they have the felicity, in the
next world, to have successful operations performed
upon them to all eternity!"

His greatest fear of doctors was that they would
prolong his life beyond his period of usefulness.
" Strange that a harp of a thousand strings should keep
in tune so long!" he would muse. He did not long
to die; but he longed to go down " with all sails set."
He dreaded being a burden to those about him; being
"mewed up at home" like an "old fogy." "A
man, as he grows old, must take care not to grow
rusty or fusty or crusty,— an old bachelor especially."
It was his daily prayer that his old age might be
lovable; that he might keep his mind and keep his
sunnyness. " Happy is he who can grow smooth as
an old shilling as he wears out; he has endured the
rubs of life to some purpose."

And he did grow smooth and tuneful and placid.
Though his voice was hoarse and his step faltering, his
gray eyes kept their twinkle and his heart was young
and singing to the end.

It was, blessedly, a sudden end — just one sharp
cry, a fall, and death. One frosty November day the
solemn bells told the farmers and sailors, the boys who
loved the apples, and all the waiting neighbors of the
glen, that the Master of Sunnyside had gone. But
the frost melted soon and gracious Indian summer
filled the air. " It 's one of his own days," thought
the loving ones who stood beside the grave.

If you take the " lazy country road " that winds its

drowsy way to Sleepy Hollow, you can find the place where Irving rests. Peter is buried there, and the mother; and Washington's grave is where he asked to have it, close to hers. If his fame had never gone beyond the " old Dutch Church " and turnpike-road, the stone could not have been more simple:

WASHINGTON

SON OF WILLIAM AND SARAH S. IRVING
DIED
Nov. 28, 1859
AGED 76 YEARS, 7 MO., AND 25 DAYS.

Sunnyside was left, as we might have expected, to Ebenezer and his daughters, " to be kept forever as an Irving rally place." But Irving left a far greater bequest: besides his books, rich in humor and kindliness, and written in " the language of the heart ", he left the dear example of one who loved and lost, and smiled, and gave; of one who sought the good and found it, whether in music or pictures, free country, books, or people; and of one who sheds a constant blessing, even now, like the sunshine from the sky.

V
EMERSON

" We will walk on our own feet; we will work with our own hands; we will speak our own minds."

Ralph Waldo Emerson.

V

LOUISA ALCOTT'S NEIGHBOR

ONE afternoon at sundown, about a hundred years ago, a slightly-built boy in "blue nankeen",— not half so blue as his own eyes,— might have been seen driving his mother's cow from pasture, along the streets of Boston. He was eating a big, juicy pear. When the cow came to the old, wooden parsonage, at the corner of Summer and Chauncy Streets, near the place where Hovey's store now stands, she turned in naturally, jangling her bell and switching her tail, and Ralph Waldo Emerson turned in after her.

It was a peaceful home. though everything was simple and many things were poor. From the windows you could see the harbor and the ships that came and went; and there were wide, empty fields, neighborly barns and sheds, and always the open sky, and the changing tide, and the salt smell of the sea. It was very near here that, a hundred years before, Benjamin Franklin and his friends had built their fishing-wharf of "borrowed" stones; and the five Emerson brothers had the same chance as Franklin to catch "tom-cod and flounders."

Let us guess that this night, however, when the cow had been milked and stabled, the boy, Ralph Waldo, did not think of the sweet, familiar view, nor even of the morrow's fishing, but of the new book which he had just drawn from the circulating-library for the great payment of six cents. It was a novel, and he was part way through. But to-night his Aunt Mary found him reading, and talked to him so seriously of his extravagance and of his mother's need, that, we are told, "He left the story unfinished and did not take out the second volume."

Yet it must not be thought that the Emerson boys did not love their Aunt Mary, or that she did not love them. She was the "family sibyl", determined that the boys should be defrauded of nothing real, and determined that, poor as they were, they should have not only school but college,— for, she said, they were "born to be educated." She, herself, trained in them "all the powers of the mind and heart." She gave them the sturdy maxim: "Always do what you are afraid to do." And no one knows how much that maxim may have braced the hearts of Ralph and Edward, when, sharing as they did the same "great-coat," other boys would call out, jeeringly: "Whose turn is it to wear the coat to-day?" "My grand-father," Emerson says, "prayed every night that none of his descendants might ever be rich," and surely his prayer was answered in the case of that one family.

When Ralph was only eight, his father died, leaving six children, all under ten. His mother took boarders, struggling through the crowded days, rising early and working late, with the hope throbbing in her heart that her boys might have every chance. Perhaps those boys shared her care too early and were over-serious; but, anyway, they were not selfish and irre-sponsible, thinking of no one but themselves: they sympathized with her lovingness and her weariness. Ralph told his older brother, William, that he thought it would be his " happiest earthly moment " when he had " a home comfortable and pleasant to offer to mother."

Though Boston winters are long and snowy, and coasting is fine on the hills, Ralph Emerson never owned a sled. But when we remember that in the winter of 1814, when he was only eleven, the family were in actual need of bread, it is good to know that he did not whimper for playthings. That year, too, his baby sister died, the only girl of the family. And so circumstances combined to give him a serious face and a serious heart, which all his comrades felt.

Perhaps he cared less than other boys for athletics because he was never physically strong; but he was no " Miss Nancy ", and no " saint ", and once, at least, he played truant from Mr. Webb's school " to romp on the common."

There was one school, however, from which Emerson was willingly excused after a day's attendance. It was a singing-school, and Ralph Waldo had not the slightest ear for music. When his turn came to sing, the master said to him " Chord."

"What?" said the child.

"Chord! Chord! I tell you," repeated the master.

"I don't know what you mean." The blue eyes looked puzzled.

"Why, sing! Sing a note." So the boy made "some kind of a noise", as he called it, and the singing-master said: "That will do, sir. You need not come again."

To know that many of our greatest men have been lacking in some particular, as Emerson was in music, seems to make them human, like ourselves; and it is always inspiring to know that most of them overcame handicaps.

The handicap of poverty is one of the simplest to overcome. It makes men of fiber. Every one of the Emerson boys was fitted for college, except Bulkley, who had to be cared for all his life because he "never grew up in mind." Each of the others helped himself to an education. Ralph Waldo wrote from Harvard: "I am to wait in the Junior Hall. I do like it, and yet I do not like it; for which sentiments you can easily guess the reason." And so it happened that the boy of brains was servant to the boys of money; while he brought them coffee and rolls, he was bringing himself character.

Meanwhile, matters were simplified at home by his step-grandfather, Dr. Ezra Ripley, inviting Mrs. Emerson and her sons to live with him in Concord. That made Ralph Waldo's climb to culture happier, because less burdened.   Some one has said, " The best of his education he gave himself in rambling reading and incessant practice in writing, and by that note-book in which, from his junior year, he began the process of storing thoughts, phrases, suggestions, for future use."   Emerson himself said, " A chamber alone, that was the best thing I found at college." And ever after, when he gave advice to young men, it was, " Sit alone; and keep a journal."

He was younger than most of his class, and not physically strong; but, if he failed in athletics (which, in truth, he hardly attempted) he won in other re-spects, and did it, too, without being a " regular grind."

There were three specially happy days at college: the days he won honors.   Although he was made class-poet only after seven others had been asked, he was perfectly delighted, and describes himself as walking up and down his lonely little room " flushed and proud of a poet's fancies."   Another year, he took a second prize for a composition " On Ethics ", and the Boyls-ton prize in declamation.   He sent the Boylston prize-money straight home, joyfully hoping that his mother would spend it on a new shawl, and he was bitterly disappointed when a letter came from the eighteen-year-old brother William, " the care-worn head of the family," saying he had used it for the baker's bill.

The years following college were among the hardest of Emerson's life.   He tried to teach school, to make money to study for the ministry, which he had chosen

for his profession and which had been the profession
of seven generations before him. But, though he attempted several different schools, he was utterly miserable in them, and by no means successful. At first,
when he taught boys and won their love, he seemed
to manage fairly well; but, when it came to assisting
his brother William in a school for "fashionable
young ladies", a school held in his mother's house, that
was a different story. Let him tell it:

"I was nineteen, and had grown up without sisters,
and, in my solitary and secluded way of living, had no
acquaintance with girls. I still recall my terrors at
entering the school and my timidities at French."
Though he carried on the school for more than a year,
he never overcame his bashfulness, or his powerless-
ness to discipline those young ladies of Boston, some
of them older than himself. "They would ask him on
Election Day to give them a holiday while he voted,"
knowing all the time he was a minor. "They liked
to make him blush." When they got entirely beyond
his control, he would send them to his mother's room
for study. Here is part of a sympathetic letter written
by him to a friend who was teaching: "How my
heart bleeds for you! Better tug at the oar, dig the
mine, or saw wood; better sow hemp, or hang with it,
than sow the seeds of instruction." He called it
"keeping school", and found his only comfort in the
afternoons when he could get into the speechless company of trees and flowers, and where he was unblush-
ingly at home.

"A woodland walk,
A quest of river-grapes, a mocking thrush,
A wild-rose, or rock-loving columbine,
Salve my worst wounds."

It seems strange that Emerson, who heartily hated
the official task of teaching, should have been so great
and so understanding a friend to the countless young
people who sought his sympathy and advice years
later under the elms of Concord. If we could have
run in on him in his Concord home, like his child-
neighbor, Louisa May Alcott, we should have known
him much better than we know him through any
books. Louisa Alcott went to school in his barn, and
played there with his children, gathered moss from
the woods for his arbor, ate pears from his laden trees,
and grew up under his kindly eyes to be her brave,
natural self. His library was always open to her;
and sometimes, when she browsed among its shelves,
"for a new and very interesting book", he would
wander in and tell her which books she might like, and
which she had better wait to know. When she was a
little girl, she sang the song of *Mignon* under his window, and, at fifteen, wrote him many letters — her
thoughts, her feelings — all her growing-up ideas; but
she never got the courage to send them. All through
life, however, he was her idol and her hero.

Not only was he the strongest influence on her character, but he was the best friend her dreamy, unprac-
tical, business-failure of a father ever had. Knowing
that Bronson Alcott could never earn anything, Emer-

son had a way of leaving money under a book on the Alcott table, or behind a candlestick. He gave Mrs. Alcott five hundred dollars to buy a place in Concord, and he offered his own home as her husband's lecture-hall. In Louisa's "Journal" we read: "Father had four talks at Emerson's; good people came, and he enjoyed them much; made $30. R. W. E. probably put in 20."

Not only in business stress was Emerson a master of sympathy; he helped Louisa in even sadder times. When her dear young sister died — the "Beth" of Little Women — he helped carry the beloved body "out of the old home to the new at Sleepy Hollow." And long years after, when Louisa's precious mother had smiled her last good-bye, with "A smile is as good as a prayer", he was near the daughter to comfort her. The telegram announcing the death of May Alcott (Amy), in Paris, was sent to Mr. Emerson, to " soften the blow." When Louisa came downstairs, she found him looking at May's portrait, "pale and tearful with the paper in his hand." "My child," he began, "I wish I could prepare you; but alas, alas!" Then his voice failed, and he gave her the telegram. Though she was a woman over forty, she was still his " child ", to be deeply helped by a wordless grasp of his hand.

His love for her father, Bronson Alcott, had, it may be, increased his love for that child, but he always had a genial way with young people, and a rare understanding of their thoughts. To her he would say: " What is true for your own private heart is true for others." His essays on "Self-Reliance", "Character", "Nature", and "Spiritual Laws" helped her to fathom herself; and his life and companionship helped her to be strong. On his part, he must have admired that "Spartan spirit." Content to wear cast-off clothes, eager to sew, and teach, and write, and work, able to sing and pray over the wash-tub, or to mother sick soldiers in war — that was Louisa Alcott. While he liked the books she wrote for children, he loved her growing, sturdy proof that "though an Alcott she could support herself."

We have let ourselves wander a little from Emerson's own life to his neighbor's, but we have known him better for the wandering. He soon gave up the hated teaching, and, four years after he left college, when he was twenty-three, began to preach. He was too frail, however, for the work. As Professor Woodberry puts it: "He read if his eyes allowed; he walked if his hip permitted; he preached if his lungs held out; he went slow." Yet, somehow, he found time and strength to help Dr. Taylor found a Sailors' Mission, and to keep up his own preaching, too, though, after each attempt, he had a pain in his chest. Finally, he had to go to Florida for the winter,— a hard thing to do for a man like him, who did not know how to live lavishly, and was bored by idleness. "I stroll on the beach," he wrote miserably, "and drive a green orange over the sand with a stick."

In the shadow of great hardships, however, such petty irritations disappear. Two years later, Emer-

son's brother Edward, who had been working in Daniel
Webster's law-office and also teaching school, was suddenly taken violently insane. Edward was almost a
part of Ralph's self. As boys they had bravely shared
poverty and sympathy and love; but now Ralph carried this sorrow alone. To Edward, it meant uncon-
sciousness; to Ralph, an agony of grief. The sick
brother was sent first to an asylum in Charleston, and
then to travel on the Mediterranean and among the
West Indies. He died in 1834, after a six years' fight
to save his mind.

We pass swiftly in *words* over the long darknesses
in people's lives; perhaps because we need to seek the
sunlight, perhaps because we would not try to utter
what is unutterable. It was by bearing sorrow himself, in the death of his brothers, his wife, and his
lovely boy, that Emerson learned how to feel for
others. His brother Charles died soon after Edward,
of lung trouble, the same illness that conquered Emerson's first wife, a delicate flower of a woman who lived
less than two years after her marriage.

I am glad he learned to love again, and that he had
a home and children, for he and children always
" took " to each other. The babies held out reaching
arms, to be strongly clasped in his. Then, too, by this
marriage he realized for eighteen years, his boyish
hopes of giving his mother a home, and it was, as he
had wanted it to be, " comfortable and pleasant."

It stood among the peaceful fields of Concord, not
far from its lazy river, a big, square, hospitable house

with its thrifty orchards, and shading elms, and sweet
air full of song. Almost across the road, Alcott
mused and talked; a mile or so away, lonely Hawthorne thought; and deep in the woods near Walden
Pond, Thoreau lived in his hut, caught the fishes in
his hands, and learned the hidden secrets of the out-
door world. Emerson was Alcott's true friend and
practically his business-manager,— and if ever a man
needed a business-manager, Alcott did; Hawthorne
was too shy and Emerson too reserved for them even
to get acquainted. Though they once tried to take a
walk together, they "hit it off" but dismally.
Thoreau and Emerson were thoroughly congenial, loving the same things in the same way. When Emerson,
through his great awkwardness with tools, failed to do
all he tried, Thoreau came to the rescue; he was his
carpenter, and he planted his larches and pines. The
poet, Channing, once chopped Emerson's wood for
him.

In his fourteen acres, more or less, there were wood-
lands, fields, and a blackberry-patch. Sometimes much
to Emerson's delight, the Indians and gipsies camped
on his ground. Then there were the pines where his
mother sat; a part of the shore of Walden, where he
and his children swam and fished and skated; and his
orchard and garden. Here he worked an hour or
more a day, pruning trees, digging, and weeding.
Emerson's pears brought the highest price in the
Boston market. When he hoed his garden, "a crop
of comfort straightway sprang up." But the work of

weeding was as disheartening to him as it is to other
people. "I stoop to pick up a weed that is choking
the corn, and find there are two; close behind it is a
third, and I reach out my arm to a fourth; behind that
there are four thousand and one." His little five-year-
old boy, Waldo, worked with him, silently happy by
his father's side. Seeing that his father did not use
a spade like any one else, he would call out, "Take
care, Papa, you will dig your leg."

Emerson's habits of writing were very irregular;
he had a method all his own, and one that few would
imitate. One day a friend found him seated at his
desk with papers spread all round him on the floor.
From these, here and there, he gathered a sentence or
paragraph for his essays. Like many other writers,
however, he sometimes composed out-of-doors in the
woods or fields where he loved to be.

Most of his writing was done in the mornings; in
the afternoons, he gardened or walked; in the evenings he often read aloud to his family. "He was
a sound sleeper and never got up at night, as some
have imagined, to jot down thoughts which then oc-
curred to him." He was a good walker, "light, erect,
and strong of limb." Occasionally he hunted, but not
to shoot. Though he learned to use a rifle, his best
friends believe that he never used it on any living
thing; and though one night he paddled out to see
a deer and drew close enough to fire, he let the
sad-eyed creature have its life. To his own question,

> "Hast thou named all the birds without a gun?
> Loved the wood-rose and left it on its stalk?"

he could answer a joyful *yes.* "Anemone and chipmunk, titmouse and rhodora, black-ice and starlight, he knew and loved them all, and was almost more than Thoreau a forest citizen." With a child's love for nature he would say: "I expand and live in the warm day like corn and melons." To him there was "beauty in fog, astronomy in plants and 'punctual birds'," and song and shine in all things of the earth, for

> "In the mud and scum of things
> There alway, alway something sings."

"Look!" he seems to say, "above your desert and find a star."

> "Wilt thou not ope thy heart to know,
> What rainbows teach and sunsets show?"

Here is part of an open letter of Emerson's to his great friend, Carlyle. It gives us an indoor glimpse of his home on May 10, 1838: "My wife Lidian is an incarnation of Christianity.— My mother, whitest, mildest of ladies.— My boy, a piece of love and sunshine well worth my watching from morning to night; these and three domestic women, who cook, and sew, and run for us, make all my household." Other children followed, among them the little Ellen, for whom Louisa Alcott wrote "Flower Fables"; and always the old Aunt Mary, who had been his boyhood adviser, was welcome in his home.

Emerson managed to give more time to his children than such busy men can often give. Awkward as he was with all tools and animals, he knew well how to handle the smallest babies, and they came to him with cooing gladness. At his thoroughly New England breakfast, he liked to eat his *pie* in peace, and would say to his children, "At breakfast all must be calm and sweet; nothing must jar." And if a child cried at the table, he was apt to send it to see whether the gate was shut, or whether the clouds were in the sky, as if he trusted the " great, all-loving Day" to bring it peace. " The small ambassador, a little perplexed . . . as to why he was sent there, returned, solemnly reported, and climbed back into his high chair." " You are bound to be healthy and happy," Emerson would say; " do not have any hobgoblin of the sick sort, but live out-of-doors, and in the sea-bath, and the sailboat, and the saddle, and the wagon, and, best of all, in your shoes, so soon as they will obey you for a mile. When you have worn out your shoes, the strength of the sole-leather has gone into the fiber of your body."

Though he was a preacher, he allowed his children a great deal of liberty on Sunday. They could walk and read, and bathe in Walden Pond; but they could not have playthings, or drive, or row. They learned hymns, as he had done, and went to their grandmother's quiet room for Bible readings. Their father liked to have them go to church, and they knew it; but the church service was never insisted on. It was possible that they, like him, would find a church in the solitary wood.

Emerson thought all young people should learn to think of others. At one of the little Emersons' birthday parties, the children got into the haycocks and began throwing the hay all round, much to the distress of the hired man. Out came the father with " long strides." " ' Lads and lasses! You must n't undo hard work. The man has worked in the heat all day; now all go to work and put back the hay.' And he stayed and saw it done, working himself."

When pleasures were harmless, however, the father was heartiest of all in their encouragement. Louisa Alcott remembered many such times with his children, " when their illustrious papa was our good playfellow. Often piling us into a bedecked hay-cart, he took us to berry, bathe, or picnic at Walden, making our day charming and memorable by showing us the places he loved . . . so that when, years afterward, we read of ' the sweet rhodora in the woods ', and the ' burly, dozing humble-bee ', we recognized old friends." He called the pines " gentlemen ", praised the specially tall ones, and once he took off his hat to an extra large red rose.

There came a time, however, when Emerson's heart was robbed of its spirit of play. His little Waldo — a living sunbeam and his father's constant companion, the " deep-eyed boy " who followed him from study to garden without bothering or interrupting — was suddenly taken ill with scarlet fever. Four days later,

Louisa Alcott, then eight years old, was sent over to ask how he was. Mr. Emerson, himself, worn with watching and sorrow, opened the door. When the little girl saw how changed he was, she could hardly stammer out her question.

"Child, he is dead!" fell the hollow answer. Then the door closed, and she ran home to tell the dreadful news and never to forget that anguished face. Emerson's beautiful poem "Threnody", in memory of Waldo, gives but a hint of the father and son as playfellows and as kindred spirits.

> "I taught thy heart beyond the reach
> Of ritual, bible, or of speech."

comes like a sob from the father; but its only answer is the lonely memory of the empty "willow wagon" of Waldo's babyhood, the "painted sled" of the romping boy, and the brook which loved to be his looking-glass.

But poetry or prose could not begin to tell the story. "You can never know," Emerson wrote to Carlyle, "how much of me such a young child can take away." He was lost for the "forever of this world." Yet, even out of Emerson's bereavement, he breathed a blessing on John Thoreau who had urged him to have Waldo's daguerreotype taken. There was, at least, that part of his sunlight child to keep, besides the sacred memory of his love.

We have talked much of Emerson's home and neighbors because through them he is best understood. To many people of his time he was a mystery, a far-away enigma. Even to the world to-day he is less present than Holmes or Longfellow. And yet he was a man of many friends. Like Agassiz, he belonged to the famous Saturday Club where gathered Lowell, Holmes, Longfellow, Norton, Hawthorne, and others. There, no one thought him cold. He came regularly and sat near Longfellow. To young people, he gave himself even more freely than to men of his own age. One little girl always remembered him as the minister who "took her on his lap and showed her the barberry blossom, and how its stamens sprang up at the touch of a pin or an insect." " My special parish," Emerson once said, " is young men seeking their way." Boys and girls came to him with all their problems and confidences; college fellows asked his advice for their futures. Howells said, when as a young man, he went to see him, " His smile was the very sweetest I have ever beheld," though it was a smile given to a perfect stranger. Emerson more than any one else encouraged the Jewess-poet, Emma Lazarus, and helped her to find publishers. It was he who pushed Carlyle's works in this country, and who continued to push for twenty years; and, as we have said, he was Bronson Alcott's bank-account, and Louisa Alcott's guiding-star.

In farmers who plowed the fields, in sea-captains who hoisted sail, in boys and girls who hoped and worked, he was deeply and permanently interested, but never, never in those who shirked and sagged. " The sun grudges his light," he would say, "the air his breath, to him who stands with his hands folded in the great school of God." When a letter came, then, from a young girl, asking him to write her valedictory, we can imagine that he gave her no gentle answer. " Stand on your own feet, think your own thoughts; live your own life!" was his motto.

" To have a friend one must be one," Emerson believed. It was beautifully touching to see the eagerness of his many Concord friends to show the genuineness of their friendship. As fellow-citizen, Emerson had belonged to the fire association. " The leathern buckets and baize bag always hung over the stairs in his side entry," and at many fires in the woods he had helped beat out the flames with pine boughs. And now, in 1872, the Concord citizens were given a chance to fight a fire for him. Very early, one July morning, Mr. and Mrs. Emerson were waked by the crackling of flames, and barely escaped with their lives from the burning house. Though the whole upper half of their home was a ruin, hurrying neighbors saved many of the household goods, Louisa Alcott guarding the precious library, badly soaked by the rain. Moreover, those loving neighbors insisted, much against Emerson's will, in rebuilding the house. Perhaps they saw that the early morning work in the pouring rain had been too hard on their dear friend of nearly seventy. At any rate, the following October, while Emerson, with his daughter Ellen, took his

third trip to Europe, his Concord friends restored his
home.

He returned like a conqueror.   There were signals
to announce his coming, a triumphal arch, and a brass-
band; there were carriages to drive him and his family
to the " new " house, round which a crowd of old and
young were gathered.   Even the babies in their
wagons came out to smile a welcome.   Just before
Emerson entered his door, he turned round, and, walking back to the gate, said in his old, gracious way:
" My friends!   I know that this is not a tribute to an
old man and his daughter returned to their house, but
to the common blood of us all — one family — in
Concord! "

So far, we have thought of Emerson almost entirely as an influence on others, and have forgotten
what influence life itself had on him — Emerson, the
minister, and yet not the minister, for he preached
only three years.   In 1832, the same year in which his
first wife died, he reached a crisis in thought which
drove him to the White Hills to consider his duty.
He was a kind of " walking sincerity ", and, he was,
above all, a believer in religious freedom.   " God can
be worshiped in a barn," he said; and when some one
once remarked that she did " not trouble the church
much " he answered quietly: " Then you have somewhere a little chapel of your own."   This summer of
1832 he had reached the point where he must be as
free with himself as he had always been with others.

"It is my desire," said he, "in the office of a Christian minister, to do nothing which I cannot do with my whole heart." "I have sometimes thought that to be a good minister it was necessary to leave the ministry," he had written in his journal and now he was to write it in his life. As the years had advanced, he had concluded that prayer, to be real prayer, must come direct from a heart-felt longing to talk with "Our Father." It was a Quaker thought. With it nad come an inability to follow, sincerely, all the ceremonies of the church. Accordingly, one memorable Sunday, Emerson stood before his quiet little congregation, and made a plain statement, asking to resign unless he could be privileged to leave out certain ceremonies which to him were insincere. His resignation was accepted, and, in consequence, the man who had spent his youth in teaching which he disliked, in order to earn money for the ministry, which he hoped to love, found himself adrift, without a profession, poor and yet with a family dependent upon him, and he was too practical and too noble to shirk responsibility.

Let no one think that the decision was easy. It was reached through hours of lonely thought and through the help of the solitary hills, and of the Maker of the hills who helps us all. And it was the steep, white path of truth that he had chosen. His own gentle judgment of others may teach us a gentle judgment of him — with honor added for the sacrifice.

For it was a sacrifice. On his return from Europe,

Ralph Waldo Emerson in 1854

in the winter of 1833-34, Emerson began his life anew
as lecturer. It meant hard work in the study and
hard work on the road, traveling with those brain-
stuffs of his as peddlers travel with their wares. It
meant, also, very small pay — an average of only
twenty dollars a lecture — and Emerson was a
" shrewd, sensible Yankee " who knew that " a dollar
is a dollar and a cent a cent and that dollars and cents
are convenient things to have in pocket. He was no
crank, no dreamer."

He gave more than he got; for to all who heard him
lecture, he was an inspiration. He taught parents
that children had a right to individual growth. " Get
off that child! " he cried, " you are trying to make
him another you." To young men he taught the
hardy doctrine, drawn perhaps from his own defeat,
that " a good failure is always a good experience."
He made them ashamed of frivolity, uselessness, and
untruth; it was as if he prayed with them that they
might always " know what is sacred."

Moreover his lectures were full of artistic touches
giving them an added charm. Once, in speaking of
Washington, he took up a glass of water, held it for
a moment, and then spilt a little as if to typify that
great man's " purity and cleanliness of soul."

Over six feet tall, Emerson stood before his
audience, slender, graceful, erect, with a smooth face
and clear, almost ruddy complexion, and a wonderful
smile that warmed. As he spoke in that deep, musical
" ground-swell of a voice ", he was at once rousing

and restful. Though by many he was less understood than felt, he gave courage and strength like a mountain wind.

"Do you understand Mr. Emerson?" asked one.

"Not a word, but I like to go and see him stand up there and look as if he thought every one was as good as he was."

Another nudged his neighbor and asked: "Don't you think we could understand him better if we stood on our heads?"

The impressions of Lowell, who heard him as a young man, are interesting: "It was as if, after vainly trying to get his paragraphs into sequence and order, he had at last tried the desperate expedient of shuffling them . . . Did you say he was disconnected? So were the stars." And later, in a letter to Norton· "Emerson's oration was more disjointed than usual, even with him. It began nowhere and ended everywhere, and yet, as usual with that divine man, it left you feeling that something beautiful had passed that way — something more beautiful than anything else. . . . Every possible criticism might have been made on it but one,— that it was not noble . . . He boggled, he lost his place, he had to put on his glasses; but it was as if a creature from some fairer world had lost his way in our fogs, and it was our fault, not his. . . . All through it I felt something in me that cried, 'Ha, ha! to the sound of the trumpets!'"

It is sad that a man with such a mind as Emerson's should have lost it during the last years, and sadder

still that he was conscious of the loss.   He never re-
covered from the exposure and shock of the Concord
fire,— slowly his power of memory slipped away and he
knew that it was slipping.   " I have lost my mental
faculties," he told a friend, " but I am perfectly well."
At Longfellow's funeral he looked down at the placidly
strong face which had so often brightened beside his
own at the Saturday Club, and said: " That gentleman was a sweet, beautiful soul, but I have entirely
forgotten his name."   And during his last illness,
when his eyes fell on Carlyle's picture,— rough old
Carlyle, who had an " Emerson's room " at the top
of his little Chelsea home — he only half knew his
friend, sighing out, " That is my man, my good
man ! "

Emerson died of pneumonia in 1882, a few weeks
before his seventy-ninth birthday.   It was early spring,
too early for many of the wild flowers he had loved.
But his friends placed vases of lilies of the valley,
red and white roses, and arbutus on the mantel in
the Concord home; and Louisa Alcott made a harp of
yellow jonquils.   She and others softened the church
pulpit with boughs of pine and hemlock and the tender
coral of the maple blossoms,— wild things which many
do not see, but which his love had welcomed every
year.   Then he was laid to rest in Sleepy Hollow,
close to his own little Waldo, and a few steps from
Beth Alcott, Thoreau, and Hawthorne.   There is a
great rock of rough rose quartz over his grave; mating
birds come in the spring to nest in the tall grass, and

violets blossom underneath the pines. It is all as peaceful as it should be,— the resting-place of a " royal soul " who had fulfilled his kingship, and a captain who had kept his " rudder true."

VI

AGASSIZ

" No one can warp Nature to suit his own views. She brings us back to absolute truth as often as we wander."

Louis Agassiz.

VI

A SWISS BOY AND HIS WANDERINGS

ONE May, over a hundred years ago, there was born in a low cottage, in the Swiss village of Motier, a baby boy who was given the long name of Jean Louis Rudolphe Agassiz. This name did not burden the child, however. He was a lusty, rollicking baby,— an out-of-doors boy from the very first; and, no doubt, he knew much better how to coo than how to cry. His parents, who spoke French, might have nicknamed him " Le soleil " or " Le bonheur ",— French names for sunshine and for happiness; but they called him simply Louis.

The manse where Louis lived, for his father was a clergyman, was very pleasant. There was a vine-yard, an orchard, and a garden, and, behind the house, a great stone basin made Louis' first aquarium,— a home for fish. Very near, too, was the beautiful Lake Morat,— a swimming-pool in summer and a skating-rink in winter; and seemingly near was Mont Vully, vine-clad or snow-clad with the seasons' change.

Until Louis was ten years old, he had no other teachers but his parents, his own good little brain, and " Mother Nature." He had no special love for study;

147

but he loved everything that was alive. He loved
the blossoms that spangled the moist Swiss meadows,
— the glistening buttercups, and crowding blue-bells,
and scores of other frail flowers blowing nameless in
the valley. And yet, much as he loved flowers, he
loved animals still more. He and his younger brother,
Auguste, had all kinds of pets —" birds, field-mice,
hares, rabbits, and guinea-pigs." He described his
own room as a " little menagerie." He " searched the
neighboring woods and meadows for birds," and raised
caterpillars and " fresh beautiful butterflies." Besides this, there was the aquarium in the big stone
basin. Like some other boys, Louis and Auguste
needed nothing to catch fish with but their active hands,
and they usually cornered their fish between the rocks
while they were in bathing.

One might think from this story that these brothers
had one unbroken life of play; but they were learning many useful things. It was a curious custom in
Switzerland, at that time, for the cooper to come just
before grape-gathering season, to fit up the wine-cellar
with barrels and hogsheads; for the tailor to come to
make clothes; and for the shoemaker to call three
times a year at all the Swiss homes, and practically
shoe the entire family. These visits were events in
the home life, and Louis, with a child's instinct for
imitation, made the most of them, watched closely, and
then tried to do the same things,— till he could make
a tiny barrel, perfectly water-tight, could tailor well,
and could make a fine pair of shoes for his little sister's

doll. And so he learned many things which he could not learn from books.

Naturally willing though he was to work with his small hands, Louis Agassiz, a Swiss boy in every fiber, had breathed in from the Swiss mountains a love of freedom,— of the wisest kind of freedom,— which no cooper's or tailor's or shoemaker's bench could make him forget, and he was by no means easy to confine or to control. Growing up as he did, with an immense admiration for the daring Swiss guides, he probably dreamed, sometimes, that he himself would be a mountain-climber. He did not mind danger, and he did not mind cold. He felt almost as much at home on his skates as in his shoes; — and, one winter day, he gave his good mother a fright that she did not soon forget. That morning, Monsieur Agassiz, the boys' father, had gone to a fair, on the other side of Lake Morat, expecting to return home that afternoon. A little before noon, while Louis and Auguste were skating, Louis proposed that they should cross the lake, join their father at the fair, and have the fun of a ride back. In time for dinner, the other boys of the village came home and told Madam Agassiz where her two children were. A little worried, naturally, by the news of this scheme, the mother hurried upstairs to search the lake, and this picture greeted her : — lying on his stomach across a wide crack in the shining ice was Louis, making a kind of bridge of his young body for his little brother Auguste to crawl safely across. You may believe that Madam Agassiz lost no time in

sending a workman, who was a " swift skater ", after
the boys; and they were overtaken just in the enthusiastic heat of their enterprise, and ignominiously
brought back, hungry and tired, with no fair, and no
ride home with Father.

This is only one story of Louis and Auguste as
playmates; but it is easy to imagine that, sharing as
they did their pleasures and their disappointments,
they were fast friends, and it was hard for both boys
when, for the first time, they were separated. Twenty
miles from Motier, at a town called Bienne, there was
a " college for boys ", and Louis was sent there alone
when he was ten years old. A year later, though,
Auguste joined him, and again the brothers worked
and played together, and looked forward eagerly to
each vacation, when they would *walk home,* starting
on their long journey a good deal earlier than the sun
started on his. We can imagine them jodeling in joyous Swiss fashion for a large part of the way and
mingling their voices with the " rush of Mountain
streams " and the goat-bells tinkling from the mist-
wrapped hills.

Louis stayed at Bienne four years, till he was fourteen, and then for two years more went farther away
still, to a more advanced school,— the college at Lau-
sanne. During all this time, his interest had grown
in the very things that interested him as a little boy;
he had a passion for natural history. Though he
studied all his books with considerable faithfulness, he
only *loved* the books on science. In his room, some

forty birds flew about, a pine-tree in the corner for
their only home. In his heart was a kind of hunger
to search, to experiment, and to discover, and there was
a vague but persistent longing to write. His practical
father, however, gentle but firm, did not encourage
him in this: Louis must fit himself for some definite
work that would insure him a steady income. Accordingly, after much thought, the boy decided to be a
physician, and, with that aim, went first to a medical
school at Zurich, then to the University of Heidelberg, and finally to Munich, where he won his degree
of Doctor of Medicine.

I have called this story of Louis Agassiz' life "A
Swiss Boy and His Wanderings" because, as Longfellow said, the Swiss boy "wandered away and away
with Nature, the dear old Nurse", to many cities and
to many lands; though his purpose was as fixed as the
poles. To search and find the truth was, he believed,
"the glory of Life" and, because nature is the source
of truth, with nature he spent his youth and manhood, giving what he found to the world through his
teaching and through his books.

When a boy goes to college, he has at least two
things to consider: his parents' aims and his own; and
very often he and his parents do not agree. This was
true of Agassiz. He yearned to search the mysteries
of nature; but he was constantly and necessarily reminded by letters from home, that the supply of money
for his education was limited and that he must settle
down to something practical. And so, Agassiz'

student life gives us two separate pictures: the picture of the boy himself, away from home, and the picture of the people at home thinking about the boy.

If we had been with Agassiz at college, we should have found that, though he had infinite patience with a microscope,— so real a longing to understand the sciences that he was

> "Content to spy a sullen egg for weeks,
> The enigma of creation to surprise,"—

though he had this eagerness for knowledge, Agassiz' heart and body were almost as active as his head; he had kept his boyish love of fun and of adventure. At Heidelberg, he met a young man, named Alexander Braun, who loved plants as much as Agassiz loved animals; and a deep friendship sprang up between them, to last as long as they lived. He and Braun were room-mates at Heidelberg, and doubtless often went swimming together in the Neckar, after lectures. Carl Schimper, a special friend of Braun's, went with them on their long trips for specimens, and he and Braun taught Agassiz many things about botany, while Agassiz taught them zoölogy; for he could " recognize the birds from far off by their song, and could give a name to every fish in the sea."

It was delightful that these three friends, though they were separated for a little while after leaving Heidelberg, could join each other again at the University of Munich. Alexander Braun, in a letter to his father, gives us a little glimpse of their life: " Under

Agassiz' new style of housekeeping, the coffee is made
in a machine which is devoted during the day to the
soaking of all sorts of creatures for skeletons, and in
the evening again to the brewing of our tea."
Schimper and Braun shared Agassiz' studio, and " the
couch, the seats, and the floor were covered with
their specimens as well as his." A stranger coming in,
could hardly have told who the fellows were, for they
went by such nicknames as " Molluscus ", " Cyprinus ",
and " Rhubarb." Their whole life here, notwith-
standing their hard work, was full of happy informal-
ity, for, though men in brains, they were boys at heart.
Once, on hearing some piece of good news, Agassiz
actually " rolled himself in the snow for joy "; and,
though such youthful capers were by no means usual,
he always loved exercise of all kinds. He was a
" powerful gymnast and an expert fencer." He de-
spised the " closet student." To his natural robust-
ness, his Swiss boyhood had added a fine store of vitality. He loved to walk and climb and did " not fear
forced marches "; to get specimens for botany or
geology he sometimes walked thirty or thirty-five miles
a day " for eight days in succession ", carrying on his
back " a heavy bag loaded with plants and minerals."

In his letter home, Agassiz described all this life
vividly and honestly, for he knew that his parents were
his best friends. He realized, however, that his course
was long and expensive, and so he wrote also of the
practical side: reminded them that he was doing his
best to economize; that he had earned his own micro-

scope by writing; and that soon a book on Brazilian
fish would be out, written by their "Louis", adding:
would not that be " as good as to see his prescription
at the apothecary's? "

Agassiz' father, though a clergyman, was not without a sense of humor. His " Louis "— most lovable of
sons — seemed to him like a dreamer, with " a mania
for rushing full-gallop into the future." " If it is
absolutely essential to your happiness," wrote the
father, " that you break the ice of the two poles in
order to find the hairs of a mammoth, or that you
should dry your shirt in the sun of the tropics, at least
wait till your trunk is packed and your passports are
signed." When, the course ended and the medical
degree won, Louis finally wrote that he would come
home to practise, bringing with him all his scientific
instruments, an immense collection, and a *painter* to
illustrate his books, the news threw the family into real
consternation. Just at that time, there was excitement
enough at home. Cecile Agassiz, for whose doll the
little Louis had made shoes, was now grown up, and
the next winter she was to be married. That summer,
the house would be overrun " with a brigade of dressmakers, seamstresses, lace-makers, and milliners."
Monsieur Agassiz said that he had put up a " big nail
in the garret on which to hang his own bands and
surplice." Where could Louis stow " his fossils, all
his scientific outfit," and a *painter?* Yet, somehow,
the family made room for him, painter and all, and for
one year he practised medicine. Then, he wandered

away again, to Paris this time, to continue his studies in natural history, for he was unable to give up his great life-plan.

In Paris, Agassiz knew that there was a man who could give him what he wanted or help him to get it for himself. While he was there, however, satisfied and absorbed, studying and receiving inspiration from the great Cuvier, letters came from home urging him to take up teaching as a profession. With this in view, he returned to Switzerland, to the beautiful town of Neuchâtel, and accepted a position as teacher of natural history. He was now a man, with a man's responsibilities; his student days ended nominally, but really ended only by his death. From then on, his large life seemed to divide itself, naturally, into three parts: his life as a traveler and student; his teaching life; and the life of his heart (or home and friends); and even then, to try to tell his story is almost like trying to carry the ocean in a pail. It included the widest wanderings: up many dangerous mountains to study glaciers; years spent in America lecturing at Harvard, and, with Mrs. Agassiz, teaching in a girls' school in Cambridge; three short visits to England to study fossil fish; a year of teaching in Charleston, South Carolina; summers by the sea in a pleasant vine-covered cottage at Nahant; a trip in the United States Coast Survey steamer to the Florida reefs; a long journey to Brazil for his health; a voyage in the *Hassler,* round South America to the Pacific, for deep-sea dredging; one summer more at home, spent mostly with his mother in the shady garden of the Swiss manse; and, at last, a summer —

> " On the Isle of Penikese
> Ringed about by sapphire seas."

And there was never a journey,— there was, perhaps, never a day,— in which the great scientist did not learn something new. He was always a boy at heart — nature was his big, beautiful book,— and he must read it as long as his eyes could see, for there would not be time to read it all.

Of the subjects in this book, he loved best glaciers and fish. Wherever he went, he found traces of moraines —" polished surfaces, furrows, and scratches ", and all the other autographs which a world of ice leaves to be read by a world of men. As far as experiments went, however, no country offered him a better opportunity than his own Switzerland, and there he first worked among the white peaks that had encircled his childhood.

To discover how glaciers moved, he and one or two scientific friends, with wise, brave guides, built a rude hut on the Aar glacier. The projecting top and side of a huge boulder made a wall and roof, and a large blanket curtained off a sleeping-room big enough for six. In September 1841, they had bored holes in the ice in a straight line from one side of the glacier to the other, and in these they had planted a row of stakes, to find out which moved faster — the sides or the middle of this river of ice. The following July, when they returned to the old station, they found these stakes no longer in a straight line, but almost in the shape of a crescent, proving, for the first time, that the glacier moved faster in the middle than on the sides.

This experiment, though it took almost a year for its result, was much less exciting than the one in which Agassiz studied the condition of the ice at the base of a crevasse; and I might here add, that in all his Alpine wanderings, his eyes having been strained by microscopic work, the glitter of the sun on the unbroken "white world" was terribly painful. He did not seem to notice pain, however, nor to falter in steep or slippery climbing; he was often, of course, tied to his friends for safety; his mountain tramps as a college lad had fitted him to bear fatigue; and the same daring that prompted him to bridge an ice-crack for Auguste, when they were boys, made him unhesitatingly attempt this new feat.

Over a glacial crevasse he had a strong tripod built, and "seated upon a board firmly attached by ropes, he was let down into the well, his friend Escher lying flat on the edge of a precipice to direct the descent and listen for any warning cry." Agassiz, absorbed in watching the "blue bands in the glittering walls", did not realize how deep he had gone till he felt his feet plunged into ice-cold water. Even then, at the signal of danger, it was no easy task for his friends to draw him up, one hundred and twenty-five feet, with pointed icicles on the sides threatening to spear his head.

All this time, interested as he was in the mountains and their glaciers, Agassiz never forgot the sea with its fish. Perhaps he was answering a thousand questions which had puzzled him as a boy, beside the old stone basin in Motier. At any rate, he was learning many new things. At the seashore at Nahant and Penikese, the best aquariums were the natural, still pools, regularly deepened by the tides and pleasantly shaded by the rocks. Here were whole families of starfish, crawling crabs, and scrambling lobsters, sea-urchins with their spines, and lovely clusters of anemones that made the pool a garden of pink and purple flowers. Agassiz often went out in his dory for large fish. When he was on the *Hassler* and the cruise of the United States Survey, the deck of the vessel was a fine laboratory. He learned more there "in a day than in months from books or dried specimens." No trip, however, seems to have given him more delight than the journey to Brazil. He went there worn out with overwork, and found himself rested by the romance and novelty of a tropical country. And when he left his Cambridge home, it was with a merry, rhymed send-off from his jovial friend, Dr. Oliver Wendell Holmes:

> "Heaven keep him warm and hearty,
> Both him and all his party!
> From the sun that broils and smites,
> From the centipede that bites,
> From the hail-storm and the thunder,
> From the vampire and the condor.
>   •   •   •   •   •   •   •

God bless the great Professor,
And the land his proud possessor,—
Bless him now and evermore!"

Agassiz encountered most of the dangers that
Holmes prophesied,— and more, too; but they brought
him interest rather than fear. He loved the tangled
forest, the brilliant flowers, and fine fruits. For him
black slaves sang and danced their fandangoes. He
saw many lazy alligators lying still as logs in the
" glassy waters ", and heard the harsh cries of monkeys, that jump and swing in the trees. He and his
party slept in hammocks in huts with mud floors and
walls, rats scampering around and bats rustling overhead. Sometimes, several Indian children slept in the
same room with Agassiz' gentle wife, and once a pig
took breakfast with them in the morning. Mrs. Agassiz accepted everything very naturally, even to the
snake which, after gliding by night from her husband's
pocket, wriggled out of her shoe just as she was going
to put it on. She enjoyed the trip, like the best of
sports, and has published an interesting account of their
travels. As they journeyed, they of course collected
animals, both to "preserve" and to pet; and on the
way down the Amazon, the deck held quite a menagerie: parrots, monkeys, deer, and one lazy little
sloth, hanging as sloths do, upside down, and making
every one laugh by his perpetual sleepiness.

Though the world will perhaps remember Agassiz
best as an explorer and scientist, many of his dearest
friends will think of him as a teacher. Teaching was

his business during those twenty-seven years, when his real home was in Cambridge, Massachusetts; and his teaching life meant much to him, for, with characteristic simplicity he signed his will " *Louis Agassiz — Teacher.*" Whether his pupils were young or old, rich or poor, brilliant or stupid, he taught them freely and gladly —" His purse and knowledge all men's like the sea." He talked with farmers of their cattle, praised the fishermen's big fish, chummed it with the quarrymen and with the Indians of Brazil, gaining from all of them what they had learned just by living, and giving to all what he had learned by research. In the lecture-rooms at Harvard and in the school for young girls, his teaching was almost a chalk-talk. His attempts as a child to make small barrels and shoes, and his years of college practice in drawing, had fitted him to stand before his classes, and, with one sweep, draw a perfect egg, or, in a few lines, picture a starfish, or the beautiful mystery of resurrection from chrysalis to butterfly. Best of all, Agassiz *loved* to teach; " the things he spoke of never grew old to him "; and his lectures had added charm because, in spite of hours of practise, there was always a little touch of French in his good English. To the last, and to the delight of his hearers, he pronounced development — devil-ope-ment.

When he was in charge of laboratory-work, instead of giving his pupils help, he forced them to make their own discoveries from actual specimens. After fifteen

In the lecture-rooms at Harvard, his teaching was almost
a chalk-talk

years of teaching, he said: "My greatest success is that I have educated five observers." One student, at least, who was closeted for hours alone with a dead, blear-eyed fish will hardly forget his "lesson in looking."

"Take this fish," said Agassiz, "and look at it; by and by I will ask you what you have seen." With that, he plunged his big hand to the bottom of a huge jar of fish preserved in alcohol and drew out a specimen, dripping and none too fragrant. "Keep your fish in the tray, and moisten it often with alcohol, but be sure to put back the stopper of the jar each time." He shot a kind glance down into the would-be scientist's disheartened face, turned his broad back, and was gone.

In about ten minutes the young student, to quote his own words, "had seen all that could be seen in that fish," and, ready for further enlightenment, set off in search of his teacher: but he had left the museum! Two hours and a half dragged by; still no professor. "Sloppy" and loathsome, the fish waited dumbly in its tray. In despair, the student "turned it over and around; looked it in the face,— ghastly: from behind, beneath, above, sideways, at a three quarters' view,— just as ghastly." Time did not sweeten its fragrance nor reveal its secrets; neither the glazed eyes nor settled jaw would tell anything of its creation. An early lunch offered relief. Back into the stale, yellow alcohol went the fish and out into the fresh air and sunlight went the boy. Being a boy, sick as he thought himself, he could still eat, and eat heartily.

When he returned, he found that Professor Agassiz had been there and gone and would not be back for several hours. "Slowly I drew forth that hideous fish," says the student, "and with a feeling of desperation again looked at it." Magnifying glasses and all other instruments were forbidden. "My two hands, my two eyes, and the fish; it seemed a most limited field. I pushed my finger down its throat to feel how sharp the teeth were. I began to count the scales in the different rows until I was convinced that that was nonsense. At last a happy thought struck me — I would draw the fish."

Just then Professor Agassiz beamed in: "That is right; a pencil is one of the best of eyes. I am glad to see that you keep your specimen wet and your bottle corked." Then, after a pause, "Well — what is it like?"

The young man began to recite his discoveries, describing the head, the lips, the eyes, the fins, the tail. He thought he had seen a good deal. But when he stopped he was met with eyes full of disappointment.

"You have n't looked very carefully. You have n't even seen one of the most conspicuous features of the animal, which is as plainly before your eyes as the fish itself. Look again, look again!" And once more the broad back disappeared.

For three days this search-training continued.

Agassiz glancing in now and then, kind and wistful, but always patiently silent in the hope that the boy would make his own discoveries. " Look, look, look! " he repeated again and again. But when, at last, the young student falteringly suggested " symmetrical sides and paired organs ", the teacher's enthusiastic *yes* was well worth waiting for.

Of all Agassiz' dear schools, none was dearer to him than his out-of-doors school on the island of Penikese in Buzzard's Bay. The lecture-room was an old barn near the sea. The wide doors stood " broadly open to the blue sky and fresh fields "; and the swallows which had built in the old rafters flew in and out, making the " air glad with wings." We can imagine Agassiz standing there, big and genial and earnest, and, like Whittier, we almost hear him say:

> " We have come in search of truth;
> As with fingers of the blind,
> We are groping here to find
> What it is that hides beneath
> Blight and bloom and birth and death."

Then the great scientist who had never lost his simple, childlike faith, but believed that, even by searching, men could not *alone* find out God, asked his pupils and teachers to join him in a short, silent prayer for God's companionship. And every one *felt* this prayer, though there was no sound on the island but the call of birds and the voice of the lapsing sea.

It is impossible to tell how his pupils loved him. He drew them all to him by his warmth, his sympathy,

his hearty love of fun.   Lowell has beautifully said:
" His magic was not far to seek,— he was so human!"
When he gave up his girls' school in Cambridge, his
pupils tried to show their love by giving him a purse
of over four thousand dollars.   He always had many
birthday surprises: serenades in his own Swiss tongue;
German student-songs to recall his happy days at
Heidelberg; and, from friends, not students, one cele-
bration that touched him deeply.   It was at the Saturday Club, on his fiftieth birthday, and he was sitting,
as usual, at the head of the table —

> "Ample and ruddy
> As he our fireside were, our light and heat."

There were fourteen at dinner, among them, Holmes,
Lowell, Hawthorne, Emerson, Sumner,— and Longfellow,— who presided at the other end of the table.
None of them ever forgot that night: how Longfellow
rose, cheeks and eyes glowing, and face young in
spite of its wreath of white hair, and read in his
" modest, musical" voice " The Fiftieth Birthday of
Agassiz "; and how, plunged as the great scientist was
into a thousand memories of childhood, the tears rolled
down his cheeks at the lines

> "And the mother at home says, ' Hark!
> For his voice I listen and yearn;
> It is growing late and dark,
> And my boy does not return!'"

Agassiz lived sixteen years after this happy birthday, loving and being loved.   Even his faults seemed

to endear him to us. He was hopelessly unbusiness-like — said he had "no time to make money"; but this trait came from a nature really too large and too earnest. He was wasteful of his health, turning abruptly from weeks of mountain-climbing, to months indoors with a microscope; but he forgot himself in love for his work. Like his family and friends, we excuse and forget these little faults, in memory of his great charm and nobility. His children will remember him as working in a corner, a pleasant smile on his face, while they entertained their guests with music and dancing; his friends will remember him as tall and broad-shouldered, with "the strong step of a moun-taineer", "a boyish twinkle in his eye", a big con-tagious laugh, and a general air of joyousness. Long-fellow came back from one of his trips to Europe loaded with messages like these: "Give my love to Agassiz. Give him the blessing of an old man"; "I have known a great many men that I like; but I love Agassiz"; and, "What a set of men you have in Cambridge . . . why, there is Agassiz,— he counts for three." The Cambridge people used to say that one had "less need of an overcoat in passing Agassiz' house."

Much as his friends loved and watched him, how-ever, they could not keep him always; they could not save him from overwork. "Remember that work kills!" was Cuvier's last warning; Humboldt wrote: "Take care of your eyes, they are *ours*."

And now, in 1869, at the first bad attack "affecting

speech and motion ", his doctors ordered him " not to think." " Nobody can ever know," Agassiz exclaimed, " the torture I endure in trying to stop thinking!" and again: " My museum! My museum! always uppermost, by day and by night, in health and in sickness, always — always!"

A second stroke of paralysis, the final break, came in 1873, the winter after Agassiz founded the school at Penikese. His friend, Lowell, far off in Florence, picked up the paper one December morning, and was carelessly scanning the news when, suddenly, three small words blurred his sight —" Agassiz is dead!" No one can tell how Lowell felt so well as he, himself, in his beautiful poem, " Agassiz,"— vivid in its picture of the two friends walking back from Boston to Cambridge arm in arm, stopping on Harvard Bridge, each to find his own message in the dark water, and at last ringing out their good-nights.

"'Good-night!' again; and now, with cheated ear
"I half hear his who mine shall never hear."

Agassiz is buried in Mount Auburn, where later were borne his friends Longfellow, Holmes, and Lowell. Pine-trees from the old home surround the Swiss boy's green grave, and keep the place fragrant and musical on windy days; and the stone, a big boulder from the Aar glacier, reminds us of the Swiss man who once built there his little hut, tramped sturdily over the snow, and even danced and sang in the free air.

VII
THACKERAY

" So each shall mourn, in life's advance,
　　Dear hopes, dear friends, untimely kill'd,
Shall grieve for many a forfeit chance,
　　And longing passion unfulfill'd.
Amen! — whatever fate be sent,
　　Pray God the heart may kindly glow,
Although the head with cares be bent,
　　And whiten'd with the winter snow.

" Come wealth or want, come good or ill,
　　Let young and old accept their part,
And bow before the awful will,
　　And bear it with an honest heart.
Who misses or who wins the prize —
　　Go, lose or conquer as you can;
But if you fail, or if you rise,
　　Be each, pray God, a gentleman."
　　　　　　William Makepeace Thackeray.

A MODERN GREATHEART

A CURLY-HEADED youngster of six stood on the deck of the big ship. Across the blue water had faded from sight the land of India, where he had left his young, widowed mother, and all that was dear to babyhood and life. Before him loomed a strange English school and a strange aunt. When the little boy knelt down at night to pray, he would ask God to make him dream of his mother and let him see again, if only in his sleep, those gray eyes full of light. The thoughts that struggled in his child-heart, however, were not trusted to the black servant beside him, or even to the other little boy, Richmond Shakspear, who, like him, was leaving his India home. Nobody would understand those puzzling thoughts. Locked away very deep in William Makepeace Thackeray's young heart lay the memory of parting,— the old ghaut, or river-stair, which led down to the boat; the quaver in his mother's voice;.the blur in his sight, and the choke in his throat; and of those strange good-byes. Perhaps there floated, too, in his tender memory, a vision of his own portrait painted some years before in far-away Calcutta: a white-dressed, round-eyed boy of three perched on a pile of big books, with his arms clasped round his mother's neck. Such a beautiful, tall mother for a little boy to sail away from, to find that queer thing called " education." But he was sailing farther and farther every minute, under the long reach of sky.

At last, one morning, after many days, they came in sight of the rock-bound island of St. Helena, rising out of the sea like a great gray cone; and, harbored there, the black servant took the two boys ashore to see a famous French soldier. After they had gone a long way over rocks and hills, they came to a garden where a man with folded arms and bowed head was walking among the flowers. " There he is," said the black man, " that is Bonaparte. He eats three sheep every day, and all the little children he can lay his hands on." The cherry-cheeked William did not know what a plump, tempting morsel of a child he was; but it seemed wise, just then, to let this ogre of a French‑ man have the island to himself, and for him and Richmond and their black guardian to continue their voyage. And so, there were more long days of blue water and sky, and of sailing on and on, till, Nov. 6, 1817, they finally reached England. This did not seem at all a cheerful place to the two boys: flags were flying at half-mast, and there was black on everything, for the whole country was in mourning for Princess Charlotte.

William's aunt, however, took him immediately into her large love, and watched over him with a mother's tenderness. How frightened she was when she found out that the child's head was big enough for his uncle's hat! A good doctor told her, though, not to worry over that head, for it had " a great deal in it." Part of the time, Thackeray lived with this aunt, Mrs. Ritchie, at Chiswick, and part with a great-uncle at Hadley. Meanwhile, his young mother had not forgotten her only child. She had married again, a Colonel Smythe of India, and now she and her husband, whom Thackeray, later, loved deeply, returned to England, and the little boy was so glad to see them that he could not speak. This was in 1822, when Thackeray was eleven years old, the same year that he entered the famous Charterhouse school.

From Thackeray's own account and his *Doctor* in " Pendennis," we can imagine his first impressions of Charterhouse, and his feelings toward the principal, whose name he has gracefully changed. As the child entered with his shining, fresh face and his shining, white collar, *Dr. Crushall* thundered out in a " big, brassy voice":

" Take that boy and his box to Mrs. Jones, and make my compliments to Mr. Smiler, and tell him the boy knows nothing and will just do for the lowest form." So far as lessons went, the boy never knew a great deal; but " he read anything he could lay his hands on; he acted when he had the chance; he debated." His friends thought of him as a broad-set, lazy child, with rosy cheeks, dark hair, and blue eyes, all a-twinkle. When he should have been working sums, he was generally covering his books and papers with comical drawings which he "chucked about" among his schoolmates. His power of mimicry and sense of fun were so tremendous that no teacher was safe from his perfect imitation, his unmistakable caricatures, or his ridicule in verse. He loved to burlesque Shakespeare, and, through him, *Macbeth* became "a butcher with two blood-reeking knives", and *Lady Macbeth,* the butcher's wife, "clapping him on the shoulder to encourage him in his bloody work." There were some verses on "Violets, dark blue violets" which young Thackeray cleverly parodied in "Cabbages, bright green cabbages",— his first literary effort. He used to recite it in tenderly sentimental tones.

Like many others, Thackeray was a home-longing boy, who, except for the fun he made out of work and the friends he made through his fun, found the holidays the best things at Charterhouse. "There are 370 in the school," he wrote to his mother. "I wish there were only 369!" and another time, wistfully: "Valentine's Day, but I have had no valentines. Dr. Russell has been fierce to-day!" Once the doctor went so far as to storm: "You are a disgrace to the school and to your family, and I have no doubt will prove so in after-life to your country!"

Yet here at the Charterhouse, Thackeray made some lifelong friends: his cousin Richmond Shakspear, Alfred Gatty, George Venables, and John Leech who, when he grew up, became the humorous artist of

"Punch." How well he remembered "small John
Leech, coming first to school and being put up on a
table, in a little blue jacket and high-buttoned trousers,
and made to sing to the other boys, as they stood round
about." Still better he remembered George Venables.
One wet half-holiday, a boy named Glossip went to the
monitor to ask leave for Thackeray and Venables to
fight. That was an unlucky day for William, whose
middle name was Makepeace. Into the battle he went
with all zeal, and out of it he came with a broken nose.
Far from treasuring ill-feeling against his vanquisher,
however, he and George Venables were friends forever more, the broken nose — a life possession — acting as a kind of seal of their affection.

Drawing, acting, fighting, and studying a *little,*
Thackeray spent six years in the Charterhouse. After
that, he lived with his parents near Ottery St. Mary,
in Devonshire, reading such books as the vicar could
lend him. The next year he entered Trinity College,
Cambridge, the same fitful student, hating mathematics
and adorning the pages of his note-books with "pen
and ink drawings." In his one attempt at writing, a
poem in competition for the Chancellor's medal, he
was beaten by his friend Alfred Tennyson. With the
feeling that he was wasting time on studies useless in
life, Thackeray left the University in the spring of
1830. The best that he got from the college were his
friends: Brookfield, Fitzgerald, Moncton Milnes, and
Alfred Tennyson; the worst was a taste for gambling,
which shortly led to sad misfortune.

Since Thackeray was now well supplied with money, he decided to complete his education by travel, beginning his foreign studies at Weimar, Germany, where he seems to have lain on the sofa, read novels, and dreamed. Enough has been said to show that, like many other artists, he had not the temperament for steady, hard work. Nevertheless, in November 1831, urged by his parents to study law, he returned to England and entered the Middle Temple for that purpose. At first he seemed to look forward happily to practising at the bar; but soon he found dry law-books very hard reading and his high-stool a hard seat. So, it happened that as soon as he became of age, July 18, 1832 (the day for which he had " panted so long ", and the day on which he inherited his father's fortune) the first thing he did was to give up the study of law. " I can draw better than I can do anything else," he said to himself, and took his way to Paris, to " make believe to be a painter." Here, while he was out-of-doors, he lived the free life that he afterwards described in writing of *Clive Newcome;* but, at other times, he might have been seen, day after day, copying pictures in the Louvre, honestly trying to excel in the art he loved. As a side interest, he corresponded for the Paris papers.

His history now led to a combination of failures, which, while they were a loss in money, were a gain in commonsense and application. In the false hope of good luck, Thackeray had gambled with his newly-acquired wealth, at an immense loss, and generally,

"made a gaby" of himself. (*Mr. Deuceace* in "Yellowplush Papers" is a sketch from this memory.)
Before long the bank in India failed. Then the paper
failed in which he and his stepfather had mutual interests. This last failure came when Thackeray was
twenty-five, just six months after his marriage. As
he said, it made him "work for bread"— the best
thing that could have happened. Now he attempted to
illustrate "Pickwick Papers", but his drawings were
refused; and again the would-be artist faced failure,
and wondered what other line of work he might try.
It seems good to the book-reading world that, even in
Thackeray's extremity, his drawings were refused, and
that marriage and poverty and failure forced him to be
an author. Before we turn, however, from his artist
to his author life, let us mark that he was "the only
great author who illustrated his own books." As he
once said, when he was sick, "The artist who usually
illustrates my works fell ill with myself."

In his earliest writings, Thackeray so lacked confidence that he published his work anonymously. He
masked as *Titmarsh, Theophile Wagstaff, Fitz Boodle,
Punch's Commissioner, Yellowplush, Spec, Major
Gahagan,* and many others, shyly hiding his own face
as if not sure it would be welcome. And yet, no
matter how much he doubted his ability — and he did
doubt it — in favor of success were his robust health,
his strong brain, and his powerful love. With the high
motive of caring for a dear wife, any real *man* could
rally from a money defeat, and Thackeray was not the

one to be depressed by little things. From now on, constitutionally idle though he was, he worked night and day for those he loved, beating out his rhymes " titúmtidy, titúmtidy "; toiling at the stale old desk; writing " The Newcomes ", not for fame, but for that other entirely worthy object, money; and, slowly and with great difficulty, grinding out " Barry Lyndon."

Two years after he and his wife had faced the hardships of poverty together, he wrote: " Here have we been two years married, and not a single unhappy day.— I feel in my heart a kind of overflowing thanksgiving which is quite too great to describe in writing."

It is good he saw the sunlight through the showers, for there was real darkness ahead for both. Only the next year, their second child, their precious baby, died. Long after, in a kind of broken cry, Thackeray spoke of " that funeral which we followed, that bitter, bitter grief which we buried." The " Great Hoggarty Diamond " breathes the pathos of his baby's death.

And yet this sorrow, great as it was, could be shared. A year later fell a greater sorrow which he had to bear alone — his wife's sickness, which was more than sickness, for she was slowly losing her mind. Only Thackeray's best friends knew how he clung to her companionship, and how he fought for her cure. He tried to nurse her himself. As he said, he " used to walk out three miles to a little bowling-green and write there in an arbor, coming home and wondering what was the melancholy oppressing the poor little woman; "

and, looking back on life: "What a deal of cares and pleasures and struggles and happiness I have had since that day in the little sunshiny arbour." In a vain hope to save her, he took her home to Ireland and her people, and then went from one watering-place to another, until, finally, there was nothing to do but place her in a private asylum in Paris.

At the beginning of Mrs. Thackeray's illness, the little London home on Great Coram Street had been broken up, and the two children, Annie, a " fat lump of pure gold," and Baby Minnie, had been sent to live with their Grandmother Butler in Paris. They stayed there for some time after Thackeray had lost in the battle for his wife's reason; while the lonely father lodged near the asylum, first in one place, then in another, once more a bachelor except for his burden of love. Yet, again, only his closest friends began to know how deeply the sorrow had hewn itself into his life; like Lamb, he wore a smile for the outer world, and still sent playful letters to his children, though they were sometimes written in a trembling hand.

One of his truest friends, Fitzgerald, was constant with long, cheerful letters, and, thinking that drawing might distract the poor man more than writing, recommended him widely as an illustrator; and begged his friends " to buy copies of ' The Second Funeral of Napoleon,' as each copy puts sevenpence half-penny into Thackeray's pocket, which is not very heavy just now."

Fitzgerald was right. For a while, even sevenpence

half-penny counted with his home-loving, homeless friend. Visions of empty mugs must have haunted the dear man; he drove himself through his tasks " for beef and mutton ", and was very busy, writing hard every day, and very poor, nevertheless.

Just as soon as he was able, in the autumn of 1846, he moved to 13, Young Street, in London, and brought his babies there to live.

We can imagine him, a sort of giant of a man, " six feet two and largely built ", standing once more before his own fire, his feet spread wide, his hands crammed deep into his pockets, a smile on that pleasant face, and a twinkle shining behind the glasses; or, perhaps, as holding Annie on his broad lap and teaching her to read from the funny alphabet-pictures he had made. He used to tear out processions of paper pigs with curly tails for his children. The companionship of his little girls was the dearest thing he had left now. As they grew older, he stole many happy holidays to take them to plays or to children's parties, which were often held at the Dickens's. He loved to see " the little ones dancing in a ring ", especially his own, one with her " hair plaited in two tails ", and the other with curls and the " most fascinating bows of blue ribbon." Still better, he loved to take them driving in the country or to the Zoo. It put him in " such chirping spirits to get out of London." As for the Zoo, they used to " amuse themselves in finding likenesses to their friends in many of the animals." " Thank E'v'ns! " Thackeray once exclaimed, " both of the girls have plenty

of fun and humour." One day, as they walked along,
he made up these lines:

"First I saw the white bear, then I saw the black;
  Then I saw the camel with a hump upon his back;
  Then I saw the gray wolf, with mutton in his maw;
  Then I saw the wombat waddle in the straw;
  Then I saw the elephant a-waving of his trunk;
  Then I saw the monkeys,—Mercy, how unpleasantly they
    smelt!"

While we are thinking of Thackeray with his own
children, let us remember him, too, with the children
of others, for he had a "marvelous affection" for all
little boys and girls. Perhaps it was just this all-
fathering nature of his, or perhaps it was the memory
of the darling who slept beneath the grass and stars,
that led him, in 1853, to adopt a third daughter, Amy
Crowe, the child of one of his friends. At any rate,
he did adopt her, and made her his own forever.

During his student days at Weimar, when he was
hardly more than a boy, one of his chief delights had
been to make caricatures for children, and, years later,
he began the drawings for " The Rose and Ring " because his little girls had wanted pictures of the king
and queen in " Twelfth Night." It was while they
were traveling in Naples, when an attack of scarlatina
kept the children indoors and away from their friends,
that the story grew to fit the pictures. It was written
with the famous gold pen. In referring to this time,
Thackeray said that he wrote a " nonsensical fairy
tale " instead of collecting material for " The New-

comes." All his life, though, his chief desire had been to write "Something good for children." As soon as he had "made a competence" for his own "young-ones" he had determined to do something "for the pleasure of young-ones in general."

Our minds are full of pictures of the kind old "giant", happy with little children. Now he bends over a small, yellow head; now he simply stands still to watch a child nibble the gingerbread-man he has tucked into her hand, his spectacles growing misty at her rapture of surprise. But he is gone without thanks! Once, while he was in America, a little girl, who was too small to see a procession, found herself suddenly lifted by strong arms, and placed on a high, broad shoulder. Some days after, when that child was out walking with her mother, she stopped still, as she saw Thackeray coming, and pointing an eager finger exclaimed: "There he is; there's my big English-man!" That same Englishman wrote, from New Orleans, that the colored children "ruined him in five cent pieces." On the train for Heidelberg, he made friends with the "two children in black" described in "The Roundabout Papers"—the real account of a real holiday taken with his "little girls." How often he sat among his friends' children asking by name for all their dolls! Once he stopped a procession of schoolgirls, saying, "Four and twenty little girls! They must have four and twenty bright little sixpences." And, going over the names at Charter-house on Founder's Day, he would exclaim: "Here's

the son of dear old So and So; let's go and tip him."
As he told Dickens, he could "never see a boy without
wanting to give him a sovereign." "Ah! my dear
sir," he wrote in a "Roundabout Paper", "if you have
any little friends at school, go and see them, and do the
natural thing by them. You won't miss the sovereign.
Don't fancy they are too old,—try 'em." And again:
"It is all very well to say that boys contract habits of
expecting tips. Fudge! Boys contract habits of tart-
and toffee-eating which they do not carry into after-
life. On the contrary, I wish I did like tarts and
toffee."

A pretty story is told of him when he was once invited to stay to dinner by a family of children.
"There is nothing, my dears, you can give me," he
argued, "for I could only eat a chop of a rhinoceros or
a slice from an elephant."

"Yes, I tan," answered a little girl of three, and off
she trotted, coming back in a few moments with a
wooden rhinoceros and a wooden elephant from her
Noah's-ark.

"Ah, little rogue," exclaimed the great man, "you
already know the value of a kiss." Then, taking her
in his arms, "he asked for a knife and fork, smacked
his lips," and pretended to eat the dinner she had
brought.

With children he was always playful, like that; but
when he just stood by to *see* children, especially when
they sang,— for he was passionately fond of music,—
their young quaverings filled his old heart, and choked

his voice, and flooded his eyes with tears. "Children's voices charm me so," he said, "that they set all my sensibilities in a quiver." Once he entered a school-room just as the children were singing, in sweetly tune-less notes: "O Paradise, O Paradise!" "I cannot stand this any longer," he mumbled, turning away his head and moving toward the door. "My spectacles are getting very dim."

"There is one day in the year," he wrote, "when I think St. Paul's presents the noblest sight in the whole world: when five thousand charity children with cheeks like nosegays, and sweet, fresh voices, sing the hymn which makes every heart thrill with praise and happi-ness. I have seen a hundred grand sights in the world — coronations, Parisian splendors, Crystal Palace openings . . . but think in all Christendom there is no such sight as Charity Children's Day." When Thackeray and Fields went together to this beautiful service, Fields tells us that he saw "the head-cynic of literature, the 'hater of humanity,' as a critical dunce in the *Times* once called him, hiding his bowed face, wet with tears, while his whole frame shook with emo-tion."

It is strange beyond believing that so many have called this tender-hearted man a cynic and a satirist and have imagined a "satiric focus" to his tear-dimmed spectacles. The glad tips to round-cheeked school-boys, the sovereigns hidden in books or laid on white pillows seem all forgotten. Such forgetfulness is like claiming entertainment and yet condemning the en-

William Makepeace Thackeray

tertainer. " Make us laugh," cried the people, " or
you and your children starve!" That was Thackeray's own feeling. " What funny things I 've written
when fit to hang myself!" he said, for very sadness
losing " sight of the text " under his eyes; and this
is the testimony of the famous gold pen:

> " I 've helped him to pen many a line for bread,
> To joke, with sorrow aching in his head,
> And make your laughter when his own heart bled."

To be sure, Thackeray himself laughed at all fal-
sity, and laughed heartily; he could not endure an
affected person or a person who posed; he had to have
a man all-honest like himself. And because he laughed
at life's shams, some of the people who heard him
laugh forgot his wonderful sympathy. They forgot
that the very man who painted *Becky Sharp* could
paint, in tender colors, the lovable *Dobbin* and the
benevolent *Colonel Newcome*. As a still further proof
that Thackeray loved reality and nobleness, there
shines in the false, scheming crowd, the face of the
beautiful rector in " Dennis Duval."

Thackeray said that his characters made themselves and that they acted without his interference.
" I don't control my character. I am in their hands,"
he repeatedly declared. When a friend asked him why
he made *Esmond* marry *Lady Castlewood*, he answered, perfectly seriously, " I did n't make him do it;
they did it themselves." Yet " Henry Esmond " was
the one novel for which he drew up a plot. Of this

favorite with many, he said: " I stand by this book, and am willing to leave it where I go, as my card." For the most part, however, he doubted his own ability, and believed that his books were failures, commenting with such impersonal frankness as, " I have just read such a stupid part of ' Pendennis.' But how well-written it is! "

His characters' homes were as real to him as his own, and their troubles almost as real. " I am going to-day to the *Hôtel de la Terrasse,* where *Becky* used to live, and shall pass by *Captain Osborne's* lodgings." The tax-collector, coming in one day, found him crying over the death of *Helen Pendennis.* " She had to die," he said, though his little daughter, Minnie, had begged him to " make her well again."

His sympathy for flesh-and-blood people was, of course, even greater than his sympathy for book-people. When he was editor of " The Cornhill Magazine," he really suffered over the sad letters of many who dreamed that they could write. " Here is a case put with true female logic. ' I am poor; I am good; I am ill; I work hard; I have a sick mother and hungry brothers and sisters dependent on me. You can help us if you will.' " Such letters wrung the kind editor's heart, and no one knows how often he answered by his own personal check. No one knows, either, how much valuable time he spent in trying to frame replies at once honest and tender. Some of the contributors asked for criticisms; others even asked him to rewrite, if he could not understand their nonsense. In fact,

the editorship of the " Cornhill " wore Thackeray out.
With great relief, in 1862, he resigned. " Oh, those
hours of madness spent in searching for Louisa's lost
lines on her dead piping bull-finch!" he sighed. " I
will send out my benediction to that printer's boy and
take t' other half-hour's doze." Jocular though this
sounds, if you would know the genuineness of his
sympathy, read " The Thorns in the Cushion."

And, if you would know Thackeray's generosity,
read any of the warm praises he heaped on his rival,
Charles Dickens. Though Charles Dickens could hardly
endure the success of " Vanity Fair," Thackeray, when
" Pendennis " was coming out, advised his friends to
get "David Copperfield." " By Jingo! it 's beautiful
— and the reading of the book has done another author
a great deal of good." " ' Pickwick ' is a capital book,"
he said ungrudgingly; " it is like a glass of good
English ale." And again, " ' Boz ' is capital this month,
some very neat, pretty, natural writing indeed, better
than somebody else's again." . . . " Long mayest
thou, O ' Boz,' reign over thy comic kingdom!" " All
children ought to love Dickens ", he wrote most heartily of all; " I know two that do, and read his books ten
times for once they peruse the dismal preachments of
their father. I know one who, when she is happy,
reads ' Nicholas Nickleby '; when she is unhappy, reads
' Nicholas Nickleby '; when she is tired, reads
' Nicholas Nickleby '; when she is in bed, reads
' Nicholas Nickleby '; when she has nothing to do,
reads ' Nicholas Nickleby '; and when she has finished

the book, reads 'Nicholas Nickleby' again. This candid young critic, at ten years of age, said: 'I like Mr. Dickens's books better than your books, Papa,' and frequently expressed her desire that the latter author should write a book like one of Mr. Dickens's books. Who can?" Though Thackeray himself failed as illustrator, he wrote of a volume of Leech's drawings, "This book is better than plum-cake at Christmas"; and so we could quote for many pages. Magnanimous, "mighty of heart and mighty of mind," Thackeray lived his belief that there was room in the world for many great men. "What, after all, does it matter," he asks, "who is first or third in such a twopenny race?"

This was his spirit toward all his rivals. In Anne's diary we read of his failure in the election to the House of Commons: "Papa came home beaten, in capital spirits." And we know that he shook his opponent's hand, with all his big heartiness. When he found that his "very two nights" for lecturing in Baltimore had been chosen by a large opera company, he exclaimed: "They are a hundred wanting bread,— shall we grudge them a little of the butter off ours?"

Yet Thackeray bitterly needed the money from those lectures, that is, he needed it for his wife and children. For them and them alone, he had taken the trip to America, hating the miles of ocean between himself and home; hating still more the horror of speaking before an audience. Like Irving, he had an in-born timidity; he had often broken down on trying to make a public speech. An hour before one of these lectures, he besought a friend: " Don't leave me,— I 'm sick at my stomach with fright." To strengthen his voice he had recited the multiplication-table to a waiter in a restaurant; but how could he strengthen his courage? Night after night, that attack of fear returned; and night after night, the beloved giant went through his painful task, for money for the children. When at last he sailed for England, he went off in a rush, the very morning he saw the ship advertised. It was easier to scribble, " Good-bye, Fields; good-bye, Mrs. Fields; God bless everybody, says W. M. T.," than to utter that hard farewell. Thackeray reached the *Europa* at the cry, " Hurry up, she 's starting! " Let us sail on with him.

From his own " White Squall " we get a peep into his home-seeking heart, on days of storm at sea:

> "I thought, as day was breaking,
> My little girls were waking,
> And smiling, and making
> A prayer at home for me."

His daughter Anne lets us welcome him with the family: " My sister and I sat on the red sofa in the little study, and shortly before the time we had calculated he might arrive came a little ring at the front doorbell. My grandmother broke down; my sister and I rushed to the front door, only we were so afraid that it might not be he that we did not dare to open it, and there we stood, until a second and much louder ring brought us to our senses. ' Why did n't you open the door?' said my father stepping in, looking well, broad, and upright, laughing. In a moment he had never been away at all."

His greeting at another time, from the dog, Gumbo, is hardly less picturesque. When the little black-and-tan saw the cab driving up the street with Thackeray inside, "with one wild leap from the curbstone, he sprang" into the carriage and landed safe on his master's knees, "knocking off his spectacles, and licking his face all over."

Through the eyes of other folks we see him in all these ways — the beneficent, tender-hearted man, "whose business was to 'joke and jeer.'" And we like to thumb his old letters, filled as they are with comic pictures and with purposely misspelled words (to be pronounced lispingly or Englishly or through the nose, for Thackeray was as whimsical as Charles Lamb). "Did you 2 have a nice T?" is characteristic, and such signatures as "Bishop of Mealy Potatoes," "Yours Distractedly, Makepeace," "G. B. Y." (for God Bless You), or any of a hundred others. Sometimes he drew a pair of spectacles instead of signing his name.

Since this "big Cornish giant" loved his meals, of course we would even rather dine with him than read his letters; but we must take our chances with all his other friends of his missing his appointment. He once neglected a dinner with a "very eminent person" because he saw beans and bacon on the menu of the Reform Club,— his grounds for declining the dinner

being he had "just met a very old friend whom he
had not seen for years, and from whom he could not
tear himself."   Another time he was late to a dinner
when he himself was host.   The guests waited and
waited; no Thackeray.   At last, when the dinner was
half-spoiled, he bounded in, clapping his still inky
hands, and shouting, " Thank Heaven, the last sheet of
' The Virginians ' has just gone to the printer! "

Through J. T. Fields, we see him lunching on
American oysters; rejecting a large one because " it
resembled the High Priest's servant's ear that Peter
cut off "; and then opening his mouth very wide for
another.   After that had slipped down, and Fields
asked him how he felt, " Profoundly grateful,"
Thackeray gulped, " and as if I had swallowed a little
baby."

His appetite alarmed Charlotte Brontë.   From afar,
and out of the midst of her limited life, she had almost
worshiped his genius; now, opposite him at dinner,
with dark eyes of wonder, she watched him eat and
vainly waited to hear him speak.   When at last she
saw him take his fifth potato, she leaned imploringly
across the table and gasped, " Oh, Mr. Thackeray!
Don't! "

It was in just such convivial spirits that Thackeray
was dearest to his friends, and his Christmas-nature
was the last they expected to lose on the day before
Christmas 1863, when all England was gay with holly.
Thackeray himself must have had warnings, but he
never hinted them to any one.   He was a little weary

and a good deal shrunken, but, on the whole, his old happy self. A few days before he died, as if by a kind of presentiment, he shook hands with Dickens, whose coldness had been growing for several years; and he sent a hand-painted sketch of a singing robin to Milnes (a farewell full of joy). But he said no good-byes to his family, and when he left them on the last night, it was in just the old, tender way. Alone, early in the morning, his great soul was carried to a greater world. " As you and I send for our children, meaning them only love and kindness, how much more Pater Noster," was one of his own restful thoughts.

That evening " Penny " Mahew brought the fatal news to a party of Thackeray's jovial fellow-workers on " Punch." " I 'll tell you what we 'll do," he said, " we 'll sing the dear old boy's ' Mahogany Tree '; he 'd like it." And so they all stood up, their choking voices missing the brave, sweet tenor of their friend, and their hearts needing his warmth; but they all stood up and sang, as best they could:

> " Christmas is here:
>   Winds whistle shrill,
>   Icy and chill,—
>   Little care we;
>   .   .   .   .
> Here let us sport,
>   Boys, as we sit;
>   Laughter and wit
>   Flashing so free.

Life is but short;
When we are gone,
Let them sing on
Round the old tree!"

In Kensal Green Cemetery, a few steps from Leech, co-worker and fun-maker on " Punch ", Thackeray lies asleep. The English ivy grows thick over his grave, clothing his place of rest with a summer mantle, and keeping his memory alive beneath the snow. His friend Lord Houghton was very angry because no room was made for Thackeray in Westminster Abbey. Happily our greatness is not measured by our graves, but by our monuments in human hearts.

VIII

LIVINGSTONE

" Go anywhere —*provided it be* FORWARD.

David Livingstone.

VIII

MRS. LIVINGSTONE stood in the doorway looking down on her sleeping boy. With his towsled hair dark against the white pillows and his eyelashes dark against his pale cheeks, he lay there in the feeble light of the winter dawn, looking particularly small and particularly glad to dream. Indeed, the mother wished she did not have to wake her little David. He was o'er young to work! Hardly more than a *bairn,* after all. But it had to be done.

No one has told us just how she waked him. Perhaps, with characteristic Scotch reserve, she did it swiftly, like any other stern duty. But Blaikie says she was a " very loving mother." And that " her love had no crust to penetrate, but came beaming out freely like the light of the sun." She was the one to " put out the candle " when her boy was studying too late, and we can imagine that, when she had to rouse him in the bleak morning, first she called, then she touched him gently, then she put her cheek down close to his and tried by her warm understanding to soften the hard news — that morning had really come, and he must rub his blue eyes open, dress, and reach the fac-

tory by six o'clock. This was ninety years ago, before there was much talk about that cruel thing, Child
Labor. The Livingstones were poor. There were
many children and Davie was next to the oldest. He
expected to help, and his father and mother expected
it of him.

The lad must be in his place at six. Then, with a
short time out to rest and eat, his little hands would tie
broken threads till eight at night. Fixed to the spin-
ning-jenny, was a Latin grammar, bought with his first
wages, so that while his fingers were busy with their
mechanical task, his brain could keep pace with the
boys at school. No doubt those boys were yawning
over their verbs that very minute; and no doubt all
the boys, including little David, would rather play on
the banks of the singing Clyde. Its music suited a
child's spirit a great deal better than the whirr of
wheels; and the winter wind blowing over its waters,
nipping though it was, was better for a child's blood
than the dust-filled air of the factory. As for sunshine, David hardly knew its flicker any more; he who
had loved so much to gather shells and flowers! He
would plod home by star-light or no light, as the
weather decreed, so that, if the school of darkness was
the best preparation for life in the " Dark Continent ",
his training was indeed rare.

Lives of most of the great men prove that those with
the least time hold time at the highest value. It is
with time as with money. The poor man, if he is
wise, values five cents more than the millionaire; David

Livingstone valued a minute more than did the boy
of endless leisure. Free time was dear to him. But
after the long factory day was over, bed was the place
for a child of ten. For his golden minutes of freedom, sound sleep was the best investment. As the lad
grew older, however, he felt compelled to wrench from
life something besides drudgery and dreams, and so,
in those precious leisure moments, he studied history,
politics, and literature, puzzled out creation's secrets
locked away in flowers and stones, and at nineteen had
saved enough money and stored up enough knowledge
to go to Glasgow and enter the University. As a boy,
he had hated to read religious books. Deacon Livingstone would fain have had his son love his catechism;
but up to this time, David had loved nothing of the
sort — not until he made up his mind to devote his
life to making men better, and went to Glasgow to
study for the ministry. Here, as Dr. Hillis puts it
" He hired a garret, cooked his oatmeal and studied
made a little tea and studied, went forth to walk but
studied ever."

One of his first attempts at preaching was enough
to make a weaker man give preaching up for life. He
was sent to Stanford to supply a sick minister's place;
but no sooner had he given out his text, than something
queer happened. " Midnight darkness came upon
him."

" My friends," he said, with his frank straightfor-
wardness, " I have forgotten all I had to say." Then
down he came from the pulpit and out he went at the

chapel door. We can imagine it perfectly: his young
face crimson, his shoes creaking with each fatal step,
and the little congregation, some laughing, some pity-
ing, but almost all remembering the failure for years
to come.

But Livingstone was not to be beaten by one defeat. Because he longed above everything else to
be a missionary, he studied surgery at the medical
college; he would want to heal men's bodies as well
as save their souls. To his commonsense, it seemed
much easier to win confidences by curing pain or
saving life than by preaching strange doctrines, no
matter how good. If his commonsense had not told
him this, the example of the world's great Healer
would have done it. And David Livingstone needed
no better example than Christ's.

As soon as he had decided on Africa as the land
for his work, the whole world tried to scare him,—
no, not his family, and not Dr. Moffat, but most of
those outside his family. When Dr. Moffat, himself an African missionary, looked into the young
man's fearless eyes, he read there the courage Africa
would need. But people in general did their best to
frighten him. Death, they said, would meet him at
every turn; between African fever, savage natives,
and the merciless power of the sun, he would be cut
off in the prime of his youthful hopefulness. The
Missionary Board, itself, would not be held responsible for any such risk. If he went, he could go independently.

In the face of all these threats and warnings the
strong heart was unshaken. A steamer would sail
for Africa almost immediately and on that steamer
Livingstone would go. He hurried home to say
good-bye. It was evening before he reached the dear
old door, and in the early morning he must leave
again. So till midnight he and his father and
mother, three understanding hearts, talked over the
fears and hopes of his journey — steadfast, all three,
yet finding the parting bitterly hard. When the sun
flushed the sky with the light of dawn, David read,
with brave simplicity, " Thou shalt not be afraid for
the terror by night, nor for the arrow that flieth by
day." Then, leaving his mother in the open doorway, he set out on his seven-mile walk to Glasgow.
His father strode beside him till they reached the
top of one of the high hills. Then the good-bye of
their life was said.

If David Livingstone had been a cold-hearted man,
the bravery needed for his African exploration would
have been purely physical. Whether he was to meet
fever, savages, or sunstroke, or even all three, physical
bravery alone would have been enough ; but he took
with him into the desolation a great, warm heart
pounding with love of home. I suppose the very
poorness of that home was dear : the old sofa ; the
faded carpet ; the fire that had not always kept them
warm ; dearest of all, the faces round the fire. David
Livingstone needed a great deal more than physical
courage to face that life of loneliness.

Since most of us would find it tiresome to follow Livingstone's long journeys even on the map, we will pay little attention to geography. It is better to remember that, to him, every name and every mile meant an experience,— those names and miles that are too tedious for us to *read* about. As he traveled, not only was he *making* geography (seeking to discover the source of the Nile), but he was trying to rid the land of slavery, and to teach the people a happy religion. These were his three great aims. But to us his story is so full of poetry and action that it reads like a wonderful book of adventure. Sometimes, as we follow his hair-breadth escapes, we forget entirely that he was a missionary, and think he must have explored for excitement or fame. We must not do this. While he was as daring as the bravest explorer, he never faltered in his purpose; he had, above all else, the motive of redeeming Africa.

Before he could do anything for the Africans, however, he had to learn their language. This took seven months. After landing at the Cape of Good Hope, the very southern tip of Africa, he struck into the forest, and there he lived, the one white man among the half-naked black savages, learning their speech and their ways. If a man from another planet should suddenly stand before you in the center of your city, he would not seem as queer as David Livingstone seemed to these black natives. We can have no idea what they thought of him, whether he was a miracle, or just a new kind of animal. But night after night he lay down to sleep among them with a fearlessness that was, in itself, power. " I trust you," his placid face would say, without speech. And, without speech, armed and wondering, they would answer, " We are worthy of your trust." They were not, except as his trust had made them so. They themselves did not know why they did not kill him as he slept there among them unprotected.

He first won their confidence as a " rain-maker." By leading " runnels from the river " he taught them to irrigate; the desert changed to a fruitful valley. " He is a wizard," they said. " He brings water to dry ground." As time went on, he taught them to make gardens, raise cattle, and build houses. He taught their young people everything practical, from carpentry to taking care of the sick. After his marriage to Dr. Moffat's daughter, his wife taught the girls dressmaking. She was as brimful of bravery as her husband. She and the children spent many years in England for the children's health and education; but all the time she was in Africa, she was a strong help to the Doctor. And Livingstone's short holidays at home were very precious. With a child on each knee, he loved to turn his dangers into stories, and see the young eyes grow big with terror, while all the time he and the children knew that he got away safely.

Truly the swamps and jungles, where he spent his brave life, were fearsome enough. Trees a hundred feet high, festooned with tangled vines, shut out the

sun, and snakes wriggled round in the tangle. Now
Livingstone was stung by nettles, now, for days together, drenched with rain. At night his only shelter
was an overturned canoe. Thirst, sunstroke, and
famine, all threatened death, just as the friends in
Scotland had prophesied. "A mole and two mice"
do not seem, to us, like a tempting supper. One evening Livingstone and his men were glad enough to
get that. When he was starving, he wished he would
not dream of "savory viands." "Took my belt up
three holes to relieve hunger," reads one day's journal. His cattle died, his goods, including his precious
medicines, were stolen. The rivers they swam or
waded were the homes of many crocodiles. Not only
was he attacked by serpents, lions, buffaloes, and hippopotami, but he was constantly harassed by tsetse-
flies and ants.

"The Majestic Sneak" was Dr. Livingstone's
nickname for the lion. Drawn by the smell of meat,
a lion would come near the camp and roar. The natives, who believed that lions were disguised chiefs,
would answer his roaring:

"You a chief, eh?" Tuba would call. "What kind
of a chief are you to come sneaking round in the dark
trying to steal our buffalo meat? Are you not
ashamed of yourself?"

"Why don't you kill your own beef?" another
would cry. "Go and hunt for yourself. There is
plenty of game in the forest."

If "lions attacked the herds in open day, or leaped

into the cattle-pens by night," one had to be killed
to scare off the others. Though it took tremendous
courage to lead lion-hunts, Livingstone was the man
who could do it. He mustered his men. Around a
group of lions hiding on a wooded hill they formed
a circle, but were afraid to throw their spears. Some
one fired. Three animals, roaring, leaped through
the line and escaped unhurt, while the panic-stricken
natives huddled back into the circle. For very
kinkiness, their hair could not stand upright; but their
knees shook, and their eyes rolled with terror. Those
who could shoot were afraid of killing their fellows.
Since the whole attack seemed as useless as it was
dangerous, the circle broke up, and the party was
about to return to the village, when, from the other
side of the hill, Livingstone made out the outline of
a tawny foe. About thirty yards away, the lion
crouched behind a bush. Livingstone took good aim
and " fired both barrels into it."

" He is shot! He is shot!" shouted the men.

" He has been shot by another man too; let us go
to him," cried others.

" Stop a little till I load again," warned Livingstone, for he saw the " lion's tail erected in anger."
Then, as he " rammed down the bullets" he " heard
a shout, and, looking half round, saw the lion springing upon him." " He caught me by the shoulder,"
reads his vivid account, " and we both came to the
ground together. Growling horribly, he shook me as
a terrier dog does a rat." Then a dreaminess like the

effect of chloroform came over the great Doctor. Though he knew what was happening, he had no " sense of pain or terror." " As he had one paw on the back of my head," the journal continues, " I turned round to relieve myself of the weight, and saw his eyes directed to Mabálwe, who was aiming at him from a distance of ten or fifteen yards. His gun, which was a flint one, missed fire in both barrels. The animal immediately left me to attack him, and bit his thigh. Another man, whose life I had saved after he had been tossed by a buffalo, attempted to spear the lion, upon which he turned from Mabálwe and seized this fresh foe by the shoulder. At that moment, the bullets the beast had received took effect, and he fell dead. The whole was the work of a few moments."

In his account, Livingstone made light of his splintered bones and of the deep prints in his arm of eleven sharp teeth. " I have escaped with only the inconvenience of a false joint," he says simply, and is thankful to his tartan jacket that partly protected him from those cruel teeth and so saved his life.

This was, perhaps, his most exciting lion-fight, but the lions were familiar neighbors all the time. In the middle of the night, one old fellow came to the camp and killed a faithful donkey. The sleepers, roused by the commotion, kindled a light by setting fire to the grass. There, in the crackling glow, they saw the great King of Cats, his forepaws buried in the donkey's back, his long mane standing out like a devil's

halo, his round eyes glittering with evil triumph.
The men fired, but the big lion was too quick for
them. He escaped, they supposed, at his usual velvet speed. But in the morning a broad track of blood
told them that he had gone away wounded, and " could
only drag himself along." The foot-prints of a second lion, however, cautioned them not to seek his
hiding-place.

We wonder, when we read stories like these, that
Livingstone could keep even for the lions a kind of
understanding friendliness. Human enough to see
their point of view, he adds to his description of
" dripping forests and oozing bogs ": " A lion had
wandered into this world of water and ant-hills, and
roared night and morning, as if very much disgusted.
We could sympathize with him."

He liked to watch all the different animals. One
day a dark green snake glided into his house to look
for mice. This is his story of the cat's reception:
" Puss approaches very cautiously and strikes her
claw into the head with a blow delivered as quick as
lightning; then holds the head down with both paws,
heedless of the wriggling mass of coils behind it;
she then bites the neck and leaves it, looking at the
disfigured head as if she knew that there had lain
the hidden power of mischief." So much space he
gives to Puss's Victory. Two sentences are enough
for his own. " I killed a snake seven feet long. He
reared up before me, and turned to fight." Evidently
bragging was not in his line.

But if it came to honoring the natives, his journal could give that generous space. "Their chief characteristic is their courage. Their hunting is the bravest thing I ever saw." Then he goes on to describe a hippopotamus-hunt. The game, if won, can be traded for maize. There are two men in each light craft. "As they guide the canoe slowly downstream towards a sleeping hippopotamus, not a single ripple is raised on the smooth water; they look as if they were holding in their breath, and communicate by signs only. As they came near the prey, the harpooner in the bow lays down his paddle and rises slowly up, and there he stands erect, motionless, and eager, with the long-handled weapon poised at arm's-length above his head, till, coming close to the beast, he plunges it with all his might in towards the heart." Surprised from sleep by sudden pain, the animal does not fight at once. But the instant the "enormous jaws appear, with a terrible grunt, above the water" the men must thrust a second harpoon, this time from directly above. Then comes the battle. In a flash, the paddlers shoot the canoe backward before hippo "crunches it as easily as a pig would a bunch of asparagus, or shivers it with a kick of his hind foot." If the canoe is attacked, the men must "dive and swim to the shore under water" playing a trick on their huge gray enemy who will look for them on the surface. Meantime the handles, tied to the harpoons by long ropes, are floating on the stream, and, from a distance, other paddlers in other canoes seize

them. Up and down and round and round they drag
the old river-horse, till weak from loss of blood,—
his frenzy changed to exhaustion,— he gives up the
fight.

Speaking of the fury of the buffaloes, Livingstone
says proudly: "Our young men never lose their
presence of mind." If a buffalo makes a charge in
the forest, they " dart dexterously out of his way behind a tree, and, wheeling round, stab him as he
passes." We catch Livingstone's admiration for the
Africans' courage when we remember that the natives wore very little clothing as protection. Their
shining dark skin had not even the buffalo's hairy
coat.

In the forest there were not only lions, serpents,
hippopotami, buffaloes, and other big foes, which any
one would have dreaded, but there were hordes of
tiny enemies: swarms of mosquitoes stinging men almost to madness; tsetse-flies killing off in a short time
" forty-three fine oxen "; pests of ants that covered
Livingstone " as close as small-pox " with a burning
agony; and leeches that flew at his white skin " like
furies, and refused to let go." He soon found that
he could not twist or tug the slippery things off; but
must give them a " smart slap " like the natives.

So much for the miseries of this jungle world. It
had its beauties — great ones, too. Livingstone has
left us a noble picture of the kingdom where animals
reign. " Hundreds of buffaloes and zebras grazed
on the open spaces, and there stood lordly elephants

feeding majestically. When we descended we found all the animals remarkably tame. The elephants stood beneath the trees, fanning themselves with their huge ears." He wrote with affection. He gloried in the crimsons and deep blues of the African tangle, and in the flowers that made a " golden carpet." It was as if the ten-year-old Scotch laddie, cheated long ago of his sunshine, found it at last through sacrifice. No vast experience in great affairs could spoil his happiness in little things — in the songs of birds; in the freshness of the morning; in everything that " God made very good." And half his heart seems at home in Scotland. There was a river " beautiful like the Clyde "; larks that did not " soar so high ", or stay " so long on the wing as *ours*"; " a tree in flower brought the pleasant fragrance of hawthorn hedges back to memory." Some days the whole world seemed steeped in clear sunshine, the air filled with the hum of insects and the " courtship " of full-throated birds. Livingstone watched them " play at making little homes," or carrying nest-feathers too heavy for their strength; and often he fed them with bread-crumbs, he who had so little bread.

Then he would fall to pondering it all. What did the savages learn from their forest-education? Did the birds teach them to make peaceful homes and the trees a quiet shelter? He could not tell. But, like Fuller's " good sea-captain " he counted the " Image of God — nevertheless his image — cut in ebony as if done in ivory." Into the tangled darkness of Africa, the Torch-Bearer carried a light; and, for the first time, eyes dull almost to blindness, saw life clean, honest, and peaceful. Like children, the savages were quick to imitate. "From nothing I say will they learn as much as from what I am," was Livingstone's great doctrine. If the life-sermon failed, no word-sermon could win. And so, for example as well as for his own comfort, he kept himself, and everything he had, scrupulously neat. He taught them to despise a man who stabbed another in the back. That was sneaky. By his own proved fearlessness and by appealing to their own bravery, he made them ashamed to be sneaks. "They never visit anywhere but for the purpose of plunder and oppression. They never go anywhere but with a club or spear in hand," he sadly admitted. "Why do you all steal from each other? Then you want to fight," he would say.

"It will be joy to sleep without dreaming of any one pursuing with a spear," one would answer.

"You have opened a path for us and we shall have sleep," said a second.

But a great chief argued: "I can make my people do nothing except by thrashing them. If you like I shall call my head-man, and with our whips of rhinoceros-hide we will soon make them all believe together."

"I wish you could change my heart," sighed another. "Give me medicine to change it, for it is proud, proud and angry, angry always. I wish to drink and have it changed at once."

But Livingstone offered no miracles. Still treating them as untaught children, he pleased them with music, and showed his magic lantern pictures of his Master's life.

"It is the Word from Heaven," they said. But most of them grasped little except that the one who bore the Word was himself good. His genius was the genius of the heart. The natives trusted him more than they could trust father or brother; and, when once their love was won, they thanked him by their faithfulness. When he was sick, one gave up his own blanket for Livingstone's bed; others carried him on their shoulders through the flood, or on a litter for the long land-journeys. If strength permitted, they traveled about two hundred miles a month. One of the stories of Livingstone's dangerous journeys through unknown bogs and woods, threatened by animals, fevers, and savages, leads us at last to the Western coast of Africa. There, coming suddenly from forest darkness to the gleaming waters of the Atlantic, the natives, who had never seen the ocean, fell on their knees in awe at its endlessness, gasping out. "The world says 'I am finished. There is no more of me.'" Their trust had kept them trudging on only to meet this strange unknown. The best Livingstone could do, as he had done all the weary way, was to renew his frequent promise to bring them back safely to their friends. Before turning back, however, he tried to complete his maps and charts and his account of their explorations. The task was nearly done when the captain of an English steamer, which was anchored in the harbor, offered Livingstone a passage home. How it tempted him! Rushing rivers, and Scotch breezes, welcoming faces, and a home-like tongue! But Livingstone had given his promise. The English-going ship sailed without him, and, keeping his word to those who had trusted, he turned eastward for another two thousand miles.

Of the horrors of the slave-trade it is enough to quote his own words: "The subject does not admit of exaggeration." His accounts, further than this, are only too vivid. "She is somebody's bairn," he would say pityingly, as he saw some poor chained creature. Three times Livingstone built for himself a house, only to have it destroyed by slave-traders, who hated him fiercely. After that, he was always home-less. What Lincoln did for America, Livingstone did for Africa. The Boers, whose chief commerce was in slaves, destroyed all he had. "They have saved me the trouble of making a will," he said. Three times in one day he nearly lost his life, for it was his life they were seeking.

Great physical courage he needed, then, but much more. For three years he heard no news from home; for two, the world heard nothing of him. "Oh, for one hour a day to play with my children!" he would think. Early in his African experience one of his babies had died in the wilderness. Years later, his boy Robert went to America, and there, like his father, spent himself for the slaves — he fought and fell at

Gettysburg. When Livingstone was on his way home from his first journey, his father died.

" You wished so much to see David," said the old man's daughter.

" Ay, very much," with Scotch strength. " But I think I 'll know whatever is worth knowing about him. Tell him I think so when you see him."

To Dr. Livingstone's delight, his wife sailed with him back to Africa. But the dreadful fever took her away. " Oh, my Mary, my Mary! how often we have longed for a quiet home since you and I were cast adrift," he sobbed. " For the first time in my life I feel willing to die." Yet, in his bitterest loneliness, he sustained himself with Christ's promise: " Lo, I am with you always, even unto the end of the world." In his original way he added, " It is the word of a Gentleman of the most sacred and strictest honour and there is an end on 't."

Long before now, the London Missionary Society had given Livingstone its strong support. His home-comings were real triumphs! medals, degrees, receptions — all the honors England showers on her heroes. Livingstone hated such a fuss. He would rather meet a lion in the jungle than be made a lion in public. With no thought of his own glory, he set forth the commercial value of Africa: its fruits, its furs, its ivory. But his strongest appeal was for the slaves. Self-forgetful always, on his careful maps were two names of his own choosing. The beautiful cataract, described by the natives as " Smoke that sounds," he

named Victoria Falls for the "Great White Queen";
and he named a lake for his hero, Lincoln.

As an acknowledged missionary, an honored " fel-
low-worker with God " as he called it, he was strikingly
level-headed and sane, and always absolutely sincere.
" Nothing will induce me to form an impure church.
Fifty added to the church sounds fine at home; but if
only five of these are genuine, what will it profit?"
Religion must be the "everyday business of life."
When he found himself too eager for visible results,
he would preach himself a little sermon: " He that
believeth shall not make haste. Surely if God can
bear with hardened impenitent sinners for thirty, forty,
or fifty years, waiting to be gracious, we may take it
for granted that His is the best way."

In September 1865, he left England for the last
time. Two years later we find him again in the heart
of Africa — a world all " froth and ooze." Again
his goods have been stolen and he himself is a mere
skeleton. Then, one bright summer morning comes a
massacre so terrific that Livingstone said it was like
" being in hell." Exhausted by exploration and sickness, with no news from home or from any one, his
" forward tread " is a poor totter. Death is the best
he can hope for; no " Good Samaritan " can possibly
pass by.— But suddenly, out of utter hopelessness, his
faithful black man, Susi, rushed in, gasping, " An
Englishman! I see him! "

One's own flag is dear to any patriot's heart. But
never was an American flag so dear to a Scotchman as

those stars and stripes to Livingstone. And never was a stage action more dramatic than Stanley's unexpected entrance — another white man in that unknown wilderness, bringing food, clothing, and medicine,— everything a desolate, dying man could need. Letters? Yes, a bagful. Livingstone read two from his children; then he demanded the news. " Tell me the news. How is the world getting on? Grant, President? Good! It is two years since I have heard a word!" The story of Stanley's and Livingstone's friendship is too beautiful to miss. Every one should read it for himself. In the joy of their companionship, Livingstone grew rapidly better: his eyes brightened; his briskness and his youthfulness came back, along with that great, sweet spirit that Stanley never forgot. Together they explored Lake Tanganyika, making what Livingstone called " a picnic " of their partnered search. But when Stanley urged him to come away with him, Livingstone steadily refused. Africa might need him yet.

But his work was nearly over. During his long, wearying illness, however, he had the comfort of seeing his "boys'" faithfulness. By his torch they had lighted theirs, and learned that brotherhood is true religion. Then, on a May morning in 1873, one watcher alarmed the rest: "Come to Bwana; I am afraid. I don't know if he is alive." Susi, Chumah, and four others ran to the tent. There, by the bedside, with his face buried in the pillow, knelt their Doctor, dead.

What to do they did not know; and he could not tell

The Meeting of Livingstone and Stanley

them any more. They wanted to keep him in Africa;
but thought that his friends would want him at home.
And so, one of them read the burial service, and they
laid his heart to rest where he had worked; but his
body, cased in tree-bark and sail-cloth, they carried
over a thousand miles to the ship that would bear it
home. Gratitude has been called " the memory of the
heart." Of all heart-memories is there a better proof
than this? The Samoans, who dug the road for
Stevenson, could count on his appreciation because he
was still alive; but Livingstone's friends, with their
dog-like fidelity, could never hope for a word, a look,
a smile of thanks. Their long, long journey to the
coast led through jungle, forest, and danger. But
they made it. And one of the boys who bore him was
a slave whom he had freed.

England gave him a place in Westminster Abbey,
with her poets and kings. On the black slab we read:

BROUGHT BY FAITHFUL HANDS
OVER LAND AND SEA
HERE RESTS
DAVID LIVINGSTONE
MISSIONARY, TRAVELER, PHILANTHROPIST
BORN MARCH 19, 1813
DIED MAY 4TH, 1873

And on the border of the stone:
" Other sheep I have which are not of this fold,
them also I must bring, and they shall hear my voice."

IX
PASTEUR

" Gentlemen, I propose a toast — To the peaceful strife of science."

Louis Pasteur.

A GREAT LIFE-SAVER

"MAD dog! Mad dog!" That cry in any country, in any street, is terrifying even to-day; but how much worse was the cry "Mad wolf!" seventy years ago through the nestling towns of the Jura Mountains! To anxious fathers and mothers looking into the faces of their little children, it brought agonizing pictures: the wildest of creatures abroad in the hills, with glittering eyes and foaming mouth, tearing on and on, and about to descend on their village and their little ones playing in the sun. Very gravely Monsieur and Madame Pasteur cautioned small Louis and his two sisters to stay in the tannery-yard close to the house. With big eyes full of reflected fear, the children listened and promised to obey. Their training in truth made them keep the promise. The fears were not groundless. Instead of the poor old wolf wearing himself out in the forest on trees and roots, he did come flying through the village; eight people in the neighborhood were bitten; and, for a long time, every one in the country round was in terror of that mad wolf.

Louis Pasteur had been a Christmas present to his

father and mother and four-year-old sister, for he was born in 1822, only two days after Christmas, in the village of Dole. I suppose no other present was half so welcome.

Though his parents had little to give him but their love, the child soon found his own playthings. We can imagine him cramming frail blue-bells into his grimy little hands for his mother and finding a world of delight in the bits of bark lying round the tannery-yard. Before long he began to feel proud of the good leather which his father made, and we can imagine him standing silently by while the ox or goat skins were unloaded from big carts, or the oak-bark was being ground for tanning. With a child's wonder he must have followed the long process from the scraping off of the hairy coats through the many soakings in the big pits, till, drained, dried, and oiled, there was a fine load of leather for the shoemaker. All this takes work and patience. It is sometimes a whole year before an ox-skin is ready to be made into a boot. In following this process, Louis's mind grew used to watching and waiting. The lessons of the tannery-yard were the beginnings of his training in science. They taught him to look for developments.

Besides this, he had regular lessons in the little school near-by. Not till he went to boarding-school, however, do we follow his education with any vivid interest.

There was storm in the sky and gloom in his heart the day he left home for the big city school. Under the flood of rain, the horses pawed restlessly. They found it cold standing still so long while bags and trunks were hoisted to the top of the coach and while Louis and his friend, Jules Vercel, said a hundred good-byes to the same dear people. They were still shouting " Au revoir! " and waving hands buoyantly from under the tarpaulin, as the heavy wheels splashed away down the road. Buoyant they seemed, but their hearts were already swelling with homesickness. Through the mist, they said a silent farewell to the gray tower of Arbois Church. Then the hills dipped down and carried them rattling onward, bound for Paris.

But this homesickness was only a taste of the homesickness to come. Jules did not suffer as much as the younger boy, who, poor fellow, though he was fifteen, lay awake night after night in the far-away city saying to himself: " ' How endless unto watchful anguish night doth seem.' "

The green trees of the tannery were far dearer to him than the glitter of Paris. We can well imagine that as the clocks chimed the hours he wondered if they were all asleep at home and if they dreamed that he was sleeping too. I suppose the moon and stars told him that they were shining down on *them*.

" If I could only get a whiff of the tannery-yard," he confided to Jules, " I feel I should be cured."

At last the head-master, Monsieur Barbet, after trying everything else, wrote a few plain facts to Louis' father.

And so, one November day, Louis Pasteur was sent for. "They are waiting for you," said a messenger, pointing to a little café on the corner. The much-puzzled boy went over to the café. There at the table, with his head in his hands, sat some one dearly familiar — his father.

"I have come to fetch you." There was no rebuke in the tanner's simple greeting. The love-longing had overwhelmed the knowledge-longing in his son's heart — that was all. The father needed no explanations.

Nevertheless, Louis' knowledge-longing was very strong, and he had no idea of giving up study. At Besançon, forty kilometers (less than twenty-five miles), from Arbois, was a college where there was plenty to learn and where he could be prepared for the "École Normale" (normal school). Several times a year his father would go to Besançon to sell his leather. That the father would combine with this business a visit to his son, Louis knew well.

At school, the boy was so careful that people thought him slow. He slighted nothing. Absolute sureness, alone, could satisfy him. "Dear sisters," he would write home, "work hard, love each other. When one is accustomed to work, it is impossible to do without it; besides, everything in this world depends on that." In one of his letters he spoke of studying mathematics till he got a "pretty bad headache." "But those head-aches never last long," he quickly added, not willing to worry any one.

At nineteen he reëntered the Barbet boarding-school

in Paris. No longer a homesick boy, he had grown
tall and self-reliant, and he soon proved himself so
capable that he was asked to help with the teaching.
By this means, his schooling cost him only one-third
of the usual price. Outside of study or teaching hours,
he and his great friend, Chappuis, had some good
times. But Louis was always in danger of overwork-
ing. "You know how we worry about your health;
you do work so immoderately," wrote his anxious
father. "Are you not injuring your eyesight by so
much night work?" Then that troubled father would
appeal to Chappuis as a kind of caretaker: "Do tell
Louis not to work so much; it is not good to strain
one's brain," adding with affection: "Remain two
good friends."

Miss Ida Tarbell gives a picture of Chappuis sitting
beside him in the laboratory stubbornly determined to
get him into the open air "until Pasteur, conquered,
jerked off his apron, saying half angrily, half grate-
fully: 'Well, let us go for a walk.'"

In the Jura home, parents and sisters waited eagerly for Louis' thick letters, all packed with lovingness and the details of his happy work. The hopes of
the whole family were centered in the boy at school.
We can picture them gathering round to read his letters aloud, and then each one taking the dear sheets to
re-read, alone, to understand them better. How worried they were during one long time of waiting:
"Eighteen days! Louis has never kept us waiting so
long! Can he be ill?"

"Don't overwork," was the father's anxious warning; "so many noble youths have sacrificed their health to the love of science — Think what a worry it is to me that I cannot be with you to look after you." Again, he wrote, after thanking Louis for his Christmas presents: "For my part, I should prefer a thousand times that this money should still be in your purse, and thence to a good restaurant, spent in some good meals that you might have enjoyed with your friends. There are not many parents, my dearest boy, who have to write such things to their son."

And now the young man, whose father had taught him his alphabet, took a turn at teaching his father and his sister, Josephine. They established a private correspondence school — that little family. "The father would often sit up late at night over rules of grammar and problems in mathematics preparing answers to send to his boy in Paris." Among other helpful things, Louis suggested a cheaper and quicker method of tanning skins; but the father did not adopt it. It was, as yet, unproved; the leather might not be so good or last so long, he argued; because he had always dealt honestly, the shoemakers trusted his goods. He would rather keep their trust than get rich. It is not hard to trace the strict honesty of Louis Pasteur, in all his scientific searchings, straight back to his tanner father.

Among the young people of to-day it is the fashion to laugh at the fellow who studies hard. "Resistance to knowledge," as Professor Phelps puts it, is a fad.

"Grind" is a term of contempt. The average boy
quails before it. But the fellow who delights in study
never grinds. A few, like Pasteur, have a real hunger
for discovery. Pasteur carried that hunger with him
when he entered the École Normale. Here, to save
time, his chemistry class did not experiment to get
phosphorus; they were merely told how to get it; and
many were satisfied to go no further. Pasteur, however, worked it out for himself: he bought bones, burnt
them to ashes, and then "treated the ashes with sul-
phuric acid." We can imagine with what pride he
wrote the label on his little bottle of home-made phosphorus. "This was his first scientific joy."

By a love for work that was almost a passion, Pasteur, so often called in the scorn of jealous rivals a
"mere chemist", went on and on, from questioning
lifeless, soulless crystals to waging war for man. His
was a long line of interests, and they seem scattered
and unrelated. That is because, whenever he found a
need, he tried to meet that need with help. Crystals,
acids, the ferments of milk and alcohol, the best way
to preserve wine and beer, the diseases of silk-worms,
hens, goats, pigs, and sheep,— cholera, fevers, and
hydrophobia. All these seized his eager attention.
Scientific zeal, patriotism, and love for service goaded
him on to further discoveries. He will be lastingly
remembered as the Conqueror of Disease.

The tanner's son, in the hidden village of Arbois —
the boy who had been called "slow," who had left the
Paris school because he was homesick, and had entered

the École Normale a little old for his class,— through working and waiting had grown very great, great enough to be known by the common people. The vine-dressers, who tended their grapes on the sunny hills of France, they knew his name. Because Pasteur had found a way to keep vines healthy, they could sell their grape juice, and bring home the shining coins to buy blue ribbons for Annette and stout shoes for Pierre. Pasteur had kept their hearts glad and their homes comfortable, and had saved one of the great industries of France.

By and by the shepherds, the goatherds, and the swineherds, even the poultry-men, heard his name. " Perhaps," one would say, " he would know what has got into our sheep." Twenty had died out of a hundred, beginning to droop only a few hours before-hand.

" It may be Pasteur could cure my hens," a second would suggest, as he leaned over the poor staggering creatures that seemed to have fallen asleep while they were trying to walk.

How much the tanner's son could do who had begun life by " curing" leather! France was his own land, and the French his own people. In the sight of his eager patriotism, service done for the French was like service done for a big family. We hope that some-times in the midst of his intensely practical discoveries he rejoiced that hundreds were happier because he had lived and because he had taught them how to get the best results from honest labor.

Of his many works there will be space, in this short sketch, to emphasize only two: his conquest of the silk-worm disease, by which he saved one of the great industries of France; and his conquest of hydrophobia, by which he saved human life.

Pasteur had never seen a silk-worm when, urged by the French government, he attacked the epidemic that had raged among the silk-worms for fifteen years. But the boy, Pasteur, had known how much depended on the making of leather and it was easy for the man, Pasteur, as he journeyed into southern France, to see that the hopes of hundreds of families depended on successful silk-worm culture. What other use had those groves of mulberry-trees? With no silk to spin what would become of the mill-workers? Strange as it may sound, Pasteur was in a land where worms seemed more important than people. Three-year-old children understood that, whatever else happened, the fires that warmed the worms must not go out; and, since the worms are the *dainty* members of the family, everything that touched them must be perfectly clean. Silk-worms will not stay on dirty mulberry leaves. Pasteur, beginning with the tiny eggs, or " seeds " as they are called, used this sure method of protection: The moth, which dies anyway soon after her eggs are laid, was " crushed in a mortar and mixed with a little water; the mixture was examined with the microscope,— and, if a germ of the disease was found, the eggs, between 300 and 700 from each moth, were immediately destroyed with everything belonging to them." It was the old, old law of the survival of the fittest.

Only the eggs from healthy moths are used for hatching, for, as some one has said, "from healthy moths healthy eggs were sure to spring, from healthy eggs, healthy worms; from healthy worms, fine cocoons," and of course from the best cocoons the best silk. Eggs are said to be "Pasteurized" when they are the eggs of a perfectly healthy moth. The word "Pasteurize" has worked into our dictionaries from Pasteur's great name and by it is meant that anything, — milk, for instance, is pure, free from living germs, health-giving. It is something for a man's name to stand in the dictionary, to the end of time, for *health*.

In Pasteur's five years' work to save the silk-worms, he had the satisfaction of seeing disease conquered. He wanted no higher pay. Creeping from millions of "seeds" came millions of worms, so tiny that at first the mulberry-leaf food had to be shredded. Soon, however, they were feeding away with a whispering noise, as if they were starved. Before long, from a moving mass of life, the separate worms showed themselves — great, grayish, velvety things as big as your little finger, fatter and fatter every day, and ravenously hungry. By and by they tried to stand on their tails in the feeding racks, and reared and stretched their necks as if asking to climb. Then it was time for little Gustave to bring bundles of brier brush — the silk-worms' ladders. And, at last, clinging to tiny branches, there

"set to work millions of spinning worms
That in their green shops weave the smooth-haired silk."

The " reels " spun by one worm are anywhere from a thousand feet to more than two miles long. In the light of Pasteur's cure, it is no wonder that, after years of failure, the silk-worm husking was a jubilee. The cocoons, "heaped in round flat baskets, ready for market, were glorified, seemingly, into heaps of golden and silvern eggs by the afternoon sun." It was a time for feasting on delicious " home-made cheese, home-grown almonds and olives, and good home-made bread." We can easily imagine that during the laughter-filled feast, Marie dreamed of a fine new jacket and Babbette of a knot of bright ribbon, a lace fichu, and a bouquet of artificial flowers.

As for Pasteur, the restorer of all these smiles, it was enough to have brought such joy to unnumbered homes. To him, home had always been sacred. Some one once said: " If you want a definition of happiness, visit the Huxley family." The same thing might have been said of the Pasteurs. Louis had known nothing but love in his father's low-roofed tannery; and he knew nothing but love in the other home which he and his wife had begun, in May 1849. Sorrows came. They came thick and fast. Three dear little girls were taken away from them, but the father and mother were strong in their belief that all would be again united. The deeper the happiness the deeper the loss, and the deeper the loss the deeper the need of faith in another life. Pasteur was one of the great scientists who kept his solid old-fashioned religion, and his comforting belief in immortality.

And, though he lost three children, a son and a daughter were left. Years later, after the son had entered the army, one bitter January day father, mother, and daughter set out to find him. In the dreadful reports of a hard fight, no news had come of their boy. Cruel suspense was almost as hard as certain sorrow. The same Jules Vercel who long ago had started with Louis Pasteur for boarding-school — Jules Vercel, now a man of fifty — was there to say good-bye to his old friend. He stood faithfully by as Pasteur helped his wife and daughter into a broken-down carriage — the only one left in the village — and set forth into the storm. Snow whirled through the air thick with flakes. It drifted the roads with great, white piles. For four days they journeyed, stopping wherever they could for the nights. Part of the way lay through a deep pine-forest, perfectly silent except when heavy masses of snow fell from the spreading boughs. By the time they reached Pontarlier, where they hoped to find their boy, the poor old carriage barely held together.

Madame Pasteur, with her face worn by cold, weariness, and fear, asked the first soldier she met for news of her son.

" All I can tell you,"— try as the soldier did, the words fell with harsh hopelessness,—" is that out of 1200 men in his batallion, only 300 are left."

But Madame Pasteur did not give up. While she was questioning another soldier, a third stepped up and said,

" Sergeant Pasteur? Yes, he is alive; I slept by him last night at Chaffois. He has remained behind; he is ill. You might meet him on the road towards Chaffois."

Chaffois? They had come right through it without knowing! It lay freezing miles behind them on the snow-banked road. But they could face again the stinging storm if their son was at the journey's end and in need. Barely had they started back when a cart labored by and from that cart some one muffled to the eyes peered into their carriages. And to that some one, — to the fellow who felt a life-time away from home — was it a miracle, or only a fevered-hope,— a beautiful delirious dream,— that his own people had come to him in the storm! Too full of feeling to speak, the little family " embraced without a word." On that bitter January day they were suddenly filled with wonderful warmth. Monsieur Pasteur took his sick son to Geneva to recover. And, no doubt, as he shared his boy's joyful surprise, he remembered how long ago, another son had been surprised by another father: he was once more a homesick boy, entering, in wonder, a corner café, staring, in half-hope at a familiar head, and rejoicing in the welcome words, " I have come to fetch you." His father had taught him fatherliness and he knew how to bestow it on his worn out soldier-boy.

Meanwhile he fathered many, not his own. Returned to his work of healing, as he entered the Zoö-
logical garden of the Institute, the children would run
to him, throw their arms around him, and bless him
with their perfect trust. And somehow the silver coins
slipped very naturally out of his pockets into theirs.

"Pasteur is a man who would find advantage from
living in a glass house," said Mr. G. M. Crawford.
It is beautiful to have such a thing true. And if Pasteur had been in a glass house, through its transparent
walls we might have seen that he not only tucked
shining presents into the children's pockets but patted
their heads, clasped their hands, and kissed their tear-
stained faces, though the tears were never there for
long.

"My child, it is all over!" he would exclaim sooth-
ingly,— "Mon enfant! Mon enfant!" It was hard
for him to see even slight suffering, particularly in animals or children,— he who had never had the "courage to kill a bird in hunting."

As his step was heard in the hospital, a halting step
because he had had a paralytic stroke, the heads on the
pillows turned toward him and the faces lighted with
smiles of gratitude. It was worth the long hours
spent in searching, the slow tests, the patient waiting;
it was worth more than medals or degrees, this great
love of thankful hearts. Pasteur had plenty of
honors; but he counted them as words and ribbons.
He was too great to think himself great. The world
was the world, full of struggle and need and woe, and

the most he could do in his full life was still very
little.

Like Agassiz, he had a passion for scientific study
and a great gift for teaching. His pupils came away
filled with his love of truth; his unwillingness to state
a fact unless proved and proved again. His teaching
seemed like inspiration, and utterly tireless. It had
been so patiently planned beforehand that all the patient preparation was concealed. It was like poured
sunlight. Nevertheless, he would never rob a student
of the joy of discovery. As a lad, it had meant much
to him to make his own phosphorus. " Where will
you find a young man," he would ask, " whose curiosity
and interest will not immediately be awakened when
you put into his hands a potato, when from that potato
he may produce sugar, from that sugar he may produce alcohol, from that alcohol ether, and vinegar?
Where is he who will not be happy to tell his family
in the evening that he has just been working out an
electric telegraph? Such studies are seldom, if ever,
forgotten." At the root of all his teaching lay the
principle of *usefulness*. It was repeated and repeated
again to hundreds. " One man's life is useless if it is
not useful to others." As he grew older and realized
too fully that the years would not grant him time to
solve all his problems, he looked to his pupils to carry
on his work. In praise of their faithful persistence he
would say: " I pointed the way; but I had only conceived hopes and you bring in solid realities." He
craved honors for them far more than for himself.

But to his list of saved lives we must add part of the credit of the lives saved by the pupils he had trained.

One of the greatest glories of a sincere teacher is the thought that there may have gone forth from his work or his personality numberless hidden influences. His influence is cumulative and eternal, whether good or bad. If his aims have been good, his influence has been good. And much that he can never have the comfort of knowing may be hidden, but living in other minds and hearts. This thought comforted Pasteur: "Our only consolation, as we feel our own strength failing us, is the consciousness that we may help those who come after us to do more and to do better than ourselves, fixing their eyes as they can on the great horizons of which we only had a glimpse." This idea he hugged for his own encouragement when, like Agassiz, he thought, "Oh, if I only had time!" In his "passion for work" and his faithfulness to teaching, he was very much like Agassiz; in his heroic struggle, under the warning hand of paralysis, he was more like Scott.

To all teachers who have known how it feels to be fretted by teasing little details, his willingness to attend to little details stands as a strengthening example. It is an example to *anyone* who is nettled by the smallness of life's concerns — the gnats that swarm around our busy heads. Pasteur was not too great to look after the "catering; to ascertain what weight of meat per pupil is given at the École Polytechnique; to order the courtyard strewn with sand; the dining-room

Louis Pasteur

door to be repaired; and to look after the ventilation of the class-rooms." He was great enough to forget his greatness if little things needed his attention.

Let us see him, at last, however, not as a teacher but as a healer. To cure hydrophobia, before he could experiment on man, he had to experiment on animals. Let those who condemn it ask and answer the question: Is it better that a guinea-pig should suffer a little or that my only child should die? Pasteur never experimented without using chloroform, and, tender-hearted man that he was, he took the greatest care to save any animal from unnecessary suffering. Never had he shot an animal of any kind for sport. But when human life was at stake "Vivisection was a dreadful necessity." Even when he had multiplied his experiments, he said, half-fearfully: "I think my hand will tremble when I go on to mankind."

In Pasteur's life, the years 1885 and 1886 were marked by wonderful strides toward the conquest of hydrophobia. The terrible memory of the mad wolf of his childhood had never worn away. It came back to him in manhood with fresh horror when, one July morning, an Alsatian mother, poorly dressed and leading a nine-year-old boy by the hand, entered his laboratory. Little Joseph Meister could hardly walk, and his small hands were fearfully bitten. In a voice full of restrained suffering and with beseeching eyes Frau Meister begged Pasteur to save her child. "He was so small!" she sobbed. "When the dog flew at him, he knew no more than to stand still and cover his face with his hands. A man, passing, beat off the beast with an iron bar. But there was my Joseph!—Oh, the dreadful blood!"

"I am no doctor," answered the scientist humbly. "I am only trying to discover cures; but I shall do my best for little Joseph." As he spoke, he gently laid his hand on the child's fair head.

When Joseph found that the treatment was no more than a pin prick, his dreary blue eyes began to shine again; he no longer dreaded the master's touch. Out in the sunny garden, among the rabbits, chickens, and guinea-pigs, he was very happy, and he generally slept more peacefully than the scientist, who tossed back and forth in the fear that the child would die.

But little Meister got well. And, furthermore, in his long stay at the laboratory he grew to be such a friend of "Dear Monsieur Pasteur" that he would run in from the garden, climb into his lap, and beg, with all kinds of childish pleadings, that some specially playful guinea-pig or pink-nosed rabbit might not be used for experiment. And little Meister had his way, like many other children who loved Pasteur as a father.

One beautiful day in the next October, six little shepherd-boys had led their flocks to a green meadow glistening in the sunlight of the Jura Mountains. Here the juicy grass drew its richness from underground streams, and here the boys found flowery places to stretch out under the blue sky-roof and talk together in their soft French voices. From time to

time they would move on to keep near their straying
sheep, while bees hummed their way into the flowers'
hearts and turned the bright cups upside down with
the weight of their velvet bodies. The children's
shepherd life was full of restful friendliness. Suddenly one of the boys, pointing to the road, shouted
"*Chien enragé! Chien enragé!*" (Mad dog! Mad
dog!) Fear raised his voice to a shriek. As the children scrambled to their feet, they saw a great creature
turn, and tear towards them. Though they ran as
fast as soft ground, wooden shoes, and fright
would let them, that was not very fast. The dog came
panting on. Then the oldest, a fourteen-year-old boy
named Jupille, turned, to save the rest, and faced their
maddened enemy, alone. With glazed eyes, and slimy
turned-back lips, the dog was close upon him. Leaping
into the air, he caught the boy's left hand between his
gleaming teeth. Jupille's mountain-training came in
play. The hills had taught him strength and swift-
ness. In his brave tussle, he managed to throw the
dog to the ground, kneel on his back, and with his
right hand force the jaws apart to set his left hand
free. Of course his right hand was terribly bitten
too; but, at last, he got a grip on the animal's neck,
and, calling to his little brother to bring him the whip,
dropped in the fight, he fastened the dog's jaws tight
with the lash. Then he worked with his wooden sabot
till the heaving creature was so nearly dead that he
could drag him to the brook and end his life.

White-faced, round-eyed, and trembling, the little

huddle of shepherd boys drooped back to the village, all of them sure that Jupille would die, and all but Jupille feeling like murderers. (His life was the price of theirs.) But the Mayor, who had heard of Pasteur, sent the great scientist swift word.

Poor Pasteur! As yet his experimenting was too new; he was not ready to risk men. Little Joseph Meister, whom he had saved, had reached him only two days and a half after the attack. Jupille's wounds would be six days old. However, Jupille would have almost no pain (only a pin-prick a day), and it might mean life. The boy was sent for; and, not only, by patient watching, was he saved, but, through the recommendation of the fatherly Pasteur, received a prize for bravery.

Some of the great scientist's experiments were not successful. He had had a chance to treat Meister and Jupille within a week of the day they were bitten. Long postponed treatment was not so sure.

The next November, Louise Pelletier, a little girl of ten, was brought to him over a month after the mad dog's attack! Pasteur did all he could; but it was useless.

" I did so wish I could have saved your little one! " he said to the father and mother. Then, as he shut the door on their sorrow, the great man, himself, burst into tears. He had not explained his bitter disappointment in failure, or his own affection for Louise, nor had he told them that their little girl was just the age

of Jeanne,— the first child given him and the first child
taken away.

Although Pasteur had this sad failure, before long
his fame was world-wide. By means of a public sub-
scription, started by the *New York Herald,* four little
Americans — children of poor laborers, were sent
across the ocean to the wonderful healer. The mother
of the youngest went with them. When her little boy,
who was only five, felt the simple needle-prick, he
asked, wonderingly, " Is this all we have come such
a long journey for?" When, healthy and smiling, the
four children came back to America, in answer to hundreds of questions about the " great man " they had
no wonderful story. The treatment had been so
easy!

But Pasteur had a story. On March 1, 1885, his
doubts smothered by success, he could tell France that
out of three hundred and fifty patients, only one had
died — Louise Pelletier. The victory was wonderful,
even taking into consideration that some of the dogs,
reported as mad, may not have been so, and that some
of the people, who were *not* treated by him, died, not
of hydrophobia, but of fear. There were men in his
time who tried to lessen his glory by these two arguments; but there were others who, during his lifetime
and since then, have called him, for the lives he saved,
the " Greatest Man of the Nineteenth Century." Napoleon, with all his military genius, was not so great,
because his business was to destroy life; Pasteur's was

to save it. A certain map of the world is dotted all over with Pasteur Institutes for the cure of hydrophobia. And there is at least one man who would call the Nineteenth Century " The Age of Pasteur."

A few days after that great report of only one case lost in three hundred and fifty, the healer's own faith was again shaken. Nineteen Russians, who had been bitten by a mad wolf, arrived in Paris. Some of them were so mangled that they had to be carried at once to the hospital. Others walked bravely along, their dark eyes gleaming — half afraid, half hopeful — under their big fur caps. They knew but one French word — *Pasteur.* As Livingstone first spoke to the Africans with eyes and heart, so Pasteur spoke to these Russians. The word Pity was written all over his face. " I 'll do my best to save you, my poor fellows," was his unspoken speech.

Yet there were, as always, ready doubters who, when three of the Russians died, began to attack Pasteur's whole method, apparently forgetting that it had taken a long time for the Russians to reach him, that they were terribly bitten, and that a mad wolf's bite is much worse than a mad dog's.

If ever any one was stimulated by obstacles it was Pasteur; but he removed obstacles for others. He made all healing free. No one was ever turned away. French, Belgians, Spanish, Portuguese, Russians, they came to him in daily crowds. Some came, as people will, just out of curiosity — just to see Pasteur — the stout little man with the short beard and black velvet

smoking-cap and the great name. He was always
hard at work. Till within a few months of the very
end, his energy went hand in hand with self-forgetfulness. Break-downs threatened him constantly; but the
saving of life — left sometimes to the power of man —
was too close to the *giving of life* — in the power of
God — for him to let one great chance slip. Even
at the last, he kept his youthful *enthusiasm,*— that pet
word of his, meaning " an inward God." There are
few things more divine than lives devoted to the hopes
of others, whether they waver over sick worms, or
sick sheep, or whether they hang on the life of a little
child.

Vallery-Radot, in his beautiful story of Pasteur,
gives a peaceful picture of the life-saver's last days.
Though he could hardly walk or speak, his eyes were
still bright, and, as he sat out of doors, " his grandchildren around him suggested young rose-trees climbing around the trunk of a dying oak." On September 28, 1895, he gave up his long battle. There was
a great national funeral: a military band, " infantry,
marines, cavalry, artillery, and municipal guards, . . .
red-robed Judges and members of University faculties in orange, red, and crimson robes." It was all
more showy than the tanner's son would have asked.
His simple grave-stone better commemorates his simple start in life. Though his name will always mean
intense energetic action, that plain stone speaks of
well-earned rest:

" Ici repose Pasteur "

X

BROOKS

"There is no man here who has not failed; but is there any man here in all this multitude who has given up?"

Phillips Brooks.

X

THROUGH FAILURE TO SUCCESS

TWO compositions lay on the dark-haired boy's desk. They were his last and hardest school efforts; they had both been written for prizes; and they had both failed. One was on "Mathematical Pursuits,"— a prose composition of five thousand words; the other was a poem on "The Shipwreck." On the back of the long envelope, the boy had written in his half-formed handwriting: "Given in for prize at the Public Latin School. But unfortunately failed. *Ah Me miserum!*"

He was only fifteen, this boy, and yet his schooldays were behind him and he was a Harvard freshman. Though he was so young, he was already six feet three inches tall. Perhaps his rapid growth had robbed him of his strength for a time, for he did not care for athletics or even for long walks; and though he entered naturally into all the college interests, this sudden manhood made him feel awkward and shy.

Longfellow was teaching modern languages at Harvard; Louis Agassiz, biology; Asa Gray, botany; Professor Child, Early English; and many other great teachers and great men stood ready to pour their glad

253

wisdom into every open mind.   And the dark-haired
fellow, Phillips Brooks, knew there was a wealth better
than gold in these men's brains, and he did not scorn
it.   Poetry he read for mere pleasure, wandering, as
in all his reading, with no guide but his fancy.   He
loved literature and the languages; he loved history
because of the men who made it.   But he hated mathematics because he could not work out the problems;
and he hated elocution because it seemed a sham.
Long years after, however, his training in elocution
proved very useful, though it never made him conquer his rapid speech.

More than any lessons, however, Brooks loved the
college life.   Jolly, cordial, true, he won his place naturally in all hearts.   During his four years, he was
made a member of six different societies, and he was
one of the commencement speakers.   Without knowing why, some of his friends almost worshiped him.
There was an intangible charm about him,— a winning playfulness,— that made them want him with
them; and yet a reserve that kept them from drawing
him out.   In college, by taking prizes for English essays, he half canceled the memory of the Latin School
disappointment.   No success or popularity could spoil
him, though, for he was too unconscious to know that
he was either brilliant or lovable.   When he was a
senior, he had a way of encouraging timid freshmen,
who might even have gone hungry through shyness.
Looking at them with his great, kind eyes, he would
push things their way at the table.   Sometimes, when

he met them alone, he would say: "The college is more for freshmen like you than for seniors like me."

When Phillips Brooks graduated, he was only nineteen, and, like many other young fellows, he had not decided on a profession. Alive in him, however, was the strong desire of most graduates — to do something at once; and this desire was strengthened by the fact that he was one of six boys, four of whom, younger than himself, were still to be educated. From his mother's side of the family, Phillips inherited a love of teaching,— his grandfather and his great-uncle having each founded a Phillips Academy, one at Andover, the other at Exeter. Ever since he was a child, he had heard of these great schools. And during his college life, the idea had dimly grown that he too might be a teacher. For the sake of experience, he thought he might take almost any position, later study abroad, and, finally, be a professor. Accordingly, when the chance came to teach in the Boston Latin School, he seized it eagerly.

No chapter in Phillips Brooks's life is so sad as this teacher chapter. None is so hopeless. And yet he began his work with hearty enthusiasm, and the first few months were happy. He had "splendid little boys," as he said, and he worked with interest. Late in the fall, however, he was given an older class, fellows only three or four years younger than himself. In letters to his friend "Top Sawyer" he wrote: "They are the most disagreeable set of creatures, without exception, that I ever met with." . . . "I am teaching them French which they don't, Greek which they won't, and Virgil which they can't understand or appreciate." In his own belief, he was not only unpopular at school, but even hated, and he said that if he met any one of his pupils socially, he would need a suit of chain-armor for protection. " I feel a little blue to-night, . . . and I come now to you and wish you with all my heart a very Happy New Year."

The truth is, his discipline was weak. Because he himself loved the subjects he taught, he took it for granted that his pupils loved them. He did not realize that much of the teaching of that day was corporal punishment; he had not had enough athletic training to enter a hand to hand fight; and he was too trusting to be a detective. These boys were mischievous and rowdyish. They had already vanquished three teachers, and, like Indians, were eager for another scalp. Besides, their boyish teacher wore glasses,— much less common then than now,— and they were not at all sure how much he could see. After plugging the thermometer with snow, they shivered and chattered, and then built an " insufferable fire." One boy threw a handful of shot in Brooks's face, and then, when the teacher looked, was sitting most innocently, perfectly still, his hand meekly raised to ask a question. Another scattered the heads of snapping-matches all over the room, and there was no way to trace the explosions. Brooks could not manage the boys himself, and he had no help from Principal Gardner, a fine athlete, who ruled by his strong right arm. According to Gard-

ner, discipline was the first mark of a good teacher, and
any one who failed in that was hopeless.

When at last, weak in heart and worn in courage,
the boy-teacher resigned, the unseeing principal met his
resignation with: " The man who fails at teaching
will fail at everything." It was a cruel shot.   Brooks
remembered those words long after the muscular Gardner had gone where fighting powers were useless.   It
is beautiful to know, however, that the boy never harbored a grudge against the man who hurt him most,
and, years later, even praised him in a public speech.
It is still more beautiful to remember that this very
defeat was the highroad to victory.   Principal Gardner lived long enough to find his own quick judgment
false, and that the boy-failure was a mighty success.

And yet, after the day of resignation, there were
hours, days, and months that spelled utter failure to
Phillips Brooks.   Inactive, empty-handed, the poor fellow went back home,— the only one in his big family
with nothing to do.   Though he secured a little private teaching to fill a few hours, the rest of the time he
had to think, to know, he was a disappointment to his
parents, to his five brothers, to every one who loved
him best.   Bitterest of all, he was a cruel disappointment to himself.   Could it be that the life which lay
before him, full of ambition, and once full of hope, was
to be a *failure?*   On his long walks he met different
class-mates; but they all seemed to be doing something, and knew what they meant to do.   When the
summer came, bringing vacation, their holidays were

earned; his were the continued indolence of an idle man.

And yet, through all this despondency, something told Phillips Brooks to hope. He seemed to realize that no one really knew him, that he did not even know himself,— boyish and commonplace conclusions enough. During those hard months his journal has one predominant thought — the loneliness of every individual; and the boy who wrote that journal longed to understand others more than he hoped to be understood himself. Loving biography as he did, every "life" he read brought him to the same conclusion: millions of hearts were lonely; millions of others would love to sympathize; but it seemed impossible. Then from the young man's soul went up a kind of prayer that he might "know the strange language in which his neighbors' lives were written"; and, finally, with this self-forgetfulness,— this great prayer for others, — there was given, slowly, strangely, a wonderful gift — the conviction that God could understand him fully, and that God knew he need not be a failure.

Up to this time, Phillips Brooks had shown no interest in religion. Sunday after Sunday he had sat half-bowed, at the end of the family pew, but neither preacher, nor parents, nor his best friends knew anything of his religion. That one part was closed to all the world. But we know that he passed through a troubled time of doubt, and that, like most others of the world's greatest believers, he found full light through the "culture of darkness."

Dr. Walker, the president of Harvard, must have had some influence over him. Phillips had heard him preach in Chapel Sunday evenings and, like other college boys, had been won by his character and power. He was a man in whom it was easy to confide, and to whom many students had bared their souls. And now one day, late in the summer, Phillips Brooks entered his study for advice. What was said behind that closed door no one knows; but the young man who came away was white and trembling.— Dr. Walker had advised him to preach.

We can no more guess the throbbings in a soul with this solemn thought of life before it than we can guess the mysteries of the ocean. Let these things be as they are made — deep, silent, and buried. After much thinking, Phillips Brooks went to his rector, Dr. Vinton, to ask what steps he should take to enter the ministry.

" Men are generally confirmed before they enter the ministry," answered Dr. Vinton, " and are supposed to be converted before they are confirmed."

" I don't know what conversion means," said Phillips Brooks.

Blessedly, Dr. Vinton did not argue or press. Here was a young man too earnest to profess what he did not know; too reverent to hurry into the most sacred relations,— a young man who, having failed in his chosen ambition, half-stunned by failure, was going to try something else. Phillips Brooks did not veil from Dr. Vinton, or his family, or himself that it was only a trial. The dismalness of failure had cut itself so deep into the young man's heart that he took up the new work at the Theological Seminary in Alexandria, Virginia, with a very wavering confidence. Because he entered a little late, he had to choose his room from the left-overs. It was a cold, dark, cheerless place in the attic, with a ceiling too low for him to stand straight, and a bed too short for him to stretch out. The students dined in a large, low room, down cellar, on such things as tomato-pies and "boiled rice with water on the brain." When "potatoes were limited", Hebrew and moral philosophy were supposed to satisfy hunger. Popular as Brooks had been at Harvard, here he made few friends,— only two in the first year; and, of all the professors, Dr. Sparrow was his only inspiration. Many nights the young man would lie awake, doubled up in his short bed, knowing well that if he were not "twenty-one, he should call himself homesick."

And yet those years in Alexandria proved one thing: that *handicaps are benefits*. In spite of bleak surroundings, friendlessness, and starvation-instruction, the Phillips Brooks who had wrung from his failure at teaching a new impetus for life, now wrung from his very leisure a new power for work. No inadequate teaching could shut from him the world of books, or the world of nature, or the world of men. His open mind could feed itself. He plunged into whatever tempted him: Greek and Latin classics, biography, history, poetry, theology, the vast beauty of the out-door world, if only caught from a car window, and always the exhaustless wonder of the human heart. Though he was sometimes impatient with the seminary and with what it did not give, he wrote in his note-book and in his soul: "We must despair of growing great unless we can feel that we are given to the cause to work for it, and not it to work for us"; and: "It must be, not what the world can do for me, but what I can do for the world." Self-forgetfulness had saved him in the Latin School failure, and it saved him now in the Virginia desert. By earnest searching he found an oasis of blessing in a strong and joyous belief,— the " new found confidence of Christian faith."

There is nothing sweeter in a strong man than un-cloaked boyishness, and this was eternal in Phillips Brooks. Home was a temple in his heart. Never in his long life did he resent the close guard of his mother nor the frank advice of his father. In his turn, he helped his younger brothers, but with no sense of aloof-ness, and no desire to pry into their souls. When he came home for vacations, he loved to go to the menag-erie with " the boys ", and begged to be excused from preaching and to sit " along side of mother " in the pew. From now on, the years had three burning in-terests for Phillips Brooks: his work, his home, and the war.

Like the other fellows at the seminary, as part of the prescribed work, he practised preaching in the small pulpit at Sharon Mission, and was nicknamed " prac-tiser " or " parsonet." At first, he did not succeed particularly well. During his senior year, however, he had a chance to teach in the preparatory department at a salary of three hundred dollars and board, and by this means he gained money and training, in addition to education. Then he went on a three months' trial to the Church of the Advent in Philadelphia; but he fell so far short of his own aims that, before the term was ended, he suggested to one of the vestrymen that perhaps he had better leave at once. His parishioners, however, were more than satisfied. Though their young preacher was reserved with individuals, he offered his whole self to his congregation. His words were alive. As his fame spread, calls to other and larger churches poured in. "Don't let it make you proud, Philly," came from the watchful mother. Proud? He did not know what that meant. Gravely he answered the invitations,— happy to be wanted; happy to be used. But he thought too much of others to have room for himself, and just now he was stirred to the depths over the problem of slavery.

In 1862, he moved to Holy Trinity Church, in Philadelphia, where his influence would be greater; but where, as before, his position as rector still hindered him from speaking his whole heart on what he felt was the sin of slavery. When news came that his younger brother George, his particular chum, had enlisted as a soldier, and his Aunt Susan had volunteered as a nurse, the young minister yearned for the good-byes and the drum-beat. Still he kept his post, hard as it was to " buckle down " to preaching in war-time.

Before long, however, when Lee threatened Philadelphia, Phillips Brooks and other clergymen, bought spades and marched out to dig trenches (rousing the slow Quaker city by their own indignant examples). Then came the news of Gettysburg — one quarter of the army dead, wounded, or taken prisoners. At that, the great man was off to the hospital, distributing clothing, writing letters, and sleeping in a tar-shop when he could find no better place. Now his heart had its double sorrow, for, just before the great battle, his brave young brother George had died in camp of typhoid-pneumonia.

We must go back a few months if we would know how deep the friendship had been between those two brothers. George was, perhaps, the least religious of all the Brooks boys; but he was a strong, athletic fellow with an instinct for farming, a joy in out-door life, and a winning lovableness that was irresistible. So far as his "inner experience" went, there seemed to have been some "hitch." For the first twenty-three years of his life, he claimed no religion and did not seem to care; he was comfortably indifferent. Again and again his mother wrote to Phillips begging him to influence George; but, as far as we know, the older brother did not interfere. There was nothing in his great nature to probe or to insist. He said it was "not fair to get a fellow in a corner and throw his soul in his face." The dearness of the Christ who dwelt in his heart could not be forced on another. He had needed time to understand it; George would need time. But the unutterable joy of being every day and all the day in the great company of his Savior was so precious that Phillips could not resist *one* letter when he heard that George was going forth to fight. That letter is closed to us; its message was carried in the soldier boy's heart to the land where it is greatly understood. But perhaps the young minister gave his brother the thought that, years later, as Bishop, he gave the world: " Christ stands before us and says ' Come to me.' You say, ' Must I ? ' And he answers, ' You may.' He will not even say, ' You must.' " Tenderly, sympathetically, without hurry and without condemnation, the older brother shared his joy, and, before George marched away, he had found the Great Love. We are sure it was a Christian's heart that beat the charge to battle and was taken home to God.

And somehow Phillips gave him up, locked away the brother-love as a sacred, lasting thing, and turned to the great, needy world. There was a day when the hand of Phillips Brooks grasped the hand of Abraham Lincoln, and it was a day for each to remember. Long before, these great men had grasped hands in purpose. When, at last the slaves were free, Phillips Brooks pleaded for the colored man, as Lincoln might have done: that he should have the " same car with us, if he is tired, and the same pew with us, if he wants to worship God." He felt the slave's weight of ignorance and our responsibility for his education. Now he was having a Christmas-tree for the little Negro Sunday-school he had started; now he was laughing at the man who left Brooks's church because he was "not black enough to go there." His speech on the life and death of Lincoln, and his prayer at the Harvard Commemoration for the soldiers, were two of his greatest utterances. Of the first we have a few beautiful fragments; but of the second, which made even Lowell's "Ode" seem small, we have only the memory of those who heard it: "Oh, that Prayer! that Prayer!" Phillips Brooks had made no notes of what he would say to God.

Like all other great lives, his was so full that it cannot be told in a few pages; it can only be suggested. He was continually sought by different churches as their rector, and by colleges and divinity-schools as president or professor. Of all the resisted calls, the chance to be Head of the Cambridge Theological Seminary was the strongest temptation. Something tugged at his heart,— the old longing for that intimate association that is given to teachers; and, like Emerson, he had to go alone among the hills for his decision, for he never made a great decision lightly. Of the thronging calls to churches, he accepted only three: two in succession in Philadelphia and one in Boston. And the changes that he made were never made for money.

In Trinity Church, Boston, he preached for twenty-two years, until he was made Bishop of Massachusetts. This gave him a chance, by taking the service at Appleton Chapel, to keep up the dear associations with Harvard College. No words can tell his power — his nfluence was far too sacred to be called "popularity."

Yet, excusing that shallow word, he was so " popular "
that his own father was afraid the congregation would
applaud him as they did Beecher,— a thing that
Brooks could not have borne.

While he was happy to be loved, he was miserable
to be worshiped, hated lionizing, and had no patience
with conventional flattery.   He laughed at the handkerchiefs of his first Christmas as a pastor, " enough
to last a lifetime "; the slippers, accumulating till they
filled barrels, and were shipped by him to the mission-
aries; and the daily flowers, which he sent to hospitals.
Too simple and too unconscious to be vain, he never
seemed to know why people loved him or to dream that
he was great.   When he preached in place of one of his
friends he exclaimed: " What a splendid congregation you have! " not seeming to realize that the congregation was " splendid " because *he* was there.   On one
of his ocean trips he wrote: " The only celebrity on
board was Mr. Froude "; and from England: " To-
morrow I go to Oxford, where I spend three days . . .
looking at all the great men."   (The mirror could have
shown him one.)   Meeting Huxley and Tennyson, being entertained by Browning and Gladstone, or preaching before Victoria,— none of these things could spoil
him.   He joked over wearing a Doctor's gown in the
procession and hired his costume because it cost too
much to buy one.   When he was asked to furnish
facts for his college class-record, he wrote: " I have
had no wife, no children, no particular honors, no serious misfortune, and no adventures worth speaking of.

It is shameful at such times as these not to have a history, but I have not got one, and must come without."
And when his photograph was sent home, he wrote:

> "And is this, then, the way he looks...
> This tiresome creature, Phillips Brooks?
> No wonder, if 't is thus he looks,
> The church has doubts of Phillips Brooks.
> Well, if he knows himself, he 'll try
> To give these doubtful looks the lie.
> He dares not promise, but will seek
> E'en as a bishop to be meek:
> To walk the way he shall be shown,
> To trust a strength that 's not his own,
> To fill the years with honest work,
> To serve his day and not to shirk,
> To quite forget what folks have said,
> To keep his heart and keep his head,
> Until men laying him to rest
> Shall say, 'At least he did his best.'"

What gave Brooks his great power,— miscalled
"popularity"? "His love of truth and his love of
souls "— his humbleness made all men his equals, and
his tolerance drew them to his heart. People remember how he left an ocean steamer, and, as he stepped
aboard the tug for the cabin-passengers, lifted his hat
to the steerage in good-bye. And they remember how
he sturdily voted against compulsory prayers at Harvard because, to him, no prayer could be compelled.

From the depths of his mighty love and sympathy,
he interpreted to all men a religion at once sane and
satisfying. Combining commonsense with uncommon

spirituality, he seems to have understood all the heart's cries and all the heart's hungers. Instead of condemning those who were " tossed up and down and back and forth in doubt ", he stretches forth an understanding hand and pleads a trusting patience. To doubters and believers, alike, he seems to say, " I know just how you feel; " and to the discouraged his tested hardihood still shouts: " There is no man here who has not failed; but is there any man here in all this multitude who has given up? "

His influence gripped men of all creeds: Jews, and Christians, Protestants and Roman Catholics. One day when two poor women in Salem, both Roman Catholics, were talking over their troubles,— the son of one had fallen into bad ways,— they decided that the thing to do was to " take him to Phillips Brooks," just as if he were a doctor of souls.

Two of this doctor's medicines were silence and companionship. When people were in trouble, he had a way of going to sit with them and letting them talk, sometimes hardly speaking at all himself. " Men like to be talked to better than to be preached at," he said. " They prefer the easy-chair to the pulpit." Thus he stood: never on a height, but shoulder to shoulder on a common ground.   Instead of driving, he took a car. Except for church, he wore the dress of a simple citizen.   " On long canoe-journeys, the guides were three weeks before they found out that he was a clergyman. On walking-trips abroad, he looked a little like a gamekeeper."

Though he never altered the service of his church, and was completely loyal to his creed, he felt the "danger of formalism and the mere piety of outside habits." Forms, titles, and robings sank into insignificance beside the high calling of truth. "I won't be called Dr. Brooks," he wrote to a friend, "and you may stop that for me when and where you can." And again: "Not a surpliced female choir, my dear friend! Almost anything but that.— The church is young-ladyish enough." Just before he was made bishop he went to New York and ordered "a set of the preposterous garments that bishops wear." "It is a pity," he said, "that one has to wear them and that the whole subject of the episcopate should be so involved with clothes."

First a man and then a clergyman, that is what he was, though he loved his life as a preacher with a deep, abiding love. "I would n't be anything but a parson for the world," he exclaimed; and, "The pulpit of Trinity is the dearest spot of earth to me,— in other words, is home."

To know this great man more perfectly, we should see him with children, go with him on his travels, read his open letters, hear him in the pulpit, and talk with him alone. Even then we can hardly catch the spirit of fun that danced over the surface of his seriousness, like phosphorus-sparkles in the sea.

Children were Brooks's special delight. Welcome as he was in hundreds of homes, the grown folks took back-places when the children were around. He some-

times told the little ones who seemed shy, that it was
" great fun to be a minister."   Once he played Goliath
for a small boy to shoot him with a sling.   When,
at the death of his parents, the old North Andover
home became his, he made it a rallying place for other
people's children.   A stove was put up in the old
corn-barn so that his nieces, Agnes, Gertie, and little
Tood, could play at cooking, and he used to take tea
with them there — big, jolly, and at home.   For the
little children he always kept a big doll, and there were
older sports for the others.   " I never see a lot of
boys," he said, " without wanting to be among them,
and wishing they would let me into their company.   I
hate to think that boys of sixteen think of me as I
used to think of men of thirty-seven when I was their
age!   Most of the wisdom of old age is humbug."

It always seems as if he should have had a wife and
children of his own instead of that house of empty
rooms kept by his faithful servant, Katie.   Though the
great preacher sought companionship in books, he was
too warm and vital to be satisfied by print.   " I cannot beg, borrow, or steal a wife and children," he said,
" so this poor working-man's heart will never leap with
joy, or at least only half-way."   Yet, like the Great
Master, his tender arms cradled the babies, and all the
children circled round his knees.   The deaf, dumb,
and blind child, Helen Keller, to whom his loving touch
was most familiar, gives her glad witness with the rest.

It is a great task to be, at once, a fine preacher and
a faithful visiting pastor.   Phillips Brooks was both.

Sometimes, for five months together, he would not have an evening free. While he was giving play-time to children and work-time to their parents, he was using up his own vitality, so that rest was indispensable. As we all know, change is the happiest rest. His journeys included the West in our own country and eleven trips abroad. He saw the palms and bamboos and bungalows of India, and the " second highest mountain in the world, blazing with snow in the sunshine "; the Swiss valleys " overrunning with water "; the " sweet green hills " on the other side of Como, " sound asleep in the sunlight which they like "; " the world of vines and oranges " near Los Angeles; the Yosemite Valley, " ringing with cataracts "; Italy, The Holy Land, and merry Japan,— besides all the places common to the tourist. The little people of Japan thought he was a strange kind of giant, and wanted to measure his hands and feet. They did not " quarrel with his bulk," however, but dragged him around in their jinrikishas as if he were a " jolly joke." Nevertheless, Phillips Brooks insisted that the coolie, who carried him across a torrent on his back, would " never forget it any more than I shall."

When he went to Berne in Switzerland, he took the trouble to hunt up an old woman who, two years before, had sold him a small wooden bear, and she was delighted to know that he had carried it in his pocket ever since. Laughingly he declared that Noah's grave was " about as long as St. Paul's Church "; but he believed in the house where Judas had lived and the wall where Paul was let down in a basket, and with deepest reverence he walked on the hills of Palestine and all the spots where Jesus must have walked.   It was on the Christmas spent in Christ's birthplace that his beautiful carol, " Oh little town of Bethlehem!" began to sing itself into his soul.   Yet the man was so closely wrapped in the minister, that even from Bethlehem he ended a letter with, " I wish I were going to bed in that backroom at home."

His letters, better than anything else, give his boyish, homesick, playful, human side.   Let us look into some of them just as they come to our hands.   For one thing, the great man with the boy heart never lost his school-boy homesickness.   He was homesick for Trip's bark, and Bridget's flapjacks, and even for his mother's stocking-bag.   On Christmas in the Holy Land he was homesick for men nailing up spruce boughs and men " carrying home turkeys by the legs."   " Who beats now on the base-ball ground? " he writes from Athens to his brother Arthur; and another time sends the combined news from America to Europe: " They have chosen Bishop Talbot to be bishop of Georgia.   Harvard beat Yale in the boat-race."   His letters are full of " God bless you all " and " Lots of love to all ", and of the superlatives of a beauty-loving nature.

He called more than one place " the most beautiful in the world," and he enjoyed " everything — hugely." No boy could have been more rollicking with fun or have panted more eagerly for the holidays, when he

was to swim and paddle, tramp and ride horseback.
"Glory, Glory, Gloriation! ten more weeks before
vacation!" is one of his jovial cries.

The nieces, who had their full share of his letters,
must have been used to his jokes. From India he
wrote: "I think I met Isaac and Jacob on two skinny
camels, just outside the gates of Aden. I asked them
how Esau was, but Jacob looked mad, and would n't
answer . . . but I feel quite sure it was they, for they
looked just like the pictures in the Bible." And to
Gertie from Jeypore: "All the little girls, when they
get to be about your age, hang jewels in their noses,
and the women all have their noses looking beautiful
in this way. I have got a nose-jewel for you, which
I shall put in when I get home, and also a little button
for the side of Susie's nose, such as the smaller children wear. Think how the girls at school will admire
you!" In one of his letters he said that a policeman
in California came running toward him shouting: "A
letter from Tood! A letter from Tood!" And in
Berlin: "Only two houses up the street lives the Emperor. He and his wife are out of town now, or,
no doubt, they would send some word to Toody."

This is his picture of Venetian bathing: "When
the little children in Venice want to take a bath, they
just go down to the front steps of the house and
jump off and swim about in the streets. Yesterday
I saw a nurse standing on the front steps, holding one
end of a string, and the other end was tied to a little

fellow who was swimming up the street. When he
went too far, the nurse pulled in the string, and got her
baby home again."

No letters are sweeter or more characteristic than
the ones which speak of presents for the children, his
great generous heart delighting in the toy-shops:

"DEAR GERTIE,

"I bought the prettiest thing you ever saw for you the
other day. If you were to guess for three weeks, making
two guesses every minute, you could not guess what it is. . . .
When you see it, you will jump the rheumatism right out of
you."

And one more. Over a month before Christmas he
sent a letter headed:

"*Very private! !*

"DEAR GERTIE,

"This letter is an *awful secret* between you and me! If
you tell anybody about it I will not speak to you all this
winter."

Then he went on to say that she was to get the
Christmas presents for him that year for all the children, finding out what they wanted in the "most secret
way," and that she could spend five dollars apiece.

"You must ask yourself what you want, but without
letting yourself know about it, and get it, too, and put it in
your own stocking, and be very much surprised when you
find it there! . . . Perhaps you will get this on Thanksgiving Day. If you do, you must shake the turkey's paw for
me."

It is no wonder that a man like that won all natures, old and young, grave and gay. While many stories of his personal kindness have been printed, many more lie buried in remembering hearts. Perhaps there are alive to-day two Harvard men who remember a call from Phillips Brooks one morning in their college room. They had been drinking the night before, and the great preacher must have known it, although he showed no signs. Instead, he sat down chummily to talk over the college interests,— the crew, the base-ball team, the coming vacation. Finally, just as he was going, he stood up, and, putting a big hand on the shoulder of each, looked down lovingly with a " Well, is it worth it?" and was gone without an answer. Yet how that heart of his must have ached, for he was the same man who, at Lincoln's death, burst out: " I go about our city and shudder (when I think of such a man as he) at the frivolous, weak, and inefficient lives our young men lead! I see them mere dawdlers in society. I see them spending their time like mere babies when there is a man's work to be done."

His wonderful tact, however, often kept him silent and gave his silence greater power than speech: those young Harvard men were more ashamed to be treated as his comrades than they would have been from many sermons.

One day a poor scrub-woman, who worked in Trinity Church, came to him to ask for the Chapel for her daughter's marriage.

" Why not take the church?" he answered.

" But that is not for the likes of me."

" Oh, yes it *is*," warmly, " for the likes of *you* and the likes of *me* and the likes of every one! "

And so the daughter was married in Trinity Church, with all its sacred majesty, and the great organ played her march of joy.

Now he was trying to keep a young girl from going on the stage; now he was late to a reception because a colored-man had " sent for " him; and now he was writing of a joy he never knew, " May the marriage-bells and skies overrun with blessings."

A working-man, who did not even attend Trinity, asked to spend the evening before a serious operation, with Phillips Brooks. Stranger though he was, the bishop welcomed him cordially, and far into the night they talked together on all sorts of subjects. The next morning the great preacher even went with him to the hospital and so was near him just before he died.

Once, before starting on a journey, he wrote to his Trinity assistant: " Will you go to see a colored-man named —— who is in the City Hospital, Boston? It is a bad case. The man shot himself some six weeks ago, in consequence of some fraudulent proceedings in which he had been caught, and now he is in a wretched state. He will probably die,— or, if he lives, will be a helpless creature . . . Do comfort the poor soul and set him right if you can."

We are not surprised that the man who had carried a spade in war-time gave material help as well as spiritual. At the time of the great Boston fire in which old Trinity was burned, Phillips Brooks, after saving a few things from the church, rushed across the street to offer his services to a great jewelry store which was in danger. With perfect trust, and asking for no certificate of deposit, one of the partners filled two large bags with pearls and diamonds, and, through the dark streets, alive with thieves, Dr. Brooks carried the treasure to a place of safety.

So much we have said of his life and so much of his helpfulness; let us go now to hear him preach. In imagination we join the vast throng that crowds its way into Trinity, filling the vestibule and the aisles and the camp-chairs in the aisles, and even pushing towards a place on the pulpit-steps. One listener has come all the way from Canada to hear this man. Many will stand through the whole service; many more cannot even get standing-room, for there are twice as many as the church can hold. Perhaps Mr. Dillon, the sexton, uses his favorite trick, in spite of the preacher's protests: he gives the young man and young woman, who come together, seats so far apart that they leave the church in disgust,— thus reducing the crowd by two.

Presently the white-robed choir sings its way into the church; the great congregation rises; and the service begins,— always a beautiful service when entered into reverently. At last the sermon. Six feet four and broadly filling his large surplice, Phillips Brooks strides up the steps and, almost before he has reached the pulpit, " shouts out " his text and has begun to preach. You have to listen very closely, for the words pour out in torrents that cannot be stayed. Whatever the Bible text, as Phillips Brooks has told us, he has " but one sermon ",—" I am come that ye might have life, and that ye might have it more abundantly." And now, as he goes on with his plea, you have forgotten yourself; you have forgotten Phillips Brooks; you are remembering God. The whole congregation is looking up into that strong, open face and those wonderful dark eyes, and young and old, rich and poor, wise and ignorant, are held as one man. The preacher stands away from the desk. Now he spreads his arms wide in " loving invitation " meant for all the world; and now, with one broad hand over his heart, throws back his head and looks up, up into the dome. You know the source of his power. There is not a particle of posing; not a thought of dramatic effect. He is telling you that you are a child of God by nature and he is begging you to be a true child of God in your life. You feel as if " God has come to live in each separate soul in the congregation and that to allow Him to live in you is the first and only thing to be thought of." While the preacher " strikes at the shirks and shams of our day with dashing pluck ", he touches with tender understanding on all sincerity, even when it means doubt or unbelief. " Waiting for the Lord is having," he says gently. You find yourself made strong,— filled with his courage for life. " It does not take great men to do great things," he says; " it takes consecrated men. . . . Be absolutely simple.

Phillips Brooks in the Pulpit

Be absolutely genuine. Never say to any one what you do not feel and believe with your whole heart." As you listen, you know that this preaching is not a " scramble for adherents " but a " Christ-like love of souls "; and you know that it is born of truth. People of "all beliefs and of no belief" are listening hungrily and Phillips Brooks, who never gave himself to a single individual, is giving himself with freedom to hundreds. Can this be the boy failure? The man, who, failing at teaching was to fail at everything? He has blessed you with his own confidingness. There are people in the church to-day who have not prayed for years, but who, filled with a sense of God's nearness and dearness, kneel down with the preacher and take the precious privilege of talking with their Greatest Friend.

So he brought men to the Divine Companion who had understood and comforted him through all his own hard training. He had had the training of failure when he tried to teach; he had had the training of doubt before he found his faith; and he had had the training of many sorrows. First came George's early death and then his brother Fred's — the bright, young clergyman, who, walking home one dark night from a sick friend's, fell through an open drawbridge and was drowned. A few years later, both father and mother had been taken home; and the loving boy, who was none the less a loving boy because he was a great man, found himself lonely for the ones he used to go to as a child.

But his reunion with those dear ones was nearer than he thought. January 17, 1893, he took a cold which developed quickly into a bad sore throat, and then into diphtheria. One night, at about eleven, the faithful servant, Katie, met him walking in the hall in a delirium; he said he was "going home." Katie gently took him to his room. Two days later, Mr. Leighton Parks called — a dear friend of Bishop Brooks.

"He's been asking for you," said Katie. "The doctor said no one was to see him; but you must go up, for he said so."

Mr. Parks went in. "The great bed was covered with books. . . . He was alone and had turned at the last, as he had done through all his lonely life, to books." Though he felt unable to eat, he promised Mr. Parks to try. That night he told Katie to leave some lemonade near him and go to bed. "I won't need you," he said. "It's late and you must go to bed."

But Katie was not the one to go to bed with him "looking like that."

Early the next morning, Monday, January 23d, Phillips Brooks entered the larger life. His books and his faithful house-servant were his only companions at the last; but a man with his faith was never really lonely.

There was a beautiful service in Trinity Church while between ten and twenty thousand stood outside in Copley Square. When the procession reached

Harvard University, eight of the tallest college seniors, walking all the way, bore the precious body on their shoulders across the grounds.   And, as they entered, the bell tolled solemnly, for Phillips Brooks had been a Harvard boy and a Harvard preacher to other boys and men.

His own two younger brothers — Arthur and John C. Brooks — both ministers — read the service at Mount Auburn, and there the lovable boy and conquering man was laid to rest close to his father and mother and Fred and George.   A faded flag flutters over the soldier's grave, and over Phillips Brooks's is cut in stone: "Him that overcometh will I make a pillar in the temple of our God."

XI
BOOTH

" Nature cast me for the part she found me best fitted for, and I have had to play it, and must play it, till the curtain falls."

Edwin Booth.

XI

IT was the thirteenth of November, but the heavens were keeping the Fourth of July: they sent forth a fall of meteors,— a glorious star-shower more beautiful than a hundred sky-rockets. On a Maryland farm, about twenty-five miles from Baltimore, the negroes gathered outside their master's cabin, and, in awed voices, began to prophesy. No one was taking notes of what they said, so the exact words are only a guess; but they were talking of the new baby born that very night.

"Sho's yo lib a rain o' stars like dat means some'n!"

"Dis yeah baby'll see ghoses, I tells yer. He'll see ghoses!" Joe's massive, black face looked almost ashen as he spoke.

"No sech ting! He's gwine ter hab de hebenly guidance ob some lucky star," declared another old darky, with convictions as strong as Joe's.

Meanwhile, the little baby Edwin Booth lay safe in his mother's arms, and never even opened his eyes to see the shower of stars. If he could have looked ahead, out of the peace of his baby-sleep, he would

perhaps have cried. Life would have shown itself not
all alight with stars, but full of gloom; and he might
have shrunk from the long fight and hard-won conquest, not only of a great art but of many sorrows.
But, by the divine plan, his child eyes were closed
both to the present and the future; and so he slept content.

The Booth farm was snuggled close to a dense forest, called the "big woods."   At the end of a crooked
lane, song-filled by mocking-birds and orioles, stood the
white-washed log house, and close to that bubbled a
clear spring of delicious water.   The cabin had been
carried by negroes, horses, and oxen across several
fields so as to be near this spring.   Mr. Junius Brutus
Booth, the father of the big family of eight, was very
particular about his children's health, and he knew
that pure water and pure food were important.   For
two reasons, he did not believe in eating meat: first,
because he thought it was less healthy than the fresh
vegetables and juicy fruits which ripened in the sun,
and second, because he was so fond of animals that
he hated to have them killed,— his brothers "In air,
and water, and the silent wood."   As his daughter
Asia put it, "Partridge, black snake, wild boar, all
alike had sacred lives."

Because Mr. Booth was an actor and most of his
time was spent among swarms of people, he loved to
steal away to the quiet of his own farm: he liked to get
out close to the earth and dig his own potatoes; he
liked to hitch up the big horse, "Captain," and the little

horse, " Peacock," and drive tandem to Richmond or
Philadelphia; he liked to tramp round over his one
hundred and fifty acres to discuss crops with Joe and
give directions for planting; he liked to " rove through
dense forests and think of wild nature." It bothered
him very little that they were " three miles from Belair
and almost as far from a store or house"; that the
post-boy, who rode round on horseback with the mail,
came only once a week to toss the letters over the
fence; and that they had to " haul twenty-five miles to
market." Though he loved his profession, and, on
the stage, seemed far more as if he were *living* a part
than *acting* one, he loved better to leave it all,— the
hundreds of upturned faces, the clapping, and the
cheers,— and be where the birds and the squirrels did
not know that he was great. At one time, Mr. Booth's
longing for solitude had been so strong that he thought
of abandoning the stage and all his brilliant success,
and keeping a lighthouse on Cape Hatteras.

We can imagine how his children enjoyed the farm.
They were intimate friends of the big green bull-
frog that lived in their water spring. To little Asia,
the forest, with its moss-carpets and waving ferns, was
a " fairy realm"; to the boys, it was the old home of
the Indians. They sloshed round in the marshes and
found arrow-heads and tomahawks. Three of these
boys we must know by name because we shall hear
more about them: Junius Brutus, the oldest, his
father's name-sake; Edwin, the star-shower baby, but,
in 1843, a dark-eyed, curly-haired active boy; and

John Wilkes. Joseph was the youngest child of all.

Whether Mr. Booth was at home or not, he expected to control his farm, his slaves, and his children. No trees were to be cut down; nothing that flew or ran was to be killed for food. " The robber of life can never give it back," he would say. This scrap from one of his letters to the children's white-haired grandfather is very characteristic:

" Tell Junius not to go opossum-hunting or setting rabbit-traps, but to let the poor devils live." He carried apples in his pockets for any horses he might meet. When he was on a sea voyage, and a storm-blown bird dropped fluttering to the deck, he fed it back to strength on corn-meal mush. Once, in an Ohio flood, he saw a horse fastened to a boat and struggling for its life. " I 'll pay $20 to any one who will go to that boat, cut the halter, and let that horse free," was his prompt offer. And, though the horse could not say thank-you, Mr. Booth had the happiness of seeing the halter cut and the worn out creature swim ashore. One day, when Mrs. Booth had the cabin all nicely scrubbed, her husband came home bringing with him a begrimed old sailor to be washed and bandaged. Kindness was his religion; though the applauding crowds who heard him take his passionate parts, may have thought that he had no religion.

They may have thought, too, that because *he* was a great actor, he wanted his children to be actors. On the contrary, much as Mr. Booth loved his profession.

he did not want one of his children to follow it. Perhaps this is the reason he seldom spoke of his stage-life at home. He thought acting was too hard on the nerves, too exhausting. Then, as he said, he wanted his boys to spend their lives on something " true ": Junius Brutus might be a surgeon; Edwin, a cabinet-maker. For John Wilkes and Joseph, the two younger boys, he had a " work-shop in the garden " with the fine old motto: " Laborare est orare." [1]

But the father's early plans failed. Not all his farm-training could cancel inherited genius. On the edge of that Maryland forest had been born a family of actors. · Added to the power of inheritance was the power of example. Without taking this immense influence into account, however, Mr. Booth let little Edwin, when he was only five or six, go behind the scenes to wait till his father finished his part. Then the child would find himself passionately caught in a pair of eager arms, hugged, tossed into the air, and perhaps treated to a song or a nursery-rhyme. Naturally the bright-eyed little fellow began to long to act too. Were not the people clapping his father? But, with childish assurance, he stoutly declared that he would be " the villain or nobody,"— no soft, loverish parts for him! Thus, as Mr. William Winter says, " The theater was Edwin Booth's schoolroom, the greatest living master of passion his tutor, and the actors his fellow pupils."

" Did you bring your school-books? " was his father's first and only welcome, for he could not for-

---

[1] " To labor is to pray."

get how much his wife had wanted Edwin left at school.

The books were in the boy's trunk; but what fascination had readers or spellers compared with his father's play-books? As Edwin said, behind the scenes he learned the "words of all the parts of every play," and, since Mr. Booth acted chiefly Shakespeare, the words, themselves, were well worth learning. Of course, when the lad went back to Maryland, he and one of his friends gave "dramatic readings" to their country neighbors. Imagine a big barn and all its windows crowded with sun-browned faces. A sheet is the curtain; a dinner-bell announces the scene. Encouraged by success, the boys decided to give an entertainment in the Belair court-house.

Colored Joe, who was sent to post the bills, "walked for miles carrying a bucket and brush" and ringing a big bell.

"Oyez, oyez, oyez," he shouted. "To-night, great tragedy!"

But that evening when the actors rode in to their star performance, they saw, to their amused disappointment, that Joe had posted every bill upside down! Such an absurd advertisement, however, did not spoil the gravity of the audience. The people came in, as Asia said, "as if going to Quaker-meeting — men on one side, women on the other." And after the performance the boys felt very rich. They had cleared thirty dollars.

When Edwin Booth finally left the farm for the theater, he left freedom for captivity. His stage life was very different from the care-free life of home. There, squatted outside the cabin, he used to strum away on his banjo. One of their musical negroes had taught him to play the banjo beautifully. He could also play the violin. The farm life, the forest walks, the abandon of music — all were holiday delights. But, when he left them, he took on his young shoulders a double responsibility. Stage life, alone, was exciting enough, with its late hours, its hurry, its nervousness; but, added to these, Edwin had the anxious care of his father. Mr. Booth not only had a " craze for drink " and was affected by a very little, but he had strange moods: he would wander away at any time, whether he had engagements or not, and without telling where he was going. The boy never felt easy when his father was out of his sight. In the faraway home his mother was trusting him, as Mr. Winter says, to be " the guide, companion, and friend of the most erratic genius that ever illumined the theater in any age. . . . The boy lived almost a servant's life in hotels, in dressing-rooms, among the wings, in constant and affectionate attendance." Late at night and sometimes far into the morning he might have been seen following that restless father, like a shadow, on, on, from street to street, with the unwearied faithfulness of utter love.

When Edwin was sixteen, a year before the Belair

court-house entertainment, he took a small part in
the same play with his father; but first he had to pass
a keen examination.

" Who was Tressel? " asked Mr. Booth.

" A messenger from the field of Tewksbury."

" What was his mission? "

" To bear the news of the defeat of the king's
party."

" How did he make the journey? "

" On horseback."

" Where are your spurs? "

Edwin looked down; he had forgotten that he needed
spurs.

" Here, take mine."

The boy unbuckled them and fastened them to his
own boots. When his part was over and he stepped
from the blaze of light to the dinginess behind the
scenes, he found his father sitting silent and thoughtful.

" Have you done well? "

" I think so," with daring frankness.

" Give me my spurs."

Cold as this dialogue seems, it is interesting. No
parrot repetition concerned the great father, who, with
the part of Shylock before him, had to be " a Jew all
day." Did his son understand who he was? That
was the point. Did he know what he was doing?
The *words* — What were the *words* compared to that?

When the play was over, however, " he coddled
me," Edwin said. He made him take gruel and wear

a worsted night-cap. And so a mother's heart may be
partner to an examiner's brain. The boy understood.

Yet, when some one asked Mr. Booth to let Edwin's
name appear with his, the father answered quietly:
" He 's a good banjo-player and might be announced
for a solo between the acts." Nevertheless, he knew
that Edwin was much more than a banjo-player; and
only two years later, with the briefest possible notice,
he forced the boy to prove his power.

At the National Theater in New York, Mr. Booth
was billed to play the part of *Richard III*. When the
carriage was at the door, however, he suddenly declared that he would not go. Edwin's entreaties could
not budge him.

" Go act it yourself," was the only answer.

The minutes were speeding on. There was only
one thing to do: carry the unwelcome news.

" Well, there is no time to change the bill," blurted
the manager distractedly. " We must close the house
— unless *you* will act the part."

And so, at seventeen, the slim fellow was hustled
into a man's clothes, and, without a particle of preparation, undertook the star part, a villain, too, before a
New York house. Nervous as any one would have
been, Edwin could hardly be heard at first.

" It 's a great pity that eminent men should have
such mediocre children," said Mr. Rufus Choate to
a friend near him.

But at the end of the play, the youthful *Richard III*
was clapped and clapped till he came before the cur-

tain. It was a night of victory: as much courage as genius had been needed to act that difficult part.

Mr. Booth called those freaks of his, "illness"; but whatever they were, they kept Edwin uncertain and bewildered, and yet, with all its anxiety, stage life had a decided fascination.

In 1852, father and son took a trip to California. They rode on mules across the Isthmus of Panama, and slept on wine-casks or barrels among familiar rats and armed natives. Often, instead of sleeping, Edwin lay awake on his blanket while around them vicious-looking men whispered in an unknown tongue and sharpened big knives.

Life was hard in California. There Edwin was left to shift for himself and "gain experience." To be absolutely without a cent, to sleep in mining-camps, to do his own cooking, washing, and mending, to be snow-bound on the mountain roads and wonder if that would mean starvation and snow-burial: all these things were his hard-won "experience." Harder still, one night, after a long tramp through mud and slush, he was met by a friend with a letter and the sharply sudden news of his father's death. It was an intense grief. There was no comfort in thinking that the years of strange watchfulness were over. Relief was swallowed up in yearning; his "care was loss of care"; most keenly he would miss the wandering father who had frayed out his youth with anxiety. And he had no impulse to tell that father's peculiarities to a curious world. Instead, there was a delicate

reverence for his reserves. "His 'oddities' were
sources of suffering to him," he wrote, "and it is not
for the son to publish what the sire — could he have
done so — would have concealed."

After his father's burial in Baltimore, Edwin returned to California to continue his hard apprenticeship. He who in childhood would be villain or nobody, now set foot on his pride, joined his eldest
brother's company, and acted in a negro farce. Not
that Edwin Booth chose drudgery and shallow comedy,
but that up those steps rose the climb to his heart's
desire. Once, in the part of *Jaffier,* he had sat down
for a moment in a black velvet suit and his father,
glancing at the grave young face, had said, " You look
like Hamlet." Again and again, Edwin remembered
those words, " You look like Hamlet." If he could
patiently trudge through his apprenticeship; bear his
brother's half-patronizing praise: " You have had a
wonderful success for a young man, but you have
much to learn "; drop, as he did, three times from
" star parts to farce," and so master the " lesson for
crushed tragedians "; paste his own posters in Honolulu because the native boys ate the paste and then
tossed away the play-bills; journey on horseback over
the western mountains with a company of strolling
players, a wagon, a brass band, and a " show "
wherever they could corral an audience; even gulp down
the fact that, abroad, one actress would not act with
him because he was " awkward "; if he could bear all
this, and still struggle on toward his mount of great-

ness, then, indeed, he was more than conqueror. The sustained courage of years is harder than a sudden charge.

Furthermore, he had his own methods to invent, though he followed Garrick's example in studying manners, attitudes, and expressions wherever he went, and though, like Kean, he practised before a mirror and marked his different positions on the stage with chalk. Of every change in expression and tone, he made a close study. Thus he harnessed genius with hard labor; neither could climb the heights of fame, alone. Though he was not tall, he carried himself commandingly. His glowing, burning eyes were greatly in his favor; so was his voice,—"clear as a bell and loud as a trumpet." He never, as Mr. Godwin says, " found it necessary to shriek like a maniac or howl like a wounded wolf."

For a brief part of Booth's stern apprenticeship he had the help of his wonderful young wife, herself a gifted actress and musician. " She delighted in my success and encouraged me in all I did. . . . Her applause was all I valued. . . . Her criticism was the most severe and just." " If my love were selfish," she would say, " you would never be great: part of you belongs to the world." The story of his first marriage is as short as it is beautiful. Mary Devlin, whom he married in July 1860, died early in 1863, leaving a year-old baby girl. At the news of her illness, Booth had started at once for their home in Dorchester, Massachusetts ; but she died a few minutes after his train left New York. "Two little years have indeed taught me much," he wrote to Dr. Osgood. "I have touched in that brief space the extremes of earthly joy and grief." . . . In his baby he still clasped a living treasure, but, his "world" was gone and so was the beauty of his art. "It is hateful to me," he cried out. "It has become a trade."

For seven months after his wife's death, Booth did not, could not, act. He moved from Dorchester to New York, and tried to fill his loneliness by making a home for his baby and his mother. Meanwhile, he completed that mastery over himself, which his wife had helped him to win. At last, he "got the control of his devil,"— an inherited taste for liquor. It was a wonderful and permanent conquest. Often, after a difficult part, he really needed a stimulant, but after his wife's death he seldom touched it even for medicine. So, his Mary still lived, in memory, in influence, and in her child. "The dear little baby is beautiful, and as full of life as her mother was," thought Booth comfortingly, "full of her sweet mother's soul . . . her eyes, voice, manner, her ringing laugh, and her joyous fun."

We can best get acquainted with Booth's personal side from reading the "Recollections and Letters" by his daughter, now Mrs. Grossman. We can see him come home from the theater, very late, and, finding his baby on the floor, lift her caressingly, and tuck her warmly back into her crib. She wakes just enough to know that he is there and she is safe: the great actor who is winning such loud and universal praise is just plain father and mother to her.

Christmas comes: her stockings are stuffed with toys; but Santa Claus was very mean. There is nothing in father's socks but shaving-brushes and razors and queer things like that. "Pop" has to kiss away the "water drops" and laugh as if he did not care, or Edwina would never have forgiven Santa Claus.

"What does little birdie say?" he recites to her — a simple poem enough, but he fills it with all its meaning so that it makes her cry. And then he is sorry. He never meant to make her cry. "I see little of my 'bird' except at meals," he says regretfully; but every night, before he goes away to act, they have a grand frolic, and the "bird" begs him not to go when it is done. "I don't want any bread and butter," she declares, when he explains his reason for acting. "All my hopes and aspirations now are clustering like a halo about my baby's head," he says. "She has grown passionately fond of her 'far-r-r-ther,' as she rolls me out of her sweet little mouth." So, their companionship blossomed,— in daily rides to the park, going to see "other little girls," and loving the big dolls.

But like Livingstone's children, Edwina had to be sent to boarding-school: her father's life was too wandering for him to give her, or himself, a real home. We can read his letters and see how now he worried over her cold, now apologized because his nervous hand could not make the writing very plain. On her eleventh birthday he began her allowance — her " sal-

ary "— and sent her, besides, a ruby ring. Fond of
animals, like his father, he wrote one letter from the
dog Pip, and another from the bird ("her little
brother St. Valentine"). When he found that she
was too anxious to win in the "Spelling Bee" he
wrote: "We can't jump into glory with a skipping-
rope."

Though his girl grew up and was married, had a
home of her own and children, she never *grew away*
from him. He adopted her babies and played with
them as he had with her. And they never guessed that
often while he crept round on the floor and romped
like a boy, he was looking for dramatic talent. All
they knew was that it was great fun to play with
grandpa; he let them pull his hair mercilessly.

This was the renowned actor of Shakespearean
tragedy,— the man who knew so much real tragedy.
His nervous care-laden boyhood and his early griefs,
the loss of his father and of his wife, were fit preparation for a heavy chain of anxieties: his darkest calamity in 1865; the burning of his theater in 1867; complete bankruptcy in 1874; a brooding sadness caused by
his second wife's "mental disturbance", and last the
fear of his own decline. Though, with the burning of
the Winter Garden Theater, Booth lost elaborate cos-
tumes, an immense amount of valuable scenery, and all
his properties including those that had been owned by
Mrs. Siddons, Kemble, and Kean,— these losses could
not down his pluck. Though, in the panic of 1873
and 1874 he failed completely, " giving up all his per-

sonal property to his creditors," this was not, as he said, " by any means the heaviest blow " his life had felt.   " He paid his debts and earned another fortune." His wife's illness and warnings of his own decline sank deeper than any material troubles.   We shall speak of these later.

In the meantime, let us go back to the gloomy night of April 14, 1865.   Southern-born though Booth was, he had cast his first and only vote for Lincoln.   With his whole warm heart he honored and loved the great, sad leader of this troubled nation.   But, in a swift moment of darkness, his own brother had taken Lincoln's life !   The national calamity broke on Edwin Booth loaded with a hundred personal sorrows.   There was his father's honorable name, dishonored ; there was his poor, dazed mother, crushed.   As he looked back over life, he had only kind things to remember of that younger brother — a good-hearted lad, perhaps the family favorite, " gentle, loving, and full of fun " ; but a poor mad fellow on this one point.   At many sacred times, John Wilkes had been one of few to stand by Edwin's side ; at his first marriage, at his first wife's burial, as fellow-actor on the stage that night of glory when the three Booth brothers played *Brutus, Cassius,* and *Antony* in " Julius Cæsar."   Edwin had always kept his brother's picture in his room.

With the terrible news of that terrible night, Booth left the stage expecting never to return.   What American could applaud his brother's brother ?   At first, warned to be cautious, he kept himself " cooped up."

Meanwhile, with characteristic tenderness, he put what heart of hope he could into his mother's broken life, though he himself was " living in a mist." " Life is a great big spelling-book ", reads one of his letters, " and on every page we turn the words grow harder to understand the meaning of. But there *is* a meaning, and when the last leaf flops over, we 'll know the whole lesson by heart." As time wore on, his friends convinced him that he need not abandon his profession forever, and that his name might yet be " free." Then there was the thought of four-year-old Edwina. To support her, he must do something, and acting was his only " trade." So, at last he determined to abandon the " aching gloom of his little red room." On January 3, 1866, he returned to the stage through what he suspected were streets of threatening. That his entrance and first sentence would betray the spirit of his hearers, he could not fail to know. It did. Nine times they cheered him, with a glorious, full-hearted, American welcome. The great audience rose, waving hands, handkerchiefs, and hats. A rain of flowers fell around him and the theater shook with thundering applause. Thank God for the forgivingness of justice! The name of Booth was " free."

From this time on, though he did not " jump into glory with a skipping-rope," he climbed there without much slipping back. Life's real tragedies must have increased his power to feel *play*-tragedies, and to make his hearers feel. For one hundred nights in succes-

sion he gave his wonderful interpretation of *Hamlet*.
In " Othello," he could alternate from *Iago's* icy scheming to *Othello's* consuming fire.   But no, the part of
Lear must have been almost anguish to him.   He was
acting in that during his second wife's pitiable illness,
playing the part of madness, and coming home to the
fear of its reality in her.   "I labored hard to forget my
troubles when I entered the theater," he said.   " The
people thought I was Hamlety all the time; whereas I
was very weary and unhappy."   But even tragedy was
a partial refuge from fact.   After years of tedious
labor, brilliant success was some satisfaction.   In
Stratford-on-Avon, Shakespeare's birthplace, he was
asked to write his name "*high up*" on the Actor's
Pillar,— some satisfaction, though the sightseers begging for autographs were a nuisance, as well as those
who   nudged   and   pointed,   whispering   audibly:
"That's him!   That's Booth!"   In Warwickshire
"the people would not let me ramble about as I liked,"
he said.   " There were entertainments, and I was
made a lion."

His reception in Germany, however, was most grati-
fying.   If the darkies who had prophesied his greatness the night of the star-shower could have been
there, how their eyes would have rolled with a positive
belief in signs!   Booth received four silver souvenirs
from the castes in different German cities.   In Berlin,
they gave him, as " the greatest master of the art," a
silver laurel-crown.   From his own description, acting
before a German audience was not easy.   " Think of

Edwin Booth as "Hamlet," 1887

acting five acts of tragedy without a hand . . . merely a subdued 'Bravo!' now and then; but when the drop falls, call after call and 'Bravos!' by the bushel make it up." As for his fellow actors, they fairly mobbed him with delight, called him "Meister! Meister!" on all sides, and hugged and kissed him with German warmth.

"The actors and actresses weep and kiss galore, and the audience last night formed a passage from the lobby to my carriage till I was in and off; yet I was nearly an hour in the theater after the play."

In Chicago, a few years before, however, Booth had learned that his fame was more dangerous than flattering. On Shakespeare's birthday, in 1879, while he was acting the part of *Richard II,* a lunatic, named Gray, shot at him three times from the first balcony. Booth never "forgot he was a king." At the third report, he stepped coolly forward and pointed Gray out to the audience. Then he asked permission to leave the stage for a moment to tell his wife that he was safe. The bullet, kept whimsically as a souvenir, made a unique watch charm. It was set in a gold cartridge and engraved "From Mark Gray to Edwin Booth, April 23, 1879."

During Booth's long life on the stage — over forty years — his high motive was to act, not what the people wanted but what the people ought to want. He called the drama "a holy art." Behind the curtain, as Joseph Jefferson said, he "conducted his theater like a church." To cultivate a taste for beauty, fine

literature, and lofty morals; to make and keep the
stage pure: this was his aim.   There was no reason,
he believed, why the pulpit and the stage should not
stand "shoulder to shoulder" in the work for
righteousness.   When a minister wrote asking if
Booth would let him enter the theater by a side or rear
door so that he could see the actor in his finest parts,
but be, himself, unseen, Booth returned the brief answer: "There is no door in my theater through which
God cannot see."

If there are still any narrow-minded people who
think that a man is bad just because he is an actor,
they should search Booth's steady, plucky life with all
its reverence for what is holy and all its faithfulness
to what is good.   Next to Booth's pluck, perhaps his
most conspicuous trait was generosity.   In the midst
of success, he could not forget the cold and hunger of
his California struggle, and that he, too, had once been
poor.   His desk was full of letters begging for large
sums of money; how many large sums he sent, in a
kind of stealthy charity, no one can ever know.   If, as
rarely happened, he spoke of them at all, it was in a
simple off-hand way, such as calling a check for $1000
"a little aid."   His friend Laurence Hutton said
Booth "gave lavishly with both hands" but "blushed
like a girl" over the letters of thanks he received.   He
was equally generous professionally,— with a big,
open graciousness as unconscious as his beautiful smile.
He praised Salvini, without bitterness; and when
Henry Irving's star of genius rose and eclipsed his

own, he was just and sweet enough to praise its shining.

The fear of his own decline, however, hung over him, and his failures through infirmity cut deep. We do not want to dwell on those sadnesses: the time when he tried to speak and could not, nor the times when, dizzy from dyspepsia, he fell flat on the stage. They were warnings, and he understood.

Nor do we want to dwell on that unexpected return to sadness so perfectly described by Mr. Howells. It was in New York at an evening party. "After we all went into the library, something tragical happened. Edwin Booth was of our number, a gentle, rather silent person in company, or with at least little social initiative, who, as his fate would, went up to the cast of a huge hand that lay upon one of the shelves. 'Whose hand is this, Lorry?' he asked our host, as he took it up and turned it over in both his own hands. Graham feigned not to hear, and Booth asked again, 'Whose hand is this?' Then there was nothing for Graham but to say, 'It's Lincoln's hand,' and the man for whom it meant such unspeakable things put it softly down without a word."

But let us see Booth on some happy occasion such as the founding of the *Players' Club* —(his cherished gift to the profession). On the last night of the old year, 1888, Booth presented the Club with the title deeds to the house at 16, Gramercy Park. According to him, everything went well that night except his speech. "I broke down toward the close." Little

difference that made! His friends loved him all the
more. That festive night, " even the log burned without smoking." "The clock, with deep, cathedral
tones, tolled twelve " just as Barrett read aloud a letter
from Booth's own Edwina, and presented the beautiful
wreath she had sent for " Hamlet, King, Father."
It is good to remember Booth that happy night. And
it is good to peep in at him many another night at
The Players', and see how the young men who may
have forgotten their manners, slip off their hats when
he comes in.

The top floor of the Club House Booth had reserved
for his home. There he lived for two years after his
quiet retirement from public life, and there, June 8,
1893, he died. He had been sick the summer before
at Edwina's home and she had cared for him with the
old-time lovingness. Taking her hand, he would say,
" Daughter, you make me like to be sick." If he realized that his life was nearly over, he did not seem depressed, although his art could not live after him like
an author's, a musician's, or a sculptor's. He had
always " thought of death as coolly as of sleep," and
as " a blessing not a loss." Like Hamlet, he would
say, " The readiness is all." It would be pleasant to
be welcomed across the " threshold of Home " by
those who had " never forgotten him, never ceased to
love and care for him." Everything seemed so very
simple that he could be buoyant, even chirk, to the end.
His daughter Edwina described his cheerfulness during
his last illness :

"How are you, dear grandpa?" her little boy called gently.

"How are you, yourself, old fellow?" came back the jovial answer. That was the last coherent thing Booth said. Like Beethoven, he passed calmly out during a wild electric storm. A glory seemed to rest on him in sleep. Regal as a crowned king he lay there, and yet placidly content, like a weary traveler who had crossed the "threshold of Home." At sunset, June 9, 1893, with many of our other kings in greatness, he was buried in America's Westminster Abbey,— the sun-steeped field of Mount Auburn.

> "A man who Fortune's buffets and rewards
> Hath ta'en with equal thanks."

XII
STEVENSON

" If I have faltered more or less
In my great task of happiness;
If I have moved among my race
And shown no glorious morning face;
If beams from happy human eyes
Have moved me not; if morning skies,
Books, and my food, and summer rain
Knocked on my sullen heart in vain: —
Lord, Thy most pointed pleasure take
And stab my spirit broad awake."

Robert Louis Stevenson.

XII

THE LIGHTHOUSE-BUILDER'S SON

IF you had lived in Edinburgh sixty years ago you might have met, coming out of the first house on Inverleith Terrace, a four-year-old boy in a blue coat, trimmed with fur, and a big beaver bonnet. You would have noticed nothing very remarkable about this child except that he had a pale, delicate, little face and enormous, shining eyes, and that he seemed very fond of his pleasant-looking nurse. This little boy was Robert Louis Stevenson, the only child of Mr. and Mrs. Thomas Stevenson.

Mr. Stevenson, Louis's father, was a lighthouse-builder, and belonged to a family of famous lighthouse-builders. His father, Louis's grandfather, built the Bell Rock Lighthouse, off the eastern coast of Scotland. How hard this was to build you can imagine when you remember that it stood on a dangerous reef, which the sea uncovered for only a few hours at low tide, so that the men had to have a special little workshop built on supports which were fixed in the rock. Then, too, as they worked on the iron foundation of the lighthouse, up would roll the sea and put out their fire. Yet Stevenson's grandfather had the determina-

tion and skill to push the work forward. He felt
the grave need of a lighthouse there, for this was the
dangerous reef described in " The Inchcape Rock."
Off the opposite coast of Scotland, on the island of
Tiree, stands another famous lighthouse which the
Stevensons built.   Eleven years before Louis was born,
his Uncle Allan had begun work on the lighthouse of
Skerryvore.   For its foundation his men had to blast
a hole forty feet square in the solid rock.   Twice,
storm and sea combined defeated Mr. Stevenson's
plans, and swept away the work of his faithful
builders.   At last, however, in 1844, the labor was
completed, and the wheeling gleam of Skerryvore-
light shines on the ocean to this day.

We want to know all this, not only because it is interesting, but because it helps us to understand Robert
Louis's life.   He loved the sea and felt at home on it;
and perhaps he would have learned to build lighthouses himself, if he had not wanted so much more to
build stories.   His love of writing must have come
from his mother's side of the family.   Although Mrs.
Stevenson did not write, she was very fond of
other people's writing, especially of poetry,— and she
taught her son to love it, too.   Besides this, her father,
Louis's other grandfather, was a minister, so that he
wrote sermons, although he did not write books.
Stevenson said of himself, however, that he was like
this grandfather in only one respect,— that he would
rather preach sermons than hear them.

From his mother's side of the family Stevenson inherited something else too, and that was a frail body and weak lungs; so that from his very babyhood he was delicate, and when he grew older he was ordered to travel and to spend much of his time out of doors, in order to live at all.

There is no better way to get the story of Stevenson's life than from his own writings. It is possible to get it almost from the beginning. His "Child's Garden of Verses", although it is not every word about himself, gives us a good idea of his sickly and lonely childhood. Nearly every poem is a little picture. If you read the "Land of Counterpane" you will see him amusing himself when he is sick; you can imagine how, with a little shawl pinned round him, he would sit up, propped against the pillows, to play with his lead soldiers. In others you find out that he was sent to bed early, and that he often lay there listening to the wind or to the people passing in the street below. In "Winter Time" you will find that he had to be all muffled up so as not to take cold. In almost every one, though, you feel how fond he was of play; how he loved the wild March wind, which did him harm, and the garden and the sunshine, which could harm no one; and how, in every way, he yearned to be as rugged as other boys.

Although he had the most loving care, still we cannot help feeling that he was often lonely, if we judge so only from the pathetic poem called "The Lamplighter." We can imagine him sitting, with his thin little face against the pane, waiting for Leerie, and saying perhaps, as many Scotch lads were taught to say, " God bless the lamplighter," and then thinking wistfully,—

" And O! before you hurry by with ladder and with light,
  O Leerie, see a little child and nod to him to-night! "

If we can take all the poems in " The Child's Garden " as true, we find that Louis was not always meek and patient. Once he even ran away, unnoticed, out under the stars, and was just delighting in his freedom, when, as he says,

" They saw me at last, and they chased me with cries,
  And they soon had me packed into bed."

His father and mother probably led in this chase, but I feel sure that his nurse, Alison Cunningham, or " Cummy ", as he called her, was not far behind. She was one of his best friends, and did much to keep him from being lonely. She read to him and told him stories; she recited poems; she took him to walk and showed him the beauty of the world; she sang, she even danced, for " her boy." Not only was she such a jolly playmate; she was a most patient nurse. Sometimes Louis would lie awake for hours coughing; then Cummy would be awake with him. " How well I remember," Stevenson wrote when he was a man, " her lifting me out of bed, carrying me to the window, and showing me one or two lit windows, where also, we told each other, there might be sick little boys and nurses waiting, like us, for the morning."

One of the things that we like best about Stevenson is that when he grew up he did not forget this nurse, but wrote her many letters, which, although he was a grown man, he often signed, " Your Laddie ", and in which, again and again, he expressed his thanks to her. Sometimes he even called her his " second mother." Although he became a well-known author, he was never ashamed of the " woman who had loved him ", but kept up the friendship; and we can imagine old Cummy with her eyes full of tears, reading and re-reading this part of a letter:—

" If you should happen to think that you might have had a child of your own, and that it was hard you should have spent so many years taking care of some one else's prodigal, just you think this: you have made much that there is in me, and there are sons who are more ungrateful to their own mothers than I am to you. For I am not ungrateful, my dear Cummy, and it is with a very sincere emotion that I write myself your little boy,

Louis."

In another letter we get a picture of them together:

" Do you remember when you used to take me out of bed in the early morning, carry me to the back windows, show me the hills of Fife, and quote to me?

' O, the hills are all covered with snaw
An' winter 's noo come fairly ! ' "

The sweetest thing that Stevenson did for Cummy, however, was the dedicating " The Child's Garden of Verses " to her. The poem of dedication is full of

love and tenderness, and all the more manly for that.
It begins,—

> " For the long nights you lay awake
> And watched for my unworthy sake,"

and ends

> " From the sick child, now well and old,
> Take, nurse, the little book you hold!
>
> And grant it, Heaven, that all who read
> May find as dear a nurse at need,
> And every child who lists my rhyme,
> In the bright, fireside, nursery clime,
> May hear it in as kind a voice
> As made my childish days rejoice ! "

Yet, with all his parents' companionship and
Cummy's sympathy and playfulness, Louis would have
missed a good deal of childish fun if he had not had
over fifty cousins.

In the summers a crowd of them visited at the
" Manse ", the home of his minister grandfather; there
were two, especially, that he loved to play with most,
a boy and a girl about his own age. One of their
favorite games was that they were fleeing from a
giant, whom in the end, of course, they always killed.
Sometimes they played that they were on exploring
tours. A favorite place for this game was a sandy isle
in Allan Water where they " waded in butter-burrs "
and where, with the plashy water all round them, they
felt delightfully secure from grown-up people. On

Sundays they went to church, where they heard the beautiful white-haired grandfather preach.   When he was in the pulpit, he seemed very great and far-away to Louis; but when he was at home the child was not afraid of him.   He tells us that once he learned a psalm perfectly, by heart, in the hope that his grandfather would give him one of the bright Indian pictures which hung on his walls and which he had brought with him from his travels.   When, after the psalm was recited, the old man only gathered him in his arms and kissed him, Louis was much disappointed. Just at that time, a picture had a real value; a kiss a most uncertain one.

Part of the summer was usually spent, not at this grandfather's manse, but at the seashore.   There, of course, Louis found the same delight that other children find in the beating and roaring of the waves, and in the natural fountains of spray that played on the rocks.   One of his friends says that he often built " sea-houses ", or great holes with the sand banked all round, in which he and his playmates would hide, there to wait, all excitement, until the creeping tide, coming ever nearer, should at last wash over their bulwark of sand and soak the children intrenched behind it.   We cannot help wondering where Mr. and Mrs. Stevenson and Cummy were when delicate little Louis led his friends in this charming game.

From these stories you will see that, on the whole, Stevenson had as much playtime as most children.

But, of course, he had to go to school. His school-
life was broken, however, because his parents, who
had to travel for their health, took him with them to
Germany, Holland, Italy, and many places in Scotland. Stevenson was sent to private schools in these
different countries, and for the rest of the time he had
tutors. There was really only one lesson, however,
that Stevenson thoroughly enjoyed, and that was
"composition." His compositions were remarkable
for their bad spelling. He could not spell well even
when he was a man, and yet writing was almost a
passion with him. When he was four years old he
had a strange dream — that he "heard the noise of
pens writing." When he was five he dictated to his
mother what he called "The History of Moses." His
uncle had offered a prize of a sovereign to the niece
or nephew who wrote the best story. Stevenson's was
not the best, and so he did not get the prize, but his
uncle gave him an extra prize because it was so good
for his age.

You will notice that Stevenson dictated his "History"; he did not write it himself. That was because he
did not know how, for he was not taught to write when
he was very young; he could not even read till he was
eight. His pretty young mother, however, and faithful Cummy read and told him stories. He said that
he lived in a "Land of Story Books." Speaking of
his love of poetry, he said that he remembered, when
he was very little, repeating these lines over and over
for their music:

"In pastures green Thou leadest me
The quiet waters by."

When he did read for himself, he read a good deal of Scott, although he was less enthusiastic than most boys over "The Waverley Novels."

Nearly everything he read made him want to write, himself. He enjoyed all his "composition" work, but he did not enjoy the writing that he did in school nearly so much as what he did of his own accord. In his other lessons, his teachers considered him thoroughly lazy. All through his boyhood, Stevenson tells us, he was "pointed out as the pattern of an idler," and yet all the time he was eagerly trying to write. When he grew older he always carried with him two books, one to read, and one to write in; and as he walked on the heathy hills, through the woods, or by the sea, his mind was busy trying to fit his thoughts to words. Sometimes he tried to describe exactly the thing he was looking at; sometimes he wrote down conversations from memory; sometimes he wrote on the same subject first in one man's style and then in another's. Thus he wrestled with his own brain; tried, criticized, and tried again. He says he practised to learn to write as boys practise to learn to whittle.

All this time, while Louis was growing from childhood to boyhood, his father was watching him closely and planning for him to follow his own profession and that of so many in the family — the brave profession of lighthouse-building. With this in view, from the time Louis was fourteen his father took him on sea-trips in the *Pharos* all among the rock-bound islands off the Scottish coast. While Mr. Stevenson inspected the lighthouses or studied the " ugly reefs and black rocks " where there was a " tower to be built and a star to be lighted," Louis talked with the captains or watched the brave builders, whom he heartily admired, — so eager they were in their perilous work. He was happy, too, tossing about on the deep water, and he knew no fear in the great storms. He felt the power of it all. He saw the shimmering beauty in the deep path of light, the beacon of safety over the black sea. These thoughts, however, did not turn his mind to lighthouse-building, but to story-building, and it was this life on the ocean which helped him to write " Treasure Island " and " Kidnapped," so popular with all young people.

We are glad Stevenson's interest turned to writing; but his father was bitterly disappointed. He thought that success in an author's profession was too uncertain. Accordingly, in the hope of rousing Louis's interest in lighthouses instead of stories, he sent him to Edinburgh University to take a course in engineering. This made not the least difference. At last his father said to himself: " It is no use to try to make a lighthouse-builder of this boy," and so he decided that Louis should study law. So it was that Stevenson, at twenty-one, began his law study; but half-heartedly.

This course, like the courses of his childhood, was hindered by much sickness. Within two years Stevenson was ordered to Italy for the sake of his nerves and lungs. Two years later he went back to England, passed examinations, and was admitted to the bar; but he never practised, because all the rest of his life was spent in searching for health in many lands. And yet, with all his weakness, he was not idle. Everywhere he went he found something worth seeing and worth writing about; and again the story of his young manhood may be read in his own books, just as the story of his childhood may be read in the " Garden of Verses." And we find him full of cheer, as a child and as a man. The little boy said,—

"The world is so full of a number of things
I'm sure we should all be as happy as kings."

The man wrote: "I have so many things to make life sweet to me, it seems a pity I cannot have that other thing, health. But though you will be angry to hear it, I believe, for myself at least, ' what is, is best.' "

The year after he left the University he took a canoeing-trip with one of his friends. This is described in " An Island Voyage." In the *Arethusa* and the *Cigarette* they paddled up the river which Stevenson said ran as though it " smelt the sea." They spent their nights and took their meals at farm-houses. Sometimes they rested on the grass beneath the trees. From a recent storm the river was unusually turbulent; trees had been uprooted, and here and there the wind had thrown them across the stream. Stevenson's canoe caught on one of these trees, capsized, and he

himself barely escaped by clinging to the tree, while
his canoe "went merrily down stream." When he
had the strength, he pulled himself ashore by the tree-
trunk, while his friend paddled off after the canoe.
Of course such a struggle, combined with a wetting,
was no help to Stevenson's health.

Two years later he took another interesting trip.
This time it was a walking-trip in France, and his only
companion was a little donkey named " Modestine."
Modestine was not taken along to ride on, but to carry
his baggage, which he describes as a big sleeping-sack,
—" a bed by night, a portmanteau by day." It was
" a long roll or sausage of green water-proof cloth
without, and blue sheep's-fur within." The sheep's-
fur made it warm and it was long enough for him to
"bury himself in it up to the neck." When he was
traveling he used it to pack things in, for he took with
him a " revolver, a little spirit-lamp and pan, a lantern,
and some half-penny candles, a jack-knife, and a large
leather flask, besides clothing, books, cakes of chocolate, and cans of Bologna sausage."

Modestine's natural pace was " as much slower than
a walk as a walk is slower than a run" and " she
stopped to browse by the way." As they journeyed
on, Stevenson met a peasant who taught him to say
" Proot!" which in French donkey-language is " Get
up!" To urge her on still more, he gave him a whip.
Another peasant, at whose house Stevenson stopped,
made him a goad, with which he " pushed Modestine
along." As their way led through the shaggy moun-

tains of France, you can imagine that they did not travel fast. Yet they went a hundred and twenty miles or so, in twelve days; and when, at the end of this time, Stevenson sold his donkey-friend, who could go no further, it was not without genuine regret, for she had been grateful, eating the black bread out of his hand, and she had been companionable. When he lay awake at night under the spicy pines, listening to the roaring wind or looking up at the glittering stars, it had been pleasant to hear Modestine pawing by his side, or walking round and round at the end of her tether.

The next year, when Stevenson was twenty-nine, he decided to go to California, and, partly to save money and partly for experience, he traveled by emigrant ship and train. In " An Amateur Emigrant " he gives his impressions of his rough companions on the sea-voyage, and also what were, perhaps, their impressions of him. The sailors called him " mate "; the officers " my man "; the workmen in the steerage considered him one of their own class; a certain mason, even, believed that he was a mason. What they all wondered at was that he should spend so much time writing.

In " Across the Plains " Stevenson pictures the trip by train to California. At night they made their beds by putting straw cushions on the boards which reached from bench to bench. Stevenson slept and " chummed " with a Dutchman from Philadelphia. These two and one other clubbed together to buy washing-materials — a tin basin, a towel, and a bar of soap.

They washed on the rear platform. They bought, too,
a few cooking-utensils and coffee and sugar, so that
they could get their own breakfasts now and then.

On this trip Stevenson found one firm friend in the
newsboy. The child had noticed how pale he looked
and that he held the door open with his foot so as to
get a little fresh air instead of the stale air of the
crowded car. So, one day when Stevenson was reading, the newsboy slipped a large juicy pear into his
hand. In fact, the little fellow " petted " him all the
rest of the way.

After he reached California, Stevenson had two
serious attacks of illness. The first was the result of
his long, tiresome journey. He was too weak to live
the life he had planned — to camp out alone in the
woods of the Coast Range. After he had been lying
for two nights in a half-stupor, under a tree, a bear-
hunter found him and carried him in his arms to a
goatherd's hut near-by. There he was taken care of
for two weeks till he grew strong enough to go on to
Monterey. From there he went to San Francisco,
where the next year he was taken sick again. This
time his illness was caused by exhausting himself with
nursing his landlady's little four-year-old child. He
saved the child's life; but it almost cost him his own.

When Stevenson was in France he had met a Mrs.
Osbourne, who was now in California with her son.
When she heard of Stevenson's illness she came to help
take care of him, and after Stevenson grew well they
were married; so it was that his next trip was taken

with her and with his stepson, Lloyd Osbourne (now himself a well-known writer).

These three camped out on Mount St. Helena, near the Silverado Mine, and called themselves by the same name which Stevenson chose for his book,—" Silverado Squatters ",— because without legal claim they had taken possession of a Silverado miner's disused house. Stevenson and his wife called themselves the King and Queen, Lloyd was the Crown Prince, and " Chuchu ", the dog, was honored as the " Grand Duke." Incidentally, the dog honored himself with their softest cushions.

After the house was cleaned and repaired it was a sweet, airy place, " haunted by the perfumes of the glen." They had filled in the doors and windows with white cotton cloth; they had brought their own stove; and they made their beds of clean hay. Though the cañons were full of rattlesnakes, none of the squatters were afraid, except " Chuchu." " Every whiz of the rattle made him bound. His eyes rolled; he trembled; he would be often wet with sweat." Stevenson, however, " took his sun-baths and open-air calisthenics, without fear, though the rattlers were buzzing all around." And he was no more afraid of the brown bears and mountain lions, though once an old grizzly visited a poultry-yard in the village below. No; none of these creatures made him leave his mountain camp; it was the old, old enemy, sickness, away off there so many miles from civilization or a doctor's help. Even " so far above the world " the seafogs found him out.

A few months later, Stevenson and his wife returned to Scotland. Mrs. Stevenson was a jolly, courageous companion, as well as a capable nurse. She had need to be both, for by this time her husband's lung-trouble had become settled. They still traveled, trying the different climates of the Scotch Highlands, the Alps, Edinburgh, and finally the South of France. Sick as he was, for the next seven years, Stevenson somehow found strength, between the attacks of illness, to write with vigor and eagerness. Besides many books for grown people, he wrote during this time his best two books for boys —"Treasure Island" and "Kidnapped." "Treasure Island" was his first book that was popular enough to pay well. Stevenson's father helped him a good deal with this, by drawing on his experiences at sea.

The death of his father, two years later, was the deepest sorrow Stevenson ever had. They had been chums together, almost like two boys, with all the added love between father and son. This grief had such a bad effect on Stevenson's health that three months later, in August, he and his family, including his mother, went to the Adirondacks in America. Until the next summer they lived there, near Lake Saranac, in a wooden house on a hilltop overlooking a stream of running water. "Highland," wrote Stevenson to one of his friends, " all but the dear hue of peat — and of many hills — Highland also but for the lack of heather."

While they were in the Adirondacks, an American

publisher offered Stevenson ten thousand dollars for
an account of a voyage in the South Seas.   The trip
might do him good; he needed the money; and, as
always, he loved the sea.   The whole family went with
him; and even his mother enjoyed it, although they
had a stormy voyage.   When Stevenson was seventeen, an old Highland sibyl had prophesied that he was
to be "very happy, to visit America, and to be much
at sea."   It had all come true.   He was happy, because he was determined to be so.   As for his life on
the sea, he tells it best himself.   "I cannot say why I
like the sea; no man can be more cynically and constantly alive to its perils; I regard it as the highest
form of gambling; and yet I love the sea as much as
I hate gambling.   Fine, clean emotions; a world all
and always beautiful; air better than wine; interest
unflagging: there is, upon the whole, no better life;"
and again: "These two last years I have been much
at sea, and never once did I lose my fidelity to blue
water and a ship."

One of the interesting things that Stevenson did on
this trip was to visit the leper-settlement on one of
the Hawaiian Islands.   None of his family went with
him.   He was one passenger in two boat-loads of
lepers.   In the boat with him were two sisters who
tried hard to be brave; but one of them could not help
crying softly all the way.   Stevenson, in his big sympathy, was soon crying with her.

A crowd of other lepers swarmed down to the shore
to meet them.   They were in all stages of the disease,

some very loathsome. Still they held out their hands in welcome. Rather than hurt their feelings by offering a gloved hand, Stevenson pretended not to see, and so did not shake hands at all. He stayed at "the lazaretto", as it was called after Lazarus in the Bible, for eight days and seven nights. The whole experience was a great drain on his sympathies, actually living with those poor people, "still breathing, still thinking, still remembering," and yet dying by inches of a most dreadful disease. But though Stevenson pitied the lepers, he did not let them see his pity. After the first break-down, he was bright as ever. He played croquet with seven leper-girls, and told stories to the old leper-women in the hospital.

His love for children never failed. From the little California boy whom he nursed through sickness at the risk of his own life, to many small waifs in city streets, his love was the same. He said himself that he almost coveted the children, he wished so much that they were his, especially "the wee ones." Once we find him formally willing his birthday to a little girl who was born on February 29, and so had only one birthday in four years; and from the island of Honolulu, he wrote to a friend of his,— another man of about forty: "The girls here all have dolls and love dressing them. You, who know so many dressmakers, please make it known it would be an acceptable gift to send scraps for doll dress-making to the Reverend Sister Mary Ann, Bishop Home, Kilaupapa, Milokai, Hawaiian Islands." This letter shows not only Stevenson's love of children, but his willingness to take trouble over little things, although by this time he was a busy and prominent man.

In April 1889, Stevenson's mother returned to Scotland, and he, his wife, and Lloyd continued their exploring tour to the Gilbert Islands, the Marquesas, the Carolines, Australia, and finally Samoa.

His life in Samoa is, in some ways, the most interesting story of all, and here again you can find that story in his own writings; this time, though, it is not in his books but in his letters. These are so vivid, that you feel as if you were right in Samoa with him. You are living in his spotless little box of a house, called *Vailima*, which means "five rivers", and so reminds you that it is within sound of flowing streams. There, from the broad veranda — and the house is almost half veranda,— you can look straight up, on one side, at the wooded Vaea Mountain; and on the other, six hundred feet below you gleams the sea, " filling the end of two vales of forest." The house is built in a clearing in the jungle. The trees about it are twice as tall as the house; the birds about it are always talking or singing, and here and there among the trees echoes " the ringing sleigh-bell of the tree toad."

During the first six months that Stevenson and his family lived at Vailima there was much to be done. They built three houses, a big barn, two miles of road (this road three times, for the roads were continually being destroyed by heavy rains), " cleared many acres of bush and made some miles of path, planted quantities of food, and enclosed a horse-paddock and some acres of pig-run."

Sometimes Stevenson calls this property a farm, and sometimes a plantation. It was a little of both. He had horses, pigs, and chickens, and raised nearly all the common vegetables. Besides these, he had the fruits of the tropics — his own banana-patch, his hedge of lemon-trees, and plenty of pineapples, bread-fruit, and cocoanuts. Stevenson enjoyed the life of a farmer as much as he had enjoyed everything else. Sometimes, as he said, he played the "game of patience" by weeding all the morning. Things often went wrong; but he took bad luck merrily. Occasionally his pigs were stolen; once his horse "kicked him in the shin" when he was taking off her saddle; once the carpenter's horse stepped in a nest of fourteen eggs and, as Stevenson said, made "an omelette of all their hopes." Still, with perfect honesty, he could sign his letter "The Well-pleased South Sea Islander"; for here in Samoa he could be out of doors, whereas in Scotland he would have been in bed. The longer he stayed there, the stronger he felt. He rode horseback for hours without getting tired, and sometimes he rode very fast.

Riding, walking, bathing, and sailing were his chief recreations. Like the natives, much of the time he went barefoot. The roads, such as they were, were cut through a forest of fruit-trees between the noisy sea and the silent mountain. Palms waved overhead;

Robert Louis Stevenson

tangled "ropes of liana" hung from the trees. The strong sun had brought out the richest, brightest colors in all the flowers; Stevenson himself was browned by its heat. Sometimes he gave himself up, like a child, to idle pleasures, such as wading for hours up to his knees in the salt water searching for shells. Once or twice he tried lawn-tennis; but after that had brought on a hemorrhage he gave it up. He usually went to bathe in the river just before lunch.

He loved his work too much, however, and was too determined to succeed in it, to spend a great deal of time even in recreation. After he had been there a few months he set himself a rigid program, and after the addition was built on the house, from his room in an out-of-the-way part of it he tells us that he saw the sunrise nearly every morning, had breakfast at six, worked till eleven, and after lunch usually worked again until four or five. Sometimes he played cards in the evening. At eight o'clock he had prayers for his own family and the Samoans of his household, a Samoan woman leading in the singing. He went to bed early, often reading himself to sleep, and sleeping on a chest covered with mats and blankets.

This program he kept so strictly that I think he must have con .ually said to himself: "Now I can see and enjoy," and "Now I must work." He did actually say that it was "hard to keep on grinding." Still he did keep on, and in addition to his work as a farmer and an author he found time to teach. He gave regular lessons to Austin Strong, his stepdaughter's little son, and taught arithmetic and "long expressions" to Henry, the son of one of the Samoan chiefs.

Henry was the first Somoan who really loved Stevenson. The affection of the natives was not very easy to win. They were naturally lazy; ignorant, of course; inclined to steal; and somewhat suspicious. Stevenson, nevertheless, saw in them not only much that was interesting, but much that was good. They were very clean people,— that attracted him in the first place,— and they were people with a genuine love of beauty. Very wisely, Stevenson saw that he could only win them by being one of them. Accordingly, he learned their language as soon as he could. He went, also, to their little church, although they were Roman Catholics and he was a Protestant, and there he knelt on the white-sanded floor among the almost naked men, the women in their gracefully draped garments of fine silk, and the little brown children with no clothing at all except girdles and large, gorgeous hats trimmed, some of them, with blue ribbon and pink roses.

When Stevenson knew their language well enough, he told them stories, and so he won from them the name of "Tusitala", which means "teller f tales"; his wife was called "Aolele" or "beautifui as a flying cloud." Thus, gradually but surely, the natives grew to know and care for their friends at Vailima. They tried to do for Stevenson what they never did for any one else,— they tried to hurry. "You never see a

Samoan run except at Vailima ", visitors would sometimes say. Occasionally, Stevenson took charge of a
big gang of road-makers, and they went through the
forest marking their path by bending down the wild
cocoa-nut trees and sitting on them to break them off.

At first many of the men were tricky and ran away;
but by and by they grew to care for the slender, white
master, with the bright eyes and winning smile, and
they really wanted to work for him. " Once Tusitala's friend, always Tusitala's friend," they would say.

When the war broke out between two chiefs, the
Samoans showed their trust in Stevenson by bringing
a bag full of coins, which they had saved for the roof
of their church, and asking him to keep them till the
fight was over. During this war Stevenson often went
to see the prisoners, told them stories, heard their
troubles, got them doctors, and was at last instrumental
in having a large number set free without having to
work out their freedom by road-building. A few days
after this, Stevenson was surprised and touched to
learn that the freed prisoners had agreed in gratitude
to work on his road as a " free gift." It was to be his
own private road, they specified, the road that led from
his house to the public way. The chiefs, themselves,
drew up the inscription in the newspaper. It was
headed " The Road of Loving Hearts " and it read as
follows:

" Considering the great love of Tusitala in his loving care of us in our distress in the prison, we have
therefore prepared a splendid gift. It shall never be

muddy, it shall endure forever, this road that we have dug."

They had given him the one thing they could give, and, as far as they knew, the one thing he wanted, and they insisted that they would not take presents of any kind, much less pay.

In a life so full of pleasure, work, and interest as this, it is sometimes hard to realize that Stevenson ever had hours of great despondency; but he often did. Although he was much better, he knew in his heart that he could never be well. It was his one great principle, however, to keep himself sunny, to wear a smiling face, "to make, upon the whole, a family happier for his presence." "The sea, the islands, the islanders, the island life and climate, make and keep me truly happier," he wrote bravely to a friend; but another time, when he had been thinking of his dear Scotland, with its "hills of sheep" and "winds austere and pure," and realizing that he could never see it again, he wrote a pathetic little poem from which these lines are taken:

"Red shall the heather bloom over hill and valley,
   .   .   .   .
Fair shine the day on the house with open door;
Birds come and cry there and twitter in the chimney,
But I go forever and come again no more."

and in a letter to a friend he wrote:

"For fourteen years I have not had a day's real health; I have wakened sick and gone to bed weary; and I have done my work unflinchingly. I have written in bed and written out of it, written in hemorrhages, written when my head swam for weakness, and for so long it seems to me I have won my wager. The Powers have so willed that my battlefield should be this dingy, inglorious one of the bed and the physic bottle. At least I have not failed but I would have preferred a place of trumpetings and the open air over my head."

During his last years he sometimes had "scrivener's cramp" so that he could not do his writing himself, but had to dictate his stories to his stepdaughter, Mrs. Strong. This, of course, was hard on his voice, and sometimes he lost the power of speech, altogether, and had to use the deaf and dumb alphabet.

One day, December 3rd, 1894, when he had felt particularly well, he came downstairs a little while before supper to help his wife make a salad, and together they set the table on the veranda. On pleasant days, they often had their meals there, for Samoa is a land of eternal summer. Stevenson had been joking with his wife about something, when suddenly he put his hand to his head with the cry: "What's that? Do I look strange?" and then he fell unconscious beside her. Doctors were quickly summoned, but they could not help him. For about two hours he lay, still unconscious, still breathing. Around the room knelt or stood a dozen or more Samoans, longing to give their service; but they, too, could do nothing. Stevenson died a few minutes past eight that night.

Half understanding that this was death and half hoping it was only sleep, the natives stayed beside him all night — some praying, some sitting in silence, others going away to return with gifts of fine, woven mats to cover him. In the morning still others came, loaded with bright flowers, till the room was glowing with color. There was nothing about that room to suggest death except the dumb, sad watchers. Among them; came an old Mataafa chief, who, crouching beside the body, broke out with "I am only a poor Samoan, and ignorant. Others are rich and can give Tusitala the parting presents of rich, fine mats; I am poor and can give nothing this last day he receives his friends."

Stevenson had asked to be buried on the summit of Vaea Mountain. There was no path to this summit, and so the chiefs assembled their men and about forty set out with knives and axes to cut a path up the steep mountain side. At one o'clock that day when all was ready, they came back, unwearied by their hard service, and a few of the strongest were chosen to carry their friend on their shoulders. Gravely and sturdily again they set out on the steep climb, followed by the family, the minister, and many Samoans and friends.

At the grave the minister read the prayer which Stevenson, himself, had offered the night before he died,—

"We beseech Thee, Lord, to behold us with favor, folk of many families and nations gathered together in the peace of this roof. Bless to us our extraordinary mercies; if the day come when these must be taken, brace us to play the man, under affliction. Go with each of us to rest and, when the day returns,

return to us our sun and comforter, and call us up
with morning faces and with morning hearts — eager
to labor, eager to be happy, if happiness shall be our
portion — and if the day be marked for sorrow, strong
to endure it."

So, his last prayer was characteristic. He had
"braced himself to play the man"; he had "awaked
with smiles, he had labored smiling." And the gathering at the grave was characteristic — the friends who
laid him there were of all classes, many, and full of
deep affection.

Even the last sleeping-place of this brave, bright,
nature-loving man was just what he had chosen —
within sight of the "besieging sea," which he had
played by as a child and never failed to love, and within
sound of God's great wind "that bloweth all day long."

"Under the wide and starry sky,

.   .   .   .   .

Here he lies where he longed to be;
Home is the sailor, home from the sea,
    And the hunter home from the hill."

XIII

SAINT-GAUDENS

" It's not the finger- but the brain-work that takes the time."

Augustus Saint-Gaudens.

XIII

THE MAGIC TOUCH

WHEN Bernard Saint-Gaudens and his young Irish wife took their six-months-old baby out of his home in Dublin and carried him on board a ship sailing for America, they had no idea what a valuable baby he was. I do not mean in money; a little family of three, they were all poor together; but I mean in brains. If babies had been dutiable, the United State Government might have exacted a tidy sum at little Augustus' entrance. But I suppose his young French father never dreamed that the small right hand clasping his own so tightly would teach stone how to speak. And I suppose even the beautiful black-haired mother, with the "generous loving Irish face", thought less of her baby's future greatness than of the famine that was driving them all to a land of strangers. Surely, to fellow-passengers, the "red-haired, whopper-jawed, hopeful" youngster did not look like a budding genius.

Nor were the New York City home and streets, where Augustus spent his boyhood, the best places to ripen genius. In the Bowery and other crowded districts, the child found no greater beauty and inspiration than the twilight-picking of flowers in a near-by graveyard. His young mind was a contented clutter of all kinds of city impressions: the smell of cake from the bakery and of peaches stewed by Germans in his tenement; "races round the block"; the racket and joy of street fights; and the greater joy of boy-invented games. In the darkness of night they stretched strings from the houses to wagons in the road, to pluck off the hats of passers-by. It was rapture when those hats were worn by mistified policemen! In a kind of chuckling terror, the boys took flight — bursting like escaping convicts with pride in their escape.

The "Reminiscences of Augustus Saint-Gaudens" paint him as no infant saint. The culprit confesses to "lickings galore in school and out", and tells us one of his "typical crimes": "The boy by my side in the class-room whispered to me, 'Say!' As I turned to him, his extended forefinger, which was meant to hit my nose, found itself at the level of my mouth. I bit it. He howled. I was 'stood up' with my back to the class and my face close against the blackboard, immediately behind the teacher, who, turned toward the class, could not see me. To relieve the monotony of the view, I took the rubber, covered my features with white chalk, and grinned around at the class. The resulting uproar can be imagined. I was taken by the scruff of the neck and sent to the private class-room, where I had the honor of a solitary and tremendous caning on parts of my body other than my hands."

He must have been very often in mischief, for Saint-

Gaudens says that, besides these whippings, he was
" kept in " for about an hour every day and he used to
look wistfully out of the window and envy the freedom of the floating clouds.

None of his teachers seemed to find anything good
either inside his fun-loving heart or his little red head.
Apparently no one but himself, or some secret crony,
admired his slate drawing of a mighty battle, or his
painting on a back fence of a negro boy with a target.
Augustus himself took great pride in that negro boy.
The hole in the boy's trousers, with the bare knee stick-
ing through, was a real stroke of genius!

The little fellow often strolled over to his father's
shop and drew pictures of the shoemakers at work.
One day, Dr. Agnew, who had come in to order a pair
of boots, saw these pen-and-ink sketches, recognized
the lifelike pose and action, talked the pictures over
with the young artist, and gave encouragement where
teachers had given only whippings.

There is a theory that the cobbler's trade offers
great chances for meditation. A man can do a power
of thinking at this steady work. But Augustus, not
being a moralizing boy, was more amused than in-
structed by his father's philosophy. Whether he was
ever told that what he did was " as much use as a mus-
tard-plaster on a wooden leg ", or that he was " as
handy with his hands as a pig with his tail " we do not
know; but those were two of his father's comparisons.
As a matter of fact, before long, the boy did many
useful things, and was particularly " handy with his

hands." As for his tongue, as soon as he learned to speak, he had to use that skilfully. At home the Saint-Gaudens children — Augustus, Andrew, and Louis — spoke French with their father and English with their mother.

On Sundays, Augustus and Andrew, the two older boys, would take the Canal Street Ferry across the North River to the New Jersey shore. There were fields and trees there, then — half a century ago, and to those city boys it was a weekly trip to heaven; with one flaw that heaven does not have,— the coming back at sunset. A mob of boys used to take the same trip. They would push their way to the bow of the boat, clamber onto a front seat, and, lords of the sea, sit there in a grinning row, their feet swinging, and their hearts big with the joy of enterprise. The Saint-Gaudens boys had five cents apiece " two to pay the ferry over, two back, and one to spend."

Hundreds of boys in the poor parts of great cities will understand this kind of a holiday better than any country boy. This is especially true if a bit of the artist is buried in their suffocated natures — a longing for space, and light, and color. Augustus had that longing, and he had a fine chance to satisfy it when, after an attack of typhoid-fever, he was sent to the country to get strong. This is the story from a long-after letter to Homer Saint-Gaudens, his only son. He called himself Nosey because of his big nose. " One night, Nosey woke up while he was sick, and he saw his mother and his mother's friend kneeling and praying by the bed.   It was very quiet, and in the little light he saw his good mother had big tears in her eyes.   And all he recollects of the sickness after that was his friend Jimmie Haddon.   He was very fond of Jimmie Haddon.   His father was a gold-beater, and he used to have four or five men with big, strong, bare arms with big veins on them, and they used to beat gold in a basement until it was so thin you could blow it away; and there was a sign over the door, of an arm just like the men's arms, and it was gold.   Well, he recollects Jimmie Haddon coming into the room and holding his mother's hand.   But they wouldn't let him go near the bed, as he might get sick too.   And then the next thing, Nosey was brought to the country, just as you are now, and it seemed so beautiful and green."   The " country " was Staten Island.

Far from the rumbling streets, the crowded buildings, the dirty smells, the little sick boy found himself once more in Paradise, only this time he did not have to leave at sunset.   There was a hill in front of the house.   For many days, he looked at that hill, so close to the loving blue, and wondered what was beyond. At last he was strong enough to climb it, and then he made the discovery that there were more hills, still farther on, all beautiful and green.   How plenteous and still it was — quite as if there was room in the world for birds and crickets, as well as for rushing people!   But, much as he loved the country, the city was to be Augustus' home for yet a long, long time.

So far, the mischievous and affectionate little boy

had not proved he had any great brain power. He drew a good deal; but what was that? Many draw who come to nothing. At thirteen, however, he changed from a pesky school-boy to an earnest little workman. To satisfy his strong art-instinct and at the same time learn a trade, he was apprenticed to a cameo-cutter named Avet. Soon after that, he entered a drawing-class in the night-school of Cooper Institute. Home from a day of cutting cameos, he would swallow a hasty supper and dash off again to draw. Either Mr. Avet, the cameo-cutter, or the drawing-teacher, must have encouraged him, for, inwardly, more in joyful hope than in conceit, Augustus believed himself a " heaven-born genius." If the people who jostled against him in stages and horse-cars had only known how great a genius, would n't they have been " profoundly impressed "? Such were his own youthful thoughts! Before long, however, he must have been too tired to care what people thought. " In the morning," as he tells us, " Mother literally dragged me out of bed, pushed me over to the washstand, where I gave myself a cat's lick somehow or other, drove me to the seat at the table, administered my breakfast, which consisted of tea and large quantities of long, French loaves of bread and butter, and tumbled me downstairs out into the street, where I awoke."

It was a rushing life for a little boy; much too rushing.

Education led him from Cooper Institute to the

Academy of Design, and then to Europe. He was in
America, however, during the exciting Civil War, and
he saw things then that, pictured on his young mind,
asked his older hands to make them live in bronze.

He saw the soldiers march by to war and in the
Draft Riots he experienced the sudden desertion of
the city streets and the more sudden sound of " men
with guns running in the distance." One April morning, when he was seventeen, he found his mother, yes,
and his father, too, crying at the breakfast-table. It
was the news of Lincoln's death. Augustus was one
of the great solemn crowd that went to see the President's tired face at rest. Like many others he looked
intently, reverently; but he did not know that the time
would come when his touch would almost make that
sad face live again.

One day early in 1867, Mr. Saint-Gaudens surprised
his boy by asking: " Would you like to go to the
Paris Exposition? "

The answer is easy to guess.

" We will arrange that," the father continued. To
the fellow who had lived such a cramped life, spending
as little as possible, always, the very idea seemed a miracle. Ever since Augustus had worked, he had regularly given his entire wages, as a matter of course, to
his parents. If he was to have a trip, it would be a
kind of present; but the father had it ready. " He
paid for my passage abroad, and gave me a hundred
dollars which he had saved out of my wages." To
most of us it seems a small enough equipment, but it

was bountiful from a poor shoemaker.   As always, the
boy was deeply touched by his parents' sacrifice.   He
had a second surprise.   An artist friend gave him a
farewell banquet, and, at the table, under Augustus'
plate, lay one hundred francs in shining gold (about
twenty dollars) " to pay for a trip to Father's village
in France."

The last night and the Sunday before sailing, Augustus was very busy.   Though his artist-heart leaped
forward, his home-loving heart tugged back.   As if to
print on his mind a better picture of two faces, very
dear, he made a bust of his father and a drawing of
his mother, those last nights in the little home he was
leaving.

Augustus Saint-Gaudens was nineteen when, in
February 1867, he sailed for Europe in the steerage.
At that bleak season, the sea seems rough enough in the
first cabin.   In the steerage, viewed with disgust by
many cabin-passengers, Saint-Gaudens was sicker than
" a regiment of dogs."   But he had with him, besides
his carpet-bag, a big cargo of youth, and ambition, and
sportsmanlike spirits.   If he ever reached the steady
shore, he was going to work hard and play hard, and
he could suffer even the miseries of that miserable voyage for the *joy that was set before him.*   It is in work
and play that we follow him, after the welcome land is
reached,— he was intense in both; he earned his vigorous play by vigorous work; and he rested himself
from work by play.

Even on his first night in Paris, as he trudged up the

brilliantly lighted Champs-Elysées, weighed down with
the immense weight of his more and more burdensome
carpet-bag, he was half laborer, half sightseer. He
hated the heavy load; but he loved the dazzling glory.
The little money his father had generously spared
would not last long, even by pinching. Augustus
would have to work as well as study. And so, a day
or two after he reached Paris, he engaged himself to
cut cameos for an Italian named Lupi. Mornings and
evenings, he worked in a modeling-school, to "learn
sculpture in nine months"; afternoons, he cut cameos
for his living. But he worked "so much at the school
and so little at the cameos", that he grew poorer and
poorer, moving from one dingy lodging to another.
The Latin Quarter must have seemed almost too home-
like to a Bowery boy. He tried sleeping on a cot without a mattress; on a mattress on the floor; with a
friend, poorer than himself, on a cot two and a half
feet wide. With merry cheer the young artists shared
their hopes and hardships. One night, he and his
chum, Herzog, moved all their little possessions in a
hand-cart hired for five cents an hour. Two cot-beds
and bedding, pitchers, basins, piles of books, a model-
ing-stand, and what few clothes they had — all were
loaded in artistic disorder on that little cart. Though
one of them "ran behind to gather the driblets", and
though they got a third friend to help, they lost a
"good quarter" of their things on the road.

Still jolly fellowship prevailed. Through all the ups
and most of the downs, Augustus whistled and sang

ear-splittingly and kept on loving " Beethoven and ice cream." It was the "regular life of a student, with most of its enthusiasms and disheartenings." Among other disheartenings, there was a nine months' delay before he was admitted to the Beaux Arts. Meanwhile, he took what he could get in smaller schools, and all the fun there was anywhere. His mimicry of Professor Jacquot is delightful. Half lispingly, half splutteringly, he would lean over the drawings and say: "'Let us shee, um-m-m! Well, your head's too big, too big. Your legsh are too short.' Then bang! bang! would come the black marks over the drawing. 'There you are! Fixsh that, my boy, fixsh that!'" The young students had a great deal of fun at Professor Jacquot's expense, and Gus Saint-Gaudens, who had been such a little scamp in the North Moore Street School long ago, had lost none of his sense of humor. It cheered him through many times of gloom.

Let us "jump" like him, from work to play. Twice we have seen him intense in labor, first as a boy in New York, cutting cameos all day and drawing at night, and then, as a young man in Paris, studying sculpture mornings and evenings, and cutting cameos in the afternoons. As a necessity, however, he snatched every chance for rest and fun. He doted on wrestling and swimming, and was a beautiful diver. So as not to interrupt his art and still get physical recreation, he would go swimming at five o'clock in the morning. He loved the consciousness of stirred blood

and strained muscles. In the gymnasium, the more
violently he exercised, the better he liked it. No one
was more eager for a holiday than he. Though the
students were poor, once in a while they allowed themselves the joy of an out-door excursion. A third-class
railway-carriage was good enough for them; much of
the time their feet were better yet. Saint-Gaudens'
friend, Monsieur Garnier, describes the delightful trip
three of them took to Switzerland. It cost from
twenty to thirty dollars. "As soon as he saw the
water, Gus had to enter. Nobody got his money's
worth so well as he. Everything seemed enchanting,
everything beautiful. We bathed in the Rhine. We
passed over it on a bridge of boats, and drank beer in
Germany. It was wonderful!" Then he went on to
tell of one day when they rose at dawn, took their tin
drinking-cups, butter in a tin box, wine and milk in
gourds, cold meat, and a big loaf of bread, and piling
them all on the top of their knapsacks, tramped forth
into the morning, poor, but happy as " escaped colts."

It seemed to be Saint-Gaudens' nature to be happy.
During his three years in Paris and his five in Rome,
hope was his best tonic. It counteracted many a dose
of disappointment, and much that was depressing.
" He was dangerously ill in a low attic in Rome," and,
though he soon proved himself a fine cameo-cutter, it
was years before his success as a sculptor was sure.
Meanwhile, he and Miss Homer had decided they
wanted to get married; but Miss Homer's father
thought an artist's trade a bit uncertain. And so,

hard as the fact was, the wedding-day hinged on *orders for statues.* They came, and so did the wedding; but Saint-Gaudens' life was a money-struggle a good deal of the way, and a health-struggle at the end. In Rome, he had to piece out his earnings for sculpture by making cameos; and in America, he had to piece out by teaching. As lives go, however, his was not sad. Love and confidence filled his childhood's poor little home. And he had, as a man, the happiness of educating his brother Louis, and of making his father proud of him. Except for the death of his parents, the shocking murder of his friend Stanford White, and the complete ruin of his Cornish studio by fire, he had, as lives go, little sorrow. Generous, free from conceit, and always fond of a good time, Saint-Gaudens was rich in friends —" bully friends who were bully men," who laughed at his singing, trembled at his fearless swims, suffered over his disappointments and illness, and gloried in his success.

The three things he had to conquer were poverty, illness, and the problems of art. It is with Saint-Gaudens, the artist, that we are chiefly concerned.

Let us scatter in disorder appropriate to a sculptor's studio a few things that increased the " toughness of his sculptor's life." After his return to America, two disappointments made him angry, and he could be *very* angry. For the Sumner statue (the only competition he ever entered) the Committee had asked for a *seated* figure. Saint-Gaudens accordingly sent in a seated model, only to have a standing one win. And he was still more furious when, a *requested* piece of sculpture sent to the Academy of Design Exhibition, was refused on the ground of "no room." It was partly "on the wrath of Saint-Gaudens" that June 1, 1877, he and his friends founded The Society of American Artists.

He described his life as "up and down, up and down all the time", and his brain, while he worked on the Farragut, as a confusion of "arms with braid, legs, coats, eagles, caps, legs, arms, hands, caps, eagles, eagles, caps." Besides this, he had to deal directly with "molders, scaffoldings, marble-assistants, bronze-men, trucks, rubbish-men, plasterers, and whatnot else, all the while trying to soar into the blue."

Except for occasional flights to Europe, the rest of his life was spent in this country: fifteen years in a New York studio on 36th Street, and seven years in Cornish, New Hampshire. Peeps into his studio give peeps at his circumstances and character. One day, amid the "clatter of molders and sculptors" and the "incessantly jangling door-bell", we find his old father and Dr. McCosh, President of Princeton, sleeping there as soundly as if they were in bed. Mr. Saint-Gaudens often took his nap at his son's studio and this day Dr. McCosh, who had come too early for his pose, had had to wait till the big horse for the Shaw Memorial had served his time as model. It was already strapped in place and "pawing and kicking" for freedom. Another day in walked Mr. Stanford White, and, glancing at Saint-Gaudens' bas-relief of Mrs. White, exclaimed:

"Oh, Gus, that's rotten!"

In an instant, Saint-Gaudens had smashed it, only to do it again. He was not, above all things, either self-controlled or patient. Once when the work had been stopped "for the thirty-fifth time, while some one looked for a lost hammer" he ordered a gross of hammers, in the hope that, out of a hundred and forty-four, one would be at hand for use.

He said to his assistants one day:

"I am going to invent a machine to make you all good sculptors.— It will have hooks for the back of your necks and strong springs.— Every thirty seconds, it will jerk you fifty feet away from your work, and hold you there for five minutes' contemplation."

"Time and distance" were two of the articles in his artist-creed.

"You delay just as your father did before you," flashed Governor Morgan. Saint-Gaudens did delay, and for this he was much criticized; but think of the discouragements that met his art, and remember, too, his *love of perfection*. Often careless molders, by neglecting some detail, would waste both time and money. When a workman broke two fingers off his "Venus of the Capitol" he had to make the whole figure again. When the Morgan monument was "within three weeks of completion" the shed which sheltered it burned down, and the statue was so badly chipped that it was ruined. Saint-Gaudens had gone into debt for this statue, and it was not insured; but the destruction of his brain- and hand-labor was worse

than the money loss. He had a hard time over one
hind leg of the Sherman horse. While he was in
Paris, something happened to the cast, and he had to
send a man to the United States to get a duplicate.
"Three weeks later the man returned — with the
wrong hind leg." Then, when the horse was enlarged,
"the leg constantly sagged." Guided by their own
judgments, the assistants "plugged up the cracks"
with the result that the leg was three inches too long at
the final measurement.

Among other stories in the charming "Reminiscences" by father and son is a confession by the son.
When he was a boy in Cornish, he had a pet goat which
he had trained to play a butting game. The goat
would butt, Homer would dodge, and then, to his great
glee, the goat would butt the wrong thing, or the air.
One day at dinner-time, when the studio barn was deserted, Homer was playing this game. Beyond the
open barn-door stood the wax model of the Logan
horse "waiting to be cast in plaster." This time,
when Homer dodged, the goat butted the back of the
horse. But since it did not fall or break, the relieved
child thought it was n't hurt and did n't tell. Before
any one noticed that "the rear of the animal was
strangely askew", the horse had been cast in plaster
and the enlargement begun. This meant the loss of a
whole summer's work — just one more of the acci-
dents and errors that increased the "toughness of the
sculptor's life." The worst of all was that great catas-
trophe, the burning of the studio in Cornish.

But instead of dwelling on that, let us look at that other cause of delay in Saint-Gaudens' work,— his love of perfection. For fourteen years, while other statues came and went, the Shaw Memorial stood in the crowded studio. A "kink in Shaw's trousers" had caught a "kink" in Saint-Gaudens' brain, Shaw's "right sleeve bothered him", and the flying figure drove him "nearly frantic." Again and again he modeled and remodeled her; he experimented with the folds of the drapery; he changed the branch in her right hand from palm to olive, to make her, as he said, less like a Christian martyr. In turn on the scaffold behind the " Shaw ", stood the Chicago " Lincoln ", the " Puritan ", The " Rock Creek Cemetery Figure ", and " Peter Cooper." Meanwhile, as Homer Saint-Gaudens says, his father returned to work on " Shaw ", "winter and summer with unflagging persistence. Even the hottest of August days would find him high up on a ladder under the baking skylight."

Besides this, Homer Saint-Gaudens says that four times his father made a new beginning for the Fish monument, before arriving at a final form and that for the McCosh relief he made "thirty-six two-foot sketches." He had to remodel by hand the enlargements of the standing Lincoln, Peter Cooper, and the Logan horse. Usually assistants do this mechanically. The inscription for the " Stevenson Memorial ", containing one thousand fifty-two letters was "modeled — not stamped — letter by letter twelve times." For a coin design Saint-Gaudens modeled seventy

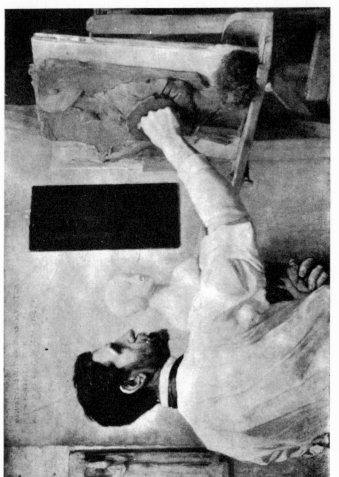

Augustus Saint-Gaudens at Work

eagles, and sometimes he would stand twenty-five of
them in a row for visitors at the studio to compare.
And for the Phillips Brooks monument he made over
twenty sketches and drew thirty angels, before he decided to use the figure of Christ instead of an angel.

"There were few objects in his later years that my
father 'caressed' as long as he did this figure," writes
Homer Saint-Gaudens of Brooks. "He selected and
cast aside. He shifted folds of the gown back and
forth. He juggled with the wrinkles of the trousers.
He moved the fingers and the tilt of the right hand
into a variety of gestures. He raised and lowered the
chin.— He shifted the left hand first from the
chest to a position where it held an open Bible, and
last to the lectern, although the lectern was *not* the
point from which Brooks spoke." And so the Brooks
statue was long delayed.

Whether Saint-Gaudens' delays were due to accident or the search for perfection, he was, as Kenyon
Cox said, "one of those artists for whom it is worth
while to wait." One committee, at least, trusted him.
That was the committee for the Shaw Memorial. It
took Gray eight years to write his perfect "Elegy."
Why not give Saint-Gaudens fourteen years for his
wonderful bas-relief?

In our search for the secret of his magic — for the
life-giving power of his touch, we find it lay where
most magic does lie, in hard work. If Christopher
Columbus could come to earth, and, standing outside
a big, darkened building, should see it suddenly blaze

with light, the touch of the electric-button would seem
to him a magic touch.   But back of that touch lay a
complex system of wires, and years of work of many
minds.   Back of the living, speaking bronze of Saint-
Gaudens lay years of struggle for perfection.   If his
Rock Creek figure fills us with the sense of mystery,
and the Shaw Memorial stirs with throbbing heroism,
if the Puritan strides before us almost comically confident, and his living Lincoln looks down, patient under
a mighty burden, it is all because the magic touch was
given through numberless experiments by the hand,
and out of the brain and heart of a devoted man.
Once given, the touch would last; he knew that "a
poor picture goes into the garret, books are forgotten,
but the bronze remains."   Saint-Gaudens' art would
not die with him, like the art of Edwin Booth.   It
would be perpetual.   And it was worth the cost, in
money and vital strength, if bronze and stone could
be made to live.

So much for the world's gain by the magic touch.
The artist had a gain, himself.   The joy of his touch
came back in many ways; although, when his statues
were unveiled, he tried to escape speech-making; and
when he was asked if his life had satisfied him, he exclaimed, in genuine modesty: "No, look at those
awful bronzes all over the country!"   When he was
traveling in the West, the sleeping-car conductor, after
painfully spelling out his name, gave his hand "a
squeeze with his big fist" and said: "Why, you're
the man who made that great statue in New York!

Well, I declare!" That little surprise brought joy. And another: One night, almost at midnight, Saint-Gaudens, his wife, and Mr. William W. Ellsworth came suddenly on an old man standing bareheaded before the Farragut monument.

"Why, that's Father!" exclaimed Saint-Gaudens. "What are you doing here at this hour?"

"Oh, you go about your business! Have n't I a right to be here?" answered the old man. So the others walked on and left him to his moonlight and his pride. It was a joy to be the cause of that pride.

And Saint-Gaudens had fun in his work, too. It must have tickled his humor to discover that four small changes in his Stevenson medallion would turn it from a thing merely characteristic of a smoking author and invalid to a half-churchly study appropriate to St. Giles in Edinburgh. "The bed gave place to a couch, the blanket to a rug — the cigarette to a quill pen, and the poem to a prayer."

Apparently the darkies, who posed for Shaw's followers, brought Saint-Gaudens the greatest merriment. He employed "countless negroes of all types", but many a time they "gave him the slip", afraid, perhaps, that he was a doctor and wanted to cut them up for experiment. Let us take a few liberties with this fact and follow an imaginary darkey: He was looking in at a bakery-window from a spot warmed by its ovens. There was the tempting array of flakey pies and luscious jelly-rolls. Judging the baggy trousers and stooping back it did not take a Saint-Gaudens imagina-

tion to know that old Zachariah Johnson was hungry.
If he could have broken the window, he would have
safely stored at least four chocolate eclairs. But, after
all, what the artist was thinking, as he looked at the
slouching figure, was that Zachariah would march well
in a company of colored soldiers. The dusky profile
showed just the right quality of determination; and the
sculptor could straighten up that back. By this time
Saint-Gaudens had reached the bakery-window.

"I 'm an artist, and would like to take your picture,"
he hesitatingly began. Then, hurrying over the explanation as fast as possible, he offered money-bait,
thinking with satisfaction, that those muggy eyes need
not be set in bronze.

At first all Zachariah saw, as he sauntered along behind, was the clear title to a good dinner. But presently he was suddenly jolted out of his pastry-dream by
sudden fear. What if this "artist" was a surgeon?
His old knees weakened. In his terrified imagination
he saw himself lying on a table, the helpless victim of
the knife. Surgeons were ogres to him. A near-by
area offered itself, and down its friendly steps he
crouchingly slunk, only his dusty old hat and one eye in
sight.

"My time ain't done come yet," he chuckled. "I 's
feelin' mighty creepy, an' I reckon I kin 'fod to lose dis
job."

Meanwhile Saint-Gaudens strode briskly on, and
never missed his model till he reached the studio door.
In time, as other attempts failed, he learned just to

offer " a job ", and " finally," he says, " I promised a
colored man twenty-five cents for every negro he would
bring me that I could use. The following day the
place was packed with them."

And so his statues brought him laughter. It was a
good gift,— with the magic touch. But not the best:
the study he put on " Brooks ", and the " Guiding Figure ", gave his heart the touch divine. During most
of Saint-Gaudens' life, religion had been only a
mystery. The boy, Augustus, had been repelled by
gloom. When his schoolmates called themselves
" miserable sinners ", or, still worse, beat their chests
exclaiming: " By my fault, by my fault, by my griev-
ous fault," he positively recoiled. Because his early
ideas of religion had been gloomy, for a long time he
had neglected the whole problem. " Only the joy of
religion had drawn from him any response." By and
by, " face to face with eternity and infinity ", the older
man had come to believe that the Great Plan was
" beneficent." And now, to make the statue of Christ,
he studied Christ's life, and, for the first time, found
the " Man of men, a teacher of peace and happiness."

The deepest gifts are often the most secret. Those
who saw Saint-Gaudens working over " Brooks "
would have guessed nothing of this. As he folded the
Bishop's robe, he was lustily singing, " Maid of
Athens ", " In the Gloaming ", or " Johnnie Jones and
his Sister Sue."

Like Stevenson he made light of pain,— this singing laborer. And yet, rheumatism, nervousness, and

dyspepsia were his steady companions. Three times he had to go to a hospital, and during those last seven years in Cornish, he fought a constant fight against illness.

He had to " work with teeth set." " He limped around behind a curtain to take medicine; — came back and worked away for hours." The last thing he touched, as an artist, was a medallion of his wife; he worked on that " when he could no longer stand."

In the little town of Cornish, brook-threaded and hill-caressed, Saint-Gaudens found a satisfying home for the last years of his life. It " smiled." For Lincoln models there were " plenty of Lincoln-shaped men." The farmers loved to see the statue in the field. And a crowd of Saint-Gaudens's friends followed him to Cornish: he had a farm; they would have farms; and they would all love the country together. So, around him grew up a little settlement of artists and writers, with gardens made to live in, pillar-like poplars, and fragrant tangles of wild-grape vines. Unknowingly the city-bred boy of long ago had craved the blossoming country, and hungered for something sweeter than the streets. The little trips to the Jersey fields, the peace of Staten Island, the overpowering grandeur of Switzerland, and the fairy-like perfection of Capri, with its " fields and fields of flowers,"— all these had made that hunger worse. Besides this, he must have learned, as most country-lovers do learn, that roughness may conceal glory: that the common potato has blossom clusters of snowy beauty; that a field lily, with.

a butterfly poised on its breast, may flame behind a bramble; and that from the blackest, slimiest mud a water-lily draws its purity. Saint-Gaudens, crying out for beauty, was weary of "work between four walls."

Then, too, as long as he was able, Cornish gave him a place to play: to ride horseback (and perhaps be thrown), to fish for trout, play golf in summer and hocky in winter, to slide down "perilous toboggan chutes", and tip out of sleighs, and to love it all — the fringing spring with its trebled brooks, and the sparkling winter with its merry bells.

As long as his strength would let him he played and worked intensely, bearing his long, unmentioned sickness with the bravest spirit till, on the third of August 1907, he died. Though he loved the world he was not afraid to leave it, and he had not counted the "mortal years it took to mold immortal forms."

XIV

THE MATTERHORN OF MEN

"With malice toward none; with charity for all; with firmness in the right, as God gives us to see the right, let us strive on to finish the work we are in; to bind up the nations' wounds; to care for him who shall have borne the battle, and for his widow, and his orphan — to do all which may achieve and cherish a just and lasting peace among ourselves, and with all nations."

Abraham Lincoln.

XIV

PART I

LINCOLN ON THE FRONTIER

IN the corridor of one of our American high
schools, two great pictures hang as companions:
that craggy peak among mountains — the Matterhorn;
that craggy peak among men — Abraham Lincoln.
The outline of his life, better known to young Americans than any other life, is given here only because
we remember that all things are new to every one
once, and that to some even the bare facts of Lincoln's great life may be new.

Abraham Lincoln was never ashamed of the log-
cabin in the Kentucky woods where he was born, on
February 12, 1809, over a hundred years ago; nor was
he ashamed of his famous coon-skin cap with the tail
hanging down behind, his bare feet, his ill-fitting,
home-spun clothes, or the hard farm work to which
he was " raised." His home training helped him more
than school; and that one-roomed Kentucky cabin
was a real home, for the young mother at the head of
it, fresh-faced and energetic, told her children Bible
stories and fairy stories and all she had ever learned
in her narrow life.

Rock Spring Farm, as Lincoln said, " lay in a valley surrounded by high hills and deep gorges." Almost as soon as Lincoln was out of babyhood, he began to help his father on their three fields, picking berries, carrying water or tools, and sturdily plodding through the daily work. His strongest memory of Rock Spring Farm was of one Saturday afternoon when he was sent to drop pumpkin-seeds. " I dropped two seeds every other hill and every other row," he said. " The next Sunday morning there came a big rain in the hills; it did not rain a drop in the valley, but the water, coming down through the gorges, washed ground, pumpkin-seeds and all clear off the field." It was only a child's disappointment, but big for a child, and one of many that this man must meet as part of his necessary training in hardihood.

Another kind of training was to come to him in bearing his father's shiftlessness. Lincoln honored and loved his young mother almost to the point of worship, not only through the first nine years of boyhood, when he had her teaching companionship and steadying love, but to the last hour of his life. His father he accepted as he would the weather, or any other unpreventable fact. As good-hearted as he was indolent, Mr. Thomas Lincoln was one of those thriftless men who blame circumstances for their own failures; and, though of course he never knew it, he was a problem in the household as long as he lived. In his contented blindness he would say comfortably, " If

Abe don't fool away all his time on his books, he may make something yet."

Moreover, being a true frontiersman, Mr. Lincoln always wanted to move on. Accordingly, when Abraham was seven years old, he took a notion to move into Indiana,— a rough journey by raft and foot through unbroken wilderness, and hard on his wife and boy and girl. They had to cut their way through the forest with axes, and cross the unbridged streams as best they could. Like the Indians, who were their only fellows, and by one of whom Abraham's grandfather had been killed, they shot or fished for their breakfasts, or gathered berries like the robins and the bears.

Nevertheless, this journey offered young Abraham more novelty than hardship. New birds flashed and sang among the trees; new animals skurried away to shadowed safety. But the new home in the wilderness was poorer and rougher than the old, and Lincoln's memory of his three years of life there was not happy. That other one-roomed cabin, back in Kentucky, had, at least, a door and window. For a long time, this Indiana one had neither; it did not even have a floor. Lincoln slept on a heap of dry leaves in a kind of loft reached by a ladder of pegs driven into the wall. The furniture was made of "rough slabs of wood." Since the forest was rich in turkeys, wild ducks, and deer, and since the streams fairly leaped with fish, it was easy to get meat; but

there were never any vegetables except potatoes; and
once, when Mr. Lincoln asked a blessing over a roasted
"mess" of these, his son added, with more truth
than reverence, "They're mighty poor blessings."

The lack of petty comforts, however, held no place
in the boy's heart beside the one great sorrow of his
Indiana experience,— the death of his mother.
Though Lincoln's father could not read, and knew
no more of writing than to struggle through his own
name, his mother fairly yearned to enlarge her own
and her children's world of thought. There had been
a satisfying sympathy between her and Abraham
which made the boy feel as if life itself was taken
away with her life. Indeed, the rude home was
darkened for all of them, used to her steadfast light.
At first, Mr. Lincoln dragged about, helplessly lonely,
but within a short time, in 1819, when Abraham was
ten years old, he was married to a Mrs. Johnston,
a widow with three children. If she had been less
fine and strong and tender,— less, we might almost
say, like Lincoln's own mother,— we can imagine how
painful her coming might have been. But she was
a capable, warm-hearted, understanding woman,
whose love answered Abe's longing from the very beginning, and lasted till the very end. "His mind and
mine — what little I had," she said, "seemed to run
together." Mrs. Lincoln not only contributed to the
home "one bureau, one table, one set of chairs, one
large clothes-chest, cooking-utensils, knives, forks,
bedding, and other articles," all novelties to her little

stepson, but she had the thrift and heart of a real
home-maker.   It was easier for the boy to wield the
ax and sickle, thresh the wheat, or plow the tawny
earth, when his tired home-coming would be welcomed by her smile.

Meanwhile, he went to school " by littles ", as he
said.   "In all, it did not amount to more than a
year."   If, as is likely, he was looked on as the home-
liest, gawkiest boy at school, he was also, perhaps, the
funniest and the warmest-hearted.   In his own plain
story to the Hon. J. W. Fell, he said nothing, of
course, of his tremendous love of reading, inherited
from his mother; his rare application, his tenderness,
or his honor, known at last to all the world.   Since
" readin', writin', and cipherin' to the rule of three "
were the only requirements of a teacher, he was
mainly self-taught.   In the museum at Springfield,
Illinois, they have kept his early copybook with its,

> " Abraham Lincoln
> his hand and pen,
> he will be good but
> god knows When."

A few fine books, well known, like a few fine friends,
are worth more than many mere acquaintances.   The
Bible, Æsop's Fables, " Robinson Crusoe ", and " Pilgrim's Progress " were Lincoln's real friends.   He
used to lie on the floor and laugh over the " Arabian
Nights."   When his stepmother saw that books meant
a great deal more to him than they did to any of her

own children, she took "particular care", as she said, "not to disturb him till he quit of his own accord." She respected his private bookcase between the logs next his bed, and the big fires he used to build to read by at night. She knew that he carried a book out to the fields so that he could read while his horse was resting, and often she would find him copying out, with his turkey-buzzard pen and briar-root ink, some favorite part to remember. "A boy like that deserves to have his chance," she would say to herself.

With as much pride as if he had been her own, she hugged the thought that, learning to spell by the good old syllable method, he beat in all the village-spelling matches; beat, indeed, so regularly that at last he was ruled out altogether. And she delighted in the further knowledge that, as Miss Tarbell puts it, he could " outlift, outwork, and outwrestle " any one. In the little village, he was the center of the husking-bees, and " raisings ", and all the rustic social life. While he helped pare apples, shell corn, and crack nuts, he would keep the whole crowd laughing at his funny stories and practical jokes. To every one he was a friend, even an old drunkard whom he found lying by the roadside one bitterly cold night and whom he carried on his back to a " shelter and a fire."

Abraham was a man now,— a great, " lathy, gang-ling " fellow, with, according to his Uncle Dennis, " suthin' peculiarsome " about him. At seventeen he stood six feet four in his stocking feet, and was a very giant for strength. "He could sink an ax deeper into the wood than any man I ever saw," said one friend. "If you heard him fellin' trees in a clearin'," said another, "you would say there were three men at work by the way the trees fell." He once lugged about a chicken-house that weighed six hundred pounds. To conquer the stubborn soil, to master the resisting timber, that was his task of youth, and it was this conquering and mastering that made the farmer's way majestic.

In Lincoln's mind the important event of 1830 was not his twenty-first birthday, but another move, this time to Illinois. And in this move the important thing was not the long caravan journey (three families of them, with all they owned, leisurely jogging along in ox-wagons), but the hard parting from all the old associations of his youth, and, dearest of all, his mother's lonely grave.

Filled as his mind was with crowding memories, nevertheless he manfully grasped, as always, the practical side of the journey. The road led onward, and he must follow it with a forward look. As a little boy he had taken a big share of life's load, as a man he must give the needed help. Accordingly, he laid in a stock of knives, forks, pins, needles, etc., and peddled them to the farmers along the road. That first year of acknowledged manhood was marked, like many other years, by his turning his hand to various things: now he was vigorously splitting hundreds of rails to earn his brown jean trousers; now tossing

the scented hay; now, in a dug-out canoe, he fought
the roaring spring currents; now ran a flat boat down
the Mississippi to New Orleans.   Arrived there, far
from being fascinated by the city life, all so new,
the forest boy, who had just come into a man's rights,
reflectively turned away.   Open to his wide-awake
mind, the roulette and whiskey and other allurements
of the Southern city were false charms, unsolid and
unlasting as bubbles; and the slave market with its
"negroes in chains — whipped and scourged " was a
horror.   "Boys, let's get away from this!" he chok-
ingly exclaimed.   "If ever I get a chance to hit that
thing, I'll hit it hard."

The next year, when Lincoln returned from New
Orleans, he went on doing odd jobs; this time, in
New Salem, Illinois.   He got a position as clerk at
the polls because, when some one asked if he could
write, he said, " I can make a few rabbit-tracks."   For
his own sake, he ground away at grammar; for
money's sake, he surveyed, or worked in a sawmill;
for the country's sake, at twenty-three, he became
captain in the Black Hawk War of the company from
Sangamon County,— quite an honor for so young a
man.   But if any one tried to glorify him as a military
hero, he would say, " I had a good many bloody
struggles with the mosquitoes and though I never
fainted from loss of blood, I was often very hungry."

He did not rise without interruption.   As he said,
he was " familiar with disappointments " and the hurts
of failures; he had almost grown to expect them.   If

he was gratified to be unanimously elected Captain just because of his "personal qualities", that gratification was to be balanced by failure in the election for the Illinois State Assembly. After this defeat, he settled down, apparently, to keeping a grocery-store in New Salem, later changing his occupation first to postmaster and then surveyor, and even thinking, for a while, of using his immense strength as a blacksmith. Meanwhile, in his inner hopes, he was looking forward to practising law, though the longed-for profession seemed almost too far off to gain. Still, as there had been time to read while the horse rested from plowing, and to study grammar when he was not surveying, so, when there were no customers, there would be time for law. He used to study for hours "stretched on the counter with his head on a cracker-box" or sprawled under an oak-tree just outside the store and "grinding around with the shade."

He read for recreation, too — for pure joy. Endeared by use, his meager stock of books fed him more richly than whole libraries feed others. Reading with mind and heart, so deeply did he know the "Life of Washington" that it was part of his own fiber. It is no wonder that he had a lifelong love for the Bible, being, as he was, moved by its literary beauty and sustained by its spirit. And it is no wonder that he loved Burns and Shakespeare. Both poets, in tune with his own understanding of men, had painted from life a score of counterparts to the rustic group that lounged with Lincoln in the village store, feet on stove and big hands pocket-deep. Both poets tickled his vital humor.

As for Burns, he and Lincoln were mates in a great many ways: one born in a clay hut, the other in a log cabin; one schooled in the Scotch hills, the other in the forest and on the prairies,— those schools of trees, and starlight, and wide spaces, teaching that men are brothers to the creatures of the grass. Surely Lincoln and Burns were kindred spirits in their tenderness, though one was so much stronger than the other in moral muscle. There was the Scotch plowman, sorry to uproot the mountain daisy and scatter the field-mouse's nest; sorry to scare the water-fowl from the dimpling Loch; himself heart-wounded when he saw the wounded hare; and, waking at night in the whirling snow-storm, thinking of the "ourie cattle and silly sheep", and the "wee, helpless", cowering birds. There was the Illinois woodsman with his hundreds of unrecorded sympathies, for he left no poems to tell them. None will ever know how often he scorned a chance to rob a nest or bring down with his gun a feathered mate; or how often, instead of the thought of cruelty, there fluttered over his rough face that look of tender understanding which always came when wood-creatures or men were at his mercy. The boy Lincoln had argued, " An ant's life is as sweet to it as ours to us," and, as his first incensed boy speeches had been against cruelty to animals, especially a custom among his playfellows of catching live turtles and putting red-hot coals on their backs, now, as a man, he would stop to hunt up a nest from which two young birds had fallen because he could not have slept otherwise; or pull a pig out of the mud " to take the pain out of his own mind." These stories are more important than they seem, because they point to Lincoln's greatest life-work, the setting at liberty those that were bound. Had the New Salem grocer never felt, as he did, the little pains of little things, it is hardly believable that he would have shared great pain with that immensity of suffering.

To go back, now, to his tradesman's prospects. Before long, Lincoln and Berry's grocery-store showed every sign of " winking out "; no wonder, when New Salem had only fifteen houses to three grocery-stores. The position of postmaster offered Lincoln more chance than this tottering business, and, as he was a man who used what was handiest, for a while he carried the mail from door to door in his hat. With the same simplicity, he stowed away what little money he had in an old blue sock; used a " long, straight grape-vine " for surveying because he could not " afford to buy a chain "; and, after he became a lawyer, wrote a deed with a tree-stump for his seat and an old shingle for his desk.

It was while Lincoln was postmaster that the pathetic romance of Ann Rutledge took hold of his great heart. Lincoln boarded at Mr. Rutledge's and knew that Ann, still only a school girl, had a lover who had gone east. Day after day the gentle little beauty

would slip into the post-office to ask for the letters
that did not come and day after day Postmaster Lincoln would have to tell her the hard truth. At last,
when even Ann had given up all hope of hearing from
her scoundrelly deserter, Abraham Lincoln told her
something which she must have known already: that
his sympathy was big enough to call love. And so
they made a plan that, the next year, when she was
through with the academy and he had been admitted to
the bar, they would be married.

But, to Ann, the next year never came. Long-
suspended hope had torn away the girl's strength,
and, even now, doubt wrestled with joy. The sweet
spring came and the summer; but, late in August, she
died.

To her young lover of twenty-six, the blow came
blindingly. The law books which had almost held a
hearth-fire when he thought of Ann, were ashes; the
very foundation of the world was straw. Meanwhile
his friends watched him closely for fear, in his desolation, he would do something desperate. Instead, like
all the greatest men, out of his grief he plucked new
strength; he returned to surveying, law, and politics,
majestic as a hero in surrender.

On the surface the man who follows many trades
seems to lead a drifting life; but Lincoln's use of spare
hours proves that he never drifted. Though he found
time to help people in hundreds of little ways, to chop
a neighbor's wood, lift a mud-locked wheel, or rock
a baby in its home-made cradle, he left time to educate

himself in the hours which other men would have wasted. He never lost sight of his purpose.

It might be called an accident, and would commonly be called luck, that he who had thought of being a blacksmith should be, instead, a lawyer, because one day, while he was still a storekeeper, he bought, for fifty cents, to help another man out, a barrel of old books and papers, and found at the bottom of the barrel Blackstone's " Complete Commentaries."

By speeches in the old log school-house, the town " square," or the harvest-fields, Lincoln began his political life. Clear-grained truth shone in every word. Sometimes, seeing such a powerful speaker spring up, as it were from nowhere, the keen country people would question his powers as a man; and then Lincoln would have to prove those powers by lifting weights, or wrestling, or cradling the russet grain in a nearby field.

In 1834, when he was twenty-five years old, he was elected to the Illinois legislature, and he was reëlected to the next assembly; but he made no particular mark. Life gave him, as yet, no promise of greatness.

To drop surveying for law; to give up a dependable income for a doubtful one; this was a hard decision for a poor man. However, in 1837, when he was twenty-eight, Lincoln made this decision; and, to further his opportunities, moved from New Salem to Springfield when he had a chance at a law-partnership. His entrance into Springfield was, at once, funny and pathetic.   One night, on a borrowed horse, he rode to Mr. Joshua Speed's country store, and, coming in with his clothes in two saddle-bags, asked the price of a single bed, blankets, and sheets.

"Seventeen dollars," answered Speed after a few minutes' figuring.

"That's cheap enough, I guess," said Lincoln, "but it's more than I can pay. If you could trust me till Christmas, and I should succeed at law, maybe I can pay you. But if I fail in this," he added sadly, "I do not know that I can ever pay."

While he spoke, Speed had studied the care-worn face and honest eyes. "I have a large room with a double bed which you are very welcome to share with me," he said.

"Where is your room?"

"Upstairs," and Speed pointed to a flight of winding stairs that led from the store.

Lincoln took his saddle-bags and mounted. Presently he came down, empty-handed, and with a broad smile announced, "Well, Speed, I'm moved."

This was the beginning of a lasting friendship. There was, perhaps, no man on earth in whom Abraham Lincoln confided as he did in this understanding storekeeper who had helped him when he was very far down.

In this humble way, with little hope and no confidence, Lincoln began his twenty odd years of life in Springfield. Slowly he worked up a practise and gained the trust of the people. Meanwhile he was never free from a heavy financial burden. The

The statue of Abraham Lincoln in
Lincoln Park, Chicago

abandoned store had left him with a big debt which he was determined to pay.   Besides this, being the man he was, he was bearing other burdens than his own.   Back in Coles County the " folks " were looking to him for help and trusting to his prosperity.   There lived his shiftless old father, his stepmother, always very dear, and a stepbrother, John Johnston, a man who was, as Mr. Herndon said, " born tired," if possible as thriftless and inert as old Thomas Lincoln, and far more like his stepfather than like his own mother.   Very likely Johnston, always willing to be lifted, looked on his brother, Abe, as a successful member of the family unwilling to share his success; whereas Lincoln knew perfectly well that Johnston would never do for himself while there was some one else to do for him.   Accordingly, we have left for our thoughtful consideration Lincoln's letters to Johnston, full of sound sense and a kind of daring frankness; full also of a rock-determination to protect his mother — letters hard alike for writer and receiver, and without doubt, though they were truly and deeply tender, Johnston thought them harsh:

Jan. 2, 1851.

" Your request for eighty dollars I do not think it best to comply with.   At the various times when I have helped you a little you have said to me, ' We can get along very well now '; but in a very short time I find you in the same difficulty again.—   You are not lazy and still you are an idler.   I doubt whether, since I saw you, you have done a good whole day's work in any one day.— Go to work for the best money wages, or in discharge of any debt you owe — that you can get; and, to secure you a fair reward for your labor, I now promise you, that for every dollar you will, between this and the first of May, get for your own labor, either in money or as your own indebtedness, I will then give you one other dollar."

(And ten months later)

"You are anxious to sell the land where you live and move to Missouri.— What can you do in Missouri more than here? Is the land any richer? Can you there, any more than here, raise corn and wheat and oats without work? Squirming and crawling about from place to place can be no good.— Half you will get for the land you will spend in moving to Missouri, and the other half you will eat, drink, and wear out.— The eastern forty acres I intend to keep for mother while she lives."

When we remember that these letters were written after he had a wife and children of his own, and his own little home to keep, such watchful care of his stepmother is all the nobler.

In October 1842, he had married Miss Mary Todd. Strangely enough, Stephen A. Douglas, from a nearby town, Lincoln's future political rival, was, for a time, his rival in love; but Miss Todd chose, as she had said she would choose, the "one who had the best chance of being President."

As she had foreseen, Lincoln, the lawyer, prospered, — not that he became suddenly rich. By his fellows he was rebuked for "pauperizing the court," but his clear brain and his integrity were recognized. He combined two things not too common in lawyers: small charges and truth. "For a man who was for a quarter of a century both a lawyer and a politician, Mr. Lincoln was the most honest man I ever knew," was one testimony. "Some things that are legally right are not morally right," was his motto. When one of his clients asked him to secure six hundred dollars, to which Lincoln thought he was not entitled, he answered coolly:

"You seem to be a sprightly, energetic man. I would advise you to try your hand at making six hundred dollars some other way."

Once, while he was collecting testimony for a murder case, he blurted out to his associate: "Swett, the man is guilty; you defend him; I can't."

Perhaps the Armstrong murder trial is the best known of all his cases. "Duff" Armstrong, son of Jack and Hannah Armstrong of New Salem, and a boy whom Lincoln had rocked in his cradle, had got into a fight with Metzker, after which a man named Norris had hit Metzker with a heavy ox-yoke. From this latter blow, in three days, Metzker died. The case was called, and Lincoln was the counsel to defend his old friend's boy. The most damaging testimony was given by a man named Allen, who declared that he had seen Armstrong strike Metzker between ten and eleven o'clock on the night of the row. By cross-questioning, Lincoln led Allen to go into details, and, among other things, to say that he had seen the fight by moonlight. This testimony sounded so clear and certain that, for a long time, every one in court believed Armstrong guilty. Then, when Armstrong's outlook was most depressing, Lincoln took out an almanac and proved that, at the time Allen had named, the moon, in its first quarter, had set. As the jury passed out, he turned to old Mrs. Armstrong who was rocking back and forth in an agony of fear, and said, "Aunt Hannah, your son will be free before sundown." When the longed-for verdict "Not guilty" had been brought in, and Mrs. Armstrong, sobbing with joy, asked the charge, Lincoln held out both his hands to her in the old way, and said: "Why, Hannah, I sha'n't charge you a cent — never. Anything I can do for you I will do willingly and without charges."

If we had followed this soft-hearted lawyer to his white house with its green lawn and children's voices, we should have found that he who had cared for fallen birds, and rocked the neighbors' babies, was the lovingest kind of a father. Little fingers explored the roughly tender features and patted the bristly black hair. No doubt he took his turn at putting the children to bed. There were three of them, all boys:

Robert, William, and Thomas. Little Edward had died in babyhood. The others, better known as Bob, Willie, and Tad, short for tadpole, will all come into this story.

In October 1846, Lincoln had written to Speed of his first boy, (Robert was then three) :

" Since I began this letter, a messenger came to tell me Bob was lost; but by the time I reached the house his mother had found him, and had him whipped; and by now, very likely, he is run away again." On bright summer mornings, he used to draw Bob up and down in a child's gig; and on cold winter ones, wrapped in a huge gray shawl, he did his own marketing, with a basket on one arm and a child on his shoulder or else pattering along beside him to keep up with his long strides.

The years rolled on, and with them pattering feet gained poise. Robert Lincoln was fifteen, Willie twelve, and Tad five in 1858, when their father took his stand in the famous debates against Stephen A. Douglas. The Democrats had named " The Little Giant " (Douglas) for a second term as United States Senator from Illinois; the Republicans had chosen a new candidate, Abraham Lincoln. And so, from August 21 to October 15, the State of Illinois had the rare treat of hearing these opposing candidates in the same town, on the same day; and never were two speakers more strikingly different: Douglas was " short and compact," Lincoln, " long and ungainly "; Douglas, handsome, Lincoln, homely and rough; one had a voice of wonderful richness, the other almost a squeak; one had been a grocery-man, the other a school-teacher. When Douglas drove to one of the debates in a coach with four white horses, Lincoln followed along in a "prairie schooner." And when the two candidates spoke, one had the air of promising assurance, while the other, a good twelve inches taller, stoopingly shambled forward, his long hands hanging out of his too short sleeves, his knees a little uncertain. How rustic he looked by comparison! But blessed be sincerity! "I was born in Kentucky, raised in Illinois just like the most of you," Lincoln captivatingly began, "and worked my way right along by hard scratching." And presently, as he came to set forth his principles, the fervor of his strong heart straightened the lank body, and the homely face was lighted to beauty by the depth of inner earnestness and by the shadows and sparkles that chased each other in those deep gray eyes.

He won another audience by humor: "My friend, Mr. Douglas, made the startling announcement to-day that the Whigs are all dead. If this be so, fellow citizens, you will now experience the novelty of hearing a speech from a dead man.

"'Hark! from the tombs a doleful sound.'"

Another time he began with a confidential twinkle: "Now I'm going to stone Stephen!" (And generally his stones hit.)

When, in turn, Douglas tried to slur his opponent's

record by saying that he had sold liquor in a country store, Lincoln quietly answered: "The difference between Judge Douglas and myself is just this that while I was *behind* the bar he was *in front* of it." And the roar of the mob was again met by a responsive sparkle in the sad gray eyes and a wonderful smile showing flashingly white teeth.

Such bits of fun, however, were only a small part of those intensely serious debates. A short time before this contest, Douglas had introduced a bill to grant the people of Nebraska and Kansas the right, if they chose, to have slaves. It was this bill that had brought Lincoln from the "court-room to the stump." By Douglas, this right to establish or reject slavery was called "the sacred right of self-government." "Slavery is a violation of the eternal right," retorted Lincoln. "That black foul lie can never be consecrated into God's hallowed truth!"— "If the negro is a man," he asked, "is it not to that extent a total destruction of self-government to say that he too shall not govern himself?"

"The white people of Nebraska are good enough to govern themselves," sneered Douglas, "but they are not good enough to govern a few miserable negroes!"

"No man is good enough to govern another man without that other's consent. I say this is the leading principle, the sheet anchor of American republicanism. This nation cannot exist half slave and half free." Thus the replies were swiftly parried by the two brilliant minds pitted against each other.

Years before, Lincoln had proved that he had no prejudice against the Southern people; he had no prejudice now; and he had no prejudice to the day of his death. " They are just what we would be in their situation," he had said. " If slavery did not now exist among them, they would not introduce it. If it did now exist among us, we should not instantly give it up. When Southern people tell us they are no more responsible for the origin of slavery than we are, I acknowledge the fact. It exists," he added, " and it is very difficult to get rid of it."— " I surely will not blame them for not doing what I should not know how to do, myself."

The key-note of Lincoln's argument, then, was not the abandonment of slavery; he was not coping with this problem yet. It was: If slavery is a bad thing it ought not to *spread*. If it spreads to the territories of Nebraska and Kansas, it will spread farther still.

Packed in the stuffy room sat boys and farmers, with mouths agape.

" Old Abe 's got a *clear* way of puttin' things," they said. " It 's hard to foller Douglas."

Indeed Lincoln's self-trained clearness, that language of almost Bible-simplicity, was counting with those country listeners.

" I felt so sorry for Lincoln while Douglas was speaking," said one, " and then I felt *so* sorry for Douglas when Lincoln replied."

" Lincoln 's a dangerous man, sir ! " stamped an old

Democrat. "He makes you believe what he says, in spite of yourself."

Before long came that famous plea, "The House Divided Against Itself," with all its daring outspokenness. "That foolish speech of yours will kill you, Lincoln; it will defeat you in the contest," said one of his friends.

"Well, doctor," was the prompt reply, "if I had to draw a pen across and erase my whole life from existence, and I had one poor gift or choice left as to which I should save from the wreck, *I should choose that speech* and leave it to the world unerased."

This was not indifference; Lincoln was eager to be Senator. But he forgot his own ambition in his fervor for the cause. At the end of the debate, he folded his hands wearily, as if he knew he had already lost.

"My friends," he said, "it makes little difference, very little difference, whether Judge Douglas or myself is elected to the United States Senate; but the great issue which we have submitted to you to-day is far above and beyond any personal interests or the political fortunes of any man. And, my friends, that issue will live, and breathe, and burn, when the poor, feeble, stammering tongues of Judge Douglas and myself are silent in the grave."

The outcome of the debate was what might have been expected: the cautious Douglas had taken the safe course, and given his words one interpretation in the South, another in the North; while Lincoln had uttered his belief with boldness, in the clear truth that was

rooted in his heart. "Lincoln," as Mr. Francis F.
Browne puts it, " won a victory for his cause and for
his party, but not for himself." By a small majority,
Douglas was reëlected.

" Abe, how do you feel after the election? " asked a
friend.

" Like the boy that stubbed his toe. It hurt too bad
to laugh, and he was too big to cry."

But Lincoln's friends were less discouraged than
he. Already they had set their hopes on him for
President. They had heard :

> " The hisses change to cheers,
> The taunts to tribute, the abuse to praise."

They believed in him more than ever, and, two years
later, when he was nominated to the highest office in
the land, they were not surprised.

We need to imagine ourselves back there in Springfield when the telegraph clicked out his nomination.
The whole town went mad with joy. Amid roaring
cheers, tooting horns, and a rush of hand-shakes, Lincoln exclaimed, " Well, gentlemen, there is a little
woman at our house who is probably more interested
in this despatch than I am." Then, with the crowd
piling along beside him, he hurried home. " Come
right in, as many as the house will hold," was his cordial invitation.

" You 'll have a larger house in Washington,"
roared the crowd.

Upstairs, two or three at a time, sprang Lincoln,

and, the good news delivered, sprang down again to
talk with the eagerly waiting mob, till little Tad
squirmed his way to his father's side, and, standing on
tiptoe, whispered behind his hand,

" Ma says, come to supper."

" It's plain this young man cannot be trusted with
secrets of State," laughed Lincoln, knowing that the
loud whisper had been heard.   And so the crowd, still
cheering, moved away : the meal schedule was sacred in
Mrs. Lincoln's eyes.

Election followed nomination; but when the day
came for good-bye, Lincoln's fellow-citizens were more
sad than proud.

" Billy," he said to his law-partner, taking Herndon's hand in both of his " you and I have been together more than twenty years, and have never ' passed
a word.' Will you let my name stay on the old sign
till I come back from Washington? "   That simplicity
was like him!   With proud affection Herndon left the
sign.

From the car-platform, in the pouring rain of a
February morning, Lincoln said good-bye to Springfield. A cold, drenched crowd thronged the station
for a last word.   He paused for a moment, and looked
down on the mass of bobbing umbrellas as if to take it
all in,— the pelting rain, the numbers, the love.
Then, sharing their wetness, hat in hand, he uttered
that greatly tender and almost prophetic farewell.

" My friends, to this place and the kindness of these
people, I owe everything. Here I have lived a

quarter of a century, and have passed from a young to an old man. Here my children have been born and one is buried. I now leave, not knowing when, or whether ever, I may return, with a task before me greater than that which rested upon Washington. Without the assistance of that Divine Being who ever attended him, I cannot succeed. With that assistance, I cannot fail. Trusting in Him who can go with me, and remain with you, and be everywhere for good, let us confidently hope that all will yet be well. To His care commending you, as I hope in your prayers you will commend me, I bid you an affectionate farewell."

There was a long whistle, a puffing cloud of black smoke, and the train slid away, taking with it Springfield's greatest treasure for the nation's need.

PART II

L INCOLN'S task, as President, required not only
all of his keen brain and responsive heart, but
all of his rugged endurance. That fine stock of health,
won by out-door training, would be needed as a brace
for the long strain of the long days. As Emerson
said, " Here was place for no holiday magistrate, no
fair-weather sailor; the new pilot was hurried to the
helm in a tornado." His story is the story not only of
the whole Civil War —" four years of battle days "
— but the story of a man besieged on every side with
numberless personal demands, and, at the same time,
the story of a man who kept himself so simply a *man,*
aside from his Presidential office, that history leaves
us a hundred memories of good times spent with Tad,
and of acts of tenderness to the " privates " in the
army.

For convenience, let us take the liberty of compress-
ing the events, sayings, and writings of several days
into one, and so follow the President's mind in its
rapidly changing problems. In reality the incidents
here given were scattered over perhaps six or seven
months; but they were all true. This imaginary day

will not be a Tuesday or Friday, which were Cabinet
days, nor a Saturday, when he sometimes held public
receptions. But, more common than any of those, it
will be what Lincoln called " A MIGHTY HARD DAY."
Many days were equally kaleidoscopic, and many days,
with him, were eighteen hours long.

A little after midnight, he was roused by a messenger with a telegram pleading for the life of a nine-
teen-year-old boy who had fallen asleep at his post,
and was to be shot the next day.

" I can't seem to say ' no ' to these things. A
farmer-boy used to going to bed at dark could n't help
it, I believe." With this half-excuse, Lincoln got up,
went into the next room, and wrote for a moment in a
careful hand. Then, folding the paper, his troubled,
gray eyes brimmed with glad light as he said: " Now
you just telegraph that mother that her boy is safe,
and I will go back to bed. There 's no harm done," in
answer to the messenger's apology for the interruption.
" I shall sleep all the better. There 's no medicine so
good for sleep as writing a soldier's pardon. Anyway," with a twinkle, " I have slept with one eye open
ever since I came to Washington; I never close both
except when an office-seeker is looking for me."

But even with that fine sleeping-potion (saving a
life) Lincoln had but a tossing night. Willie and Tad
were both sick, and two or three times he got up to see
how the little boys were resting, and then he went
back to lie awake and wonder about the halting general
who would not strike a blow.

Next morning, he came downstairs eating a big, red apple, and, loving the peaceful, eastern light and the homelike twitterings of the birds, took an early walk with Hatch to where he could see the white tents of his soldiers. Lincoln was wrapped in his big, gray shawl. As the *Reveille* sounded, he looked down on the men just waking to work, and said sadly: " That is not the Army of the Potomac; that is McClellan's body-guard."

Back at the White House by nine o'clock, he hurried through breakfast; then, as usual, he walked over to the War Department to discuss the situation and read the telegrams, mainly from McClellan. There they were: demands for more men and more supplies, excuses for delay, arguments that if he should fight and lose, it would n't be his fault. As Lincoln read them over, he said wearily, " If General McClellan does not want to use the army for some days, I should like to borrow it. He 's an admirable engineer, but he seems to have a special talent for the stationary engine." Then, after much deliberation, he despatched two telegrams: one ordering the constant protection of the important city, Washington, which McClellan seemed ready to forget; the other reminding the general that he must make sure that he was not so " over-cautious " as to be " unmanly."

McClellan had a talent for making excuses. Welcome to the President among these many made-up reasons for postponing action, lay Grant's telegram to Buckner: " No terms, except unconditional and im-

mediate surrender." That " unconditional surrender "
(later, Grant's nickname) just suited Lincoln, and,
when some busybody told him that Grant drank, he
promptly answered: "I wish I knew his brand of
whiskey. I'd recommend it to my other generals."

When the President had finished his work at the
War Department, he returned to his office and the heap
of letters piled on his desk. The crowd had already
begun to gather in the halls and anteroom: lame veter-
ans, anxious mothers of soldiers, and a multitude of
office-seekers. But Louis, who had taken their cards,
had told them that Lincoln must first attend to his
mail, which often took two or three hours. Applicants
at the White House needed patience; so did the President. In company with his private secretary, he read
and answered the most important letters at once. The
first envelope he opened this morning was a report so
long that he exclaimed in despair, "I should want a
new lease of life to read this through! If I send a
man to buy a horse for me, I expect him to tell me his
points — not how many *hairs* there are in his tail."
As he spoke, his eyes fell on a letter in Horace
Greeley's familiar hand. Greeley, the founder of the
New York Tribune, was important enough to have a
pigeon-hole in Lincoln's desk to himself. He had an
immense following. As Emerson wrote to Carlyle,
Greeley did the thinking for the American farmers
" at a dollar a head." Whatever criticisms Greeley
made were reflected in the minds of thousands. The
letter to-day held the usual suggestions: Terms of

peace ought to be drawn up; emancipation ought to be proclaimed.

Now Greeley was no more anxious for peace and emancipation than the burdened President; but Lincoln, in his wisdom, knew that the Southerners would not agree to peace-terms yet, and that the time was not ripe to proclaim emancipation. He must wait for a signal victory.

When Lincoln had carefully read Greeley's letter, his secretary pointed out a column of bitter criticism in the *Tribune*. But the President who barely had time to "skirmish" with the newspapers, gave it no more than a glance. He had a principle against reading attacks on himself. Or was it a comfortable indifference? "If the end brings me out all right," he thought, "what is said against me won't amount to anything; if the end brings me out wrong, ten angels swearing I was right would make no difference." This morning, he said cheerfully, "When I think of Greeley, I feel like the big fellow whose little wife used to beat him over the head without resistance. The man would say: 'Let her alone. It don't hurt me, and it does her a power of good.'" Then, after sitting sprawlingly still for a while and gnawing the end of his pen, he wrote the famous letter to Greeley (quoted only in part):

"My paramount object in this struggle is to save the Union, and is not either to save or to destroy slavery. If I could save the Union without freeing any slave, I would do it; and if I could save it by freeing all the slaves, I would do it; and if I could save it by freeing some and leaving others alone, I would also do that."

Many other letters he read and answered; but, before he was through, Louis came in with a handful of cards, and the mail gave place to a swarm of applicants, nine-tenths of them office-seekers. After Lincoln had seen, one at a time, the members of Congress, and others associated with the government, he belonged very truly to the people. "My rightful masters," he had called them in his First Inaugural. And now, as he heard their many demands and requests, they were masters of his time and thought. To-day, the first of the waiting crowd was an office-seeking editor, who, to help his claim, produced a yellowed, old newspaper to prove that he had been the first to name Lincoln for nomination.

"Do you really think that announcement was the occasion of my nomination?"

"Certainly," was the hopeful reply.

"Well, don't be troubled about it; I forgive you." And Lincoln politely opened the door, and the editor passed out.

Next, in solemn parade, came a committee of ministers, to tell the President that God had revealed to them his duty in regard to slavery.

"I hope it will not be irreverent in me to say that, if it is probable that God would reveal His will to others, on a point so connected with my duty, it might be supposed He would reveal it directly to me." And presently, by his silent forcefulness, the committee knew that the interview was ended, and gave place to a stormy-looking citizen who said, among other things, that Secretary Stanton had called the President a " fool."

" Did Stanton say I was a fool? " (very coolly.)

" He did, sir."

" If Stanton said I was a fool, then I must be one, for he is nearly always right."

While Lincoln waited for the next visitor, he turned to the big map of his country, always hanging in the office, and took up his perpetual war-puzzle. " In front was a solid and defiant South; behind, a divided and distrustful North." He studied the map a great deal, and between whiles, when he could snatch the time, read one of three books always at hand: Artemus Ward or Shakespeare for entertainment, and the Bible for strength.

But another committee had stalked in, confident of its right to interfere, and full of advice both un-limited and unsought.

" Gentlemen," answered the patient President, " suppose all the property you were worth was in gold, and you had put it in the hands of Blondin to carry across the Niagara River on a rope; would you shake the cable, or keep shouting out to him, ' Blondin, stand up a little straighter! — Blondin, stoop a little more — go a little faster — lean a little more to the North — lean a little more to the South '? No! You would hold your breath as well as your tongue, and keep your hands off till he was safe over. The Government is carrying an immense weight. Untold treasures are in our hands. We are doing the very best we can. Don't badger us. Keep silence, and we 'll get you safe through."

When the President had despatched this committee, he refused further calls till afternoon, " ran the gantlet " through the crowded corridors to the west end of the house, and there ate his simple lunch: a glass of milk, a biscuit, and an apple.

Before going back to his office, he glanced again at the *Tribune*, and his eye lighted on Stedman's poem, " Abraham Lincoln, give us a Man!" Though its truth stung him, he, himself, was too true to hide the sting. It was a plea for a Northern General to match the Southern hero, Robert E. Lee, and Lincoln cut it out to read aloud to his Cabinet:

> " Is there never one in all the land,
>   One on whose might the Cause may lean?
> Are all the common ones so grand,
>   And all the titled ones so mean?

> " O, we will follow him to the death,
>   Where the foeman's fiercest columns are!
> O, we will use our latest breath
>   Cheering for every sacred star!
>   His to marshal us high and far,
> Ours to battle, as patriots can,
>   When a Hero leads the Holy War!
> Abraham Lincoln, give us a Man!"

" Whichever way it ends," he sighed, his mind heavy with war, " I have the impression that I shan't last long after it's over." Then, with bowed head, he went back to his office, there to receive more visitors till four o'clock in the afternoon.

" 'Flabbiness' is the only word to express my feelings at the end of a long day open to the flood-gates of public demand," he said to his wife, as he seated himself beside her for their customary drive. " I sometimes imagine that every one picks out his *special piece of my vitality* and carries it off."

At their six o'clock dinner, Mrs. Lincoln brokenly told him that Willie was worse. Growing alarmed, Lincoln gave up the theater that evening and excused himself from every one to sit beside the sick child. That night, as for many nights before, he shared the watch with the nurse.

How he prayed for his boy's life, alone by the little bed, no one will ever know. " I have been many times driven to my knees," he once said, " by the overwhelming conviction that I had nowhere else to go." To our short vision, the longing prayers of that night were not answered: Willie died February 20, 1862; and the man who, in childhood, had lost his mother, and, in youth, Ann Rutledge, gave up his little boy, and, wan and shaken as he was by grief, gripped again the affairs of the nation.

We can imagine, however, the sweet look that crossed his face, a few days later, when he sent an officer's commission to the boy who had slept at his post, tired from carrying a double load. It was as if, for a moment, President Lincoln had assumed Di-

vine Fatherhood, and answered the prayer of some
one else for a treasured life. "The soldier who can
carry a sick comrade's baggage, and die for the deed
without a murmur, deserves well of his country," he
said.

From thus following Lincoln through this imaginary day, we can get a slight idea of four years of
such life in that hardest place — the President's.

Like a watchfully great physician, Lincoln kept
his hand on the pulse of the whole nation. There
were the armies of Tennessee, winning large tracts
under Grant's bulldog control; there was the Navy,
fighting a glorious fight. But, during the early part
of the struggle, a series of disasters to the Union
Army around the Potomac made victory almost certain for the South. Some of the Northern generals
cowered before Lee as if he were invulnerable. Long
delays and slighted opportunities; that full retreat at
the first Battle of Bull Run "to the sound of the
enemy's cannon"; even a resignation of a general
on the very eve of battle — these were a few of the
failures.

And yet, as Lincoln said, worse than this fear of
Lee, yes, the very hardest thing about the war (next
to the awful sacrifice of life), was the jealousy among
his generals, particularly the minor officers. "Family
quarrels," Lincoln called them; but they made him a
world of trouble, those refusals of general after
general to act under another's command. The President was constantly shifting his men about, trying

to find the right general-in-chief; and, hardly less important, the right leader for the Army of the Potomac. Military knowledge, stability, and courage had to be combined. We have but to read the list of "reliefs" to see how the bewildered Lincoln tried one after another, and still did not find the right man. No wonder perplexity furrowed his face; it furrowed his tired heart. . . . To hope, and hope again, and then be disappointed — that was his life. Mentally to map out a forward march, and then to get that worn-out message: "We have recrossed the Rappahannock."

"What will the country say! What will the country say!" he exclaimed at last, pacing up and down, his face ashen with grief, and the yellow bit of paper shaking in his big hand.

Meanwhile pleas poured in from sad-eyed fathers and sobbing mothers to defer the execution of boys who had deserted, or to pardon on account of youth. And, with every pardon, rained down a storm of condemnations, on Lincoln, the over-merciful.

"Let me keep alive till this great trouble is over," he sighed, "and then I will take a long rest — a very long one perhaps."

We do not wonder that he had to snatch from his labors moments of rest through humorous books, the theater, or little Tad. Robert Lincoln was no longer a child. He had entered Harvard before his father became President. But young Tad not only had the freedom of the White House; he went along on horseback when his father reviewed the troops. The President sat his horse like a general, and Tad galloped gaily behind, his cloak flying in the wind. Probably the child thought that his father was as interested in all the boy's affairs, particularly the pet goats, and Jack the turkey, as he was in the outcome of the war. Early one December, this fine, large turkey had been sent to the White House for the President's Christmas dinner. Tad immediately adopted him, fed him, and trained him to follow him about the yard. In the midst of a Cabinet Meeting, a few days before Christmas, the child flung open the door, and rushing to his father, sobbed out: "They're going to kill Jack! They're going to kill Jack!"

Official business waited. The President held the throbbing little body close for a moment, and then said, taking the tear-stained face between his hands:

"But Jack was sent to us to be killed and eaten for this very Christmas."

"I can't help it! He's a good turkey and I won't have him killed!" in passionate grief from Tad.

Then, with comical dignity, Lincoln took a small card, and wrote on it Jack's reprieve in the exact form he used for the reprieves of other condemned prisoners; and Tad, a winning lawyer, raced off, to set the turkey free.

Lincoln's children were not the only ones to feel his fatherliness. The soldiers loved to have him come to camp and shake their hands, and call them his "boys." Some he knew even by their first names.

" I can't help it! He's a good turkey and I won't have h'm killed,"
in passionate grief from Tad

"He always called me Joe," remembers one old veteran. "That coffee smells good, boys; give me a cup," he would say, or he would sit down on a campstool among them to eat˙beans. Though at one time, when he made his hospital rounds, there were from five to six thousand soldiers, he shook hands with every one, lighting the grizzled faces and sunken eyes with that tenderly sympathetic smile that almost had the power of healing. Three of the wards were full of wounded Southerners. "Mr. President, you won't want to go in there," said the escorting doctor; "they are only *Rebels*."

"You mean Confederates," was the quick reply, "Southern gentlemen." And every soldier in those three wards was greeted as cordially as all the rest. "They must always remember that we have suffered with them through all this. And when it is all over, if God gives us a victory, we must show mercy." To Lincoln the Civil War was never "The Rebellion"; it was "This Great Trouble."

When he was first made President, he had cherished a hope that the Government might emancipate the slaves by buying them from their owners. In two messages, mathematically worked out, he had set forth this dearest plan of his life. It might take thirty-seven years in its accomplishment; it would be a great cost to the nation; but, even then, it would cost less than war; and it was "much — very much that it would cost no blood at all."— "The way is plain, peaceful, generous, just," he pleaded, "a way which, if followed, the world will forever applaud, and God must forever bless."

But the plan failed. War, with its terrible cost of money and lives, continued. Lincoln was only too anxious to issue an emancipation proclamation, but he had to wait for a Northern victory. At last this came, at the battle of Antietam, following which, on September 22, 1862, the newspapers announced that, on the first of the next January, the slaves would be set free. Late on New Year's afternoon in 1863, Secretary Seward brought the Proclamation to the President for his signature. At the reception that day, standing beside Mrs. Lincoln, elegant in spreading satin, the President had shaken such hundreds of hands that his own hand was nearly paralyzed. As he took the paper, the "most vital document of the century," he waited a moment, then, slowly but strongly, wrote his name. "It looks a little tremulous," he said, "for my hand was tired; but my resolution was firm."

The following July came the terrible triumph of Gettysburg — that awful three days' battle which was called a victory. In "The Perfect Tribute" Mrs. Andrews has given us the best possible story of how Lincoln wrote his Gettysburg address on a piece of wrapping-paper, and then, after Edward Everett's two hours of eloquence, offered it to the multitude in its brief perfection. History has never given so great an example of CONFIDENCE IN THE POWER OF SIMPLICITY.

Meantime the President had found the commander he was looking for —"Unconditional Surrender"

Grant. Lincoln beamed his satisfaction. "He makes no fuss, but makes things git," he said.

"What our generals need to learn is that Lee is mortal," Grant had calmly concluded.

And now, at last, Lincoln placed unquestioning confidence in another. "The particulars of your plans I neither know nor seek to know," he wrote. And, in the summer of 1863, after the capture of Vicksburg: "I now wish to make the personal acknowledgment that you were right and I was wrong." On March 10, 1864, in an impressive ceremony, Lincoln appointed Grant to the newly-created office of lieutenant-general. The President spoke the solemn words as if he were not only knighting a hero, but consecrating him: "As the country herein trusts you, so, under God, it will sustain you."

In American history, the year 1864 is marked by a succession of calls for more troops. Twice the President issued drafts for soldiers, one for 500,000, the other for 200,000. On July 4, he called for 500,000 volunteers. That these unpopular calls might cost him his reëlection the next November, he knew perfectly well. But his integrity argued: "It is not a personal question at all. It matters not what becomes of *me*. *We Must Have the Men.* If I go down, I intend to go like the Cumberland, with my colors flying."

Though he was human enough to crave a second term, he did not expect it. His renomination was a surprise. "It reminds me of the Dutch farmer who thought it was n't best to swap horses while crossing a stream," he laughed; then added, soberly, "I am thankful to God for this approval of the people."

Indeed Lincoln had not only this approval of "the people", but the approval of many individuals who had once been enemies. Of his rival, Seward, he had made a fast-bound friend; of the inflammable Stanton, a watchful caretaker, nervous as a woman at Lincoln's propensity to go about unguarded. As long before as the First Inauguration, his old opponent, Douglas, seeing that Lincoln did not quite know what to do with his hat, had stepped forward, taken it, and humbly held it through the whole speech. That gracious self-conquest was too noble to be forgotten.

As Lincoln rose at his Second Inauguration to take again the oath of office, strangely and beautifully, out of the gloom of the winter sky burst a bright sunbeam and shone down like a blessing. It made Lincoln's heart jump. The crowd cheered and shouted, but was hushed in an instant as he raised his hand to speak. Yet, even as he said those benignant words, " With malice toward none, with charity for all, with firmness in the right, as God gives us to see the right," a dark man in the crowd was listening with smothered hate, and planning to do him harm.

And now, the war was almost over. " I beg to present you, as a Christmas gift, the city of Savannah," had been Sherman's December telegram. For months the Confederate army had lived on less than one-third rations, without blankets or shoes,— horses, mules,

and men sharing a common hunger.   The brave " gray
lines " had grown very thin.   Stonewall Jackson had
been killed at Chancellorsville.   At last, from mere
exhaustion and to save a final sacrifice of life, Lee and
his fragment of an army were starved into surrender.
On Palm Sunday, April 9, 1865, the grand old Southern general gave up his sword.   And in the North,
cannon boomed, bells rang, flags flaunted in the spring
breeze.

"Bress de Lord, dere is de great Messiah!" blub-
bered an old darky, as he fell on his knees before Lincoln in a deserted street of Richmond.

" Don't kneel to me," was the swift rebuke.   " That
is not right.   Kneel to God only, and thank him for
your liberty."

There came almost a week of strange elation.   The
President drove in his carriage; he read to Tad; he
dreamed of the end of his official life and a quiet return to the Springfield home.   " We 'll go back to the
farm, Tad.   I was happier as a boy there when I dug
potatoes at twenty-five cents a day than I 've ever been
here.   I 'll buy you a mule and a pony, and you can
have a little cart and make a little garden in a field all
your own."

On the night of April 14, rather reluctantly, he
thrust his gnarled hands into a pair of white-kid gloves
(he was never quite comfortable in gloves) and started
for Ford's Theatre.   His wife had planned a box-
party for that evening, and the whole audience
rustlingly waited their late arrival, and cheered their

entrance with free-handed, full-throated power. But in the night outside couched an enemy, skulkingly taking notes of the President's glory. He was the dark man in the crowd at the Second Inauguration. John Wilkes Booth, an actor and Edwin Booth's brother, with knowledge of " every entrance and exit ", and perfect freedom to come and go, stole through the now-deserted hall to the back of the President's box. There was a flash, a loud report, a cry. Lincoln fell forward.

On the hush of midnight following the day of glory broke the clangor of alarm-bells and the dull boom of cannon; while in a humble house, across the street from Ford's Theatre, faithful doctors and a few friends watched over our greatest national treasure in a last agonizing effort to guard it still. But the bullet had entered Lincoln's brain. In the quiet of the April morning, his great soul found its great rest. " Now he belongs to the ages! " whispered Stanton.

The shoutings of newsboys in streets too accustomed to " Extras! Extras! "; public buildings fluttering with useless black; private houses darkly shrouded; even the little children wearing their bits of mourning; these were a few of our land's vain efforts to express an inexpressible grief. Away back in Coles County, a white-faced old mother sobbed aloud at the crushing news: " I did n't want him elected President. I always knew they 'd kill him." And Tad? With the books that he and his father had shared, the pencils his father had sharpened, and all the little personal things that held such double preciousness, Tad could not even look at the silent, care-worn face of him whose cares were now laid down.

"Do you think my father has gone to heaven?" he demanded looking up at the bright sky.

"I have no doubt of it," came the sure answer.

"Then," trying his best to be sturdy, "I am glad he has gone there, for he was never happy after he came here. This was not a good place for him."

They buried President Lincoln near his old home in Springfield, Illinois; and Willie's little body was carried home with his father's over the blossom-bordered miles that sang of spring and life. There must have been a a great many friends waiting at the station who, less than five years before, had come there in the rain to say good-bye.

> "Great captains, with their guns and drums
>   Disturb our judgment for the hour,
>   But at last silence comes;
> These all are gone, and, standing like a tower,
>   Our children shall behold his fame.
>   The kindly-earnest, brave, foreseeing man,
> Sagacious, patient, dreading praise, not blame,
>   New birth of our new soil, the first
>   American."

THE END

"Gold is tried in the fire and acceptable men in the furnace of adversity."